The Portland Handbook

A practical guide for international residents

Margie Rikert
Carol Cowan

RGM Group • 2240 NW 113th Ave • Portland • Oregon • USA • 97229

ISBN 0-9704522-0-9

Artist Extraordinaire - Gary Whitley

Design Consultants - Q-BALL Creative • Portland • Oregon

Every effort has been made to keep this book accurate and up-to-date with reliable information. But as phone numbers change and businesses come and go, you may find some things are now inaccurate. Please let us know and we will incorporate changes in the next edition.

We have drawn on the resources (and patience) of many people. Our heart-felt thanks go to:

Devan Anthony
Nancy Atkinson
Holly Miller Chi
Ernie and Marilyn Cowan
Greg, Zack, Max, and Annelies Cowan
Linda Crabtree
Ana de la Rua Domenech
Julie Gatewood
Lisette Gibbons
Gerald Hoodenpyl
Leslie Kegel

Sonja Laird
Anne Larsen
Julie Resnick
Stephen Richardson
Carroll and Jane Rikert
David Rikert
Nancy Rogers
Terry Scribner
Pam Siffert
Nicki Stackhouse

Thanks to Marc Vickery of Go Graphics (503-663-3535, gomarc@teleport.com) for his line-art in Chapter 5.
Special thanks also to Tri-Met for the use of the bus service area symbols, and bus stop sign in Chapter 11.

Welcome

Moving to any new community is full of challenges, whether you stay for a short time or a lifetime. You must learn how to make a rewarding life for yourself and your family in a new place. Whether you move across the city, New York to Los Angeles, or Sidney to Portland, the basic things you need to make you feel at home will always be the same: enrolling your children in school; settling into a home; finding your favorite foods; understanding slang and idiom; being able to get help when you need it; or making friends. Moving is even harder when the language and culture are not your own.

The Portland Handbook is for non-American families and individuals who move to Portland for school or career.

This book is written by two American women who have had the experience of living outside of the United States. We remember what frustrated us while trying to make a home in a strange new place. We have tried to identify and explain some of those things that are unique to the American way of life. From banking to shopping, from driving a car to going to school, from dining out to finding a doctor, we hope that this book will help you to truly make Portland your home.

Welcome to Portland.

Margie Rikert

Carol Cowan

How to Use this Book

This book is not a tourist guide. This book is a tool to help you settle into your new home in Portland.

It is written for non-American residents in Portland. Whether you are here for a student exchange, as an immigrant, or on assignment with your company, Portland can feel uncomfortable and lonely until you understand how it works best for you.

We recognize that as American authors we have an inherent bias in our view of things. We have tried to get as many perspectives as we could from our international friends and co-workers. Please let us know if there are things we have left out, or things that have confused you. You can use the address on the last page of the book to contact us.

While written for non-Americans, if you are a U.S. citizen moving into Portland there are chapters that will be helpful to you: Finding Your Home, Local Transportation, and Education to name a few.

As you read it you will see that we often refer to two other 'tools' available to you for free.

1) The Yellow Pages. The telephone companies deliver this telephone book free to your home on an annual basis. If you are comfortable using the telephone, the Yellow Pages can save you a great deal of time. The challenge in using the Yellow Pages is finding the type of service that you need, when your vocabulary may not fit the American English used by the telephone book editors. This is why throughout this book we reference the applicable heading of the Yellow Pages with this symbol.

2) The Internet. While not everyone has access to a computer and the Internet from home, the Portland-area library systems offer free use of terminals. If you do not know how to use a computer, or feel as if you would just like some help, there are people at the library who will happily assist you. We have listed websites throughout the book for your reference.

The book is organized with a table of contents at the start of each chapter. These lists cover the main subjects of each chapter. To get started in using the book, however, the simplest strategy may be to use the book's index to find what you immediately need.

Table of Contents

Basics

Chapter 1

Basics

U.S. Basics

This chapter is an introduction to the facts of life in the United States. It also will introduce you to Oregon, the Portland area and, finally, to a few useful local resources which may make your adjustment easier.

U.S. State Abbreviations

You will often see the state names abbreviated. The United States Postal Service prefers abbreviations in all mailing addresses. Below is a list of the 50 states and the two-letter abbreviation for each.

State	Abbr.	State	Abbr.
Alabama	AL	Montana	MT
Alaska	AK	Nebraska	NE
Arizona	AZ	Nevada	NV
Arkansas	AR	New Hampshire	NH
California	CA	New Jersey	NJ
Colorado	CO	New York	NY
Connecticut	CT	North Carolina	NC
Delaware	DE	North Dakota	ND
District of Columbia	DC	Ohio	OH
Florida	FL	Oklahoma	OK
Georgia	GA	Oregon	OR
Hawaii	HI	Pennsylvania	PA
Idaho	ID	Rhode Island	RI
Illinois	IL	South Carolina	SC
Indiana	IN	South Dakota	SD
Iowa	IA	Tennessee	TN
Kansas	KS	Texas	TX
Kentucky	KY	Utah	UT
Louisiana	LA	Vermont	VT
Maine	ME	Virginia	VA
Massachusetts	MA	Washington	WA
Maryland	MD	West Virginia	WV
Michigan	MI	Wisconsin	WI
Minnesota	MN	Wyoming	WY

Addresses

When you look at an address it will be laid out in the following format:

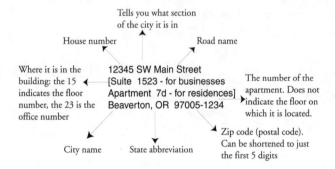

Tells you what section of the city it is in

House number

Road name

Where it is in the building: the 15 indicates the floor number, the 23 is the office number

12345 SW Main Street
[Suite 1523 - for businesses
Apartment 7d - for residences]
Beaverton, OR 97005-1234

The number of the apartment. Does not indicate the floor on which it is located.

City name   State abbreviation

Zip code (postal code). Can be shortened to just the first 5 digits

Currency

In the United States, the dollar is the only accepted currency. In paper notes there are $1, $5, $10, $20, $50 and $100. These are known as dollar bills (or simply, bills). Coins (valued in cents) include the:

Slang for a dollar is a buck or a green back.

Penny (1¢ or $.01)	one cent, worth one hundredth of a dollar, copper colored, medium size
Nickel (5¢ or $.05)	five cents, silver colored, larger than a penny
Dime (10¢ or $.10)	ten cents, silver colored, very small
Quarter (25¢ or $.25)	twenty-five cents, silver colored with a center layer of copper, heavier, larger than a nickel
Susan B. Anthony dollar ($1.00)	silver colored, bigger than a quarter
Sacajawea gold dollar	gold colored. This coin is the first step in removing paper one dollar bills from circulation.

☞ **Know your coins. Most store clerks do not count back change. The cash register calculates the amount of change you are due and the clerk will simply hand it to you in a pile. Count it yourself for accuracy.**

Date

When a date is written in the United States, it is in the format of month/day/year. For example, January 15, 2000, is written as 1/15/00.

Insurance

Insurance

*

Insurance Broker

People purchase insurance for two reasons. First, in some cases, it is required by law (as with automobiles), and second, it can protect you financially if something goes wrong. The three types of insurance that are discussed in this book:

- Homeowners Insurance (refer to Chapter 5, 'Finding Your Home')
- Automobile Insurance (refer to Chapter 11, 'Local Transportation')
- Health Insurance (refer to Chapter 8, 'Health Care')

Often all types of insurance can be purchased from the same insurance company. Companies that advertise in the yellow pages often list the types of insurances they carry. Insurance Brokers are agents who do not represent one company, but rather give you the option for policies from different companies. You may need to call on several companies and /or agents to find insurance policies that best meet your needs and are the most affordable.

Definitions

These terms are common to any insurance:

Policy - the contract between you and the insurance company that details what the insurance will do for you.

Coverage - refers to the amount of money, and for what occurrences it will be paid, if you have need of it.

Premium - the cost of the insurance policy.

Deductible - the amount of money that you must pay before the insurance policy will start to pay.

Claim - a formal demand to recover losses covered by an insurance policy.

Exclusion - event or loss that the policy does not cover.

Liability - a legally enforceable obligation.

Location in a Building

The ground level floor of a home is referred to as the first floor. The floor above the entry level is the second floor. In an office or apartment building with an elevator, the entry level may be referred to as either the ground floor or the first floor. In an elevator, the floor selection buttons usually mark the entry-level floor with a Star * but can also use the letters L (for Lobby) or G (for Ground) or M (for Main) or the number 1 (for first).

Measurements

The United States does not use the metric system.

Weight is measured using pounds and ounces. These are written as:

pounds	lb.
ounces	oz.

Liquids are measured in cups, pints, quarts, and gallons. These are written as:

teaspoons	tsp.
tablespoons	tbsp. or Tb.
cups	C.
pints	pt.
quarts	qts.
gallons	gal.

Speeds are given in miles per hour (written as m.p.h.).

Length is measured in inches, feet, yards, and miles. These are written as:

inches	in. or "
feet	ft. or '
yards	yd.
miles	m.

Temperature is given in degrees Fahrenheit (written as °F).

Conversion Calculations

Dry Measures

When you know		
	ounces	multiply by 28.35 to get grams.
	pounds	multiply by .454 to get kilograms.
	pounds	divide by 14 to get stones.

6

Liquid Measure

When you know   cups   multiply by .236 to get liters.

                               pints   multiply by .473 to get liters.

                               quarts   multiply by .946 to get liters.

                               gallons   multiply by 3.785 to get liters.

Speed

When you know miles per hour multiply by 1.609 to get kilometers per hour.

Length

When you know   inches   multiply by 2.54 to get centimeters.

                               feet   multiply by .3048 to get meters.

                               yards   multiply by .9144 to get meters.

                               miles   multiply by 1.609 to get kilometers.

Temperature

When you know Fahrenheit, subtract 32, multiply by 5 and then divide by 9 to get Celsius, $((F-32)*5)/9$ or use this chart:

	Fahrenheit	**Celsius**
Water freezes	32°F	0° C
	40	4.4
	50	10
	60	15.6
	70	21.1
	80	26.7
Body temp	98.6	37
	100	37.8
Water boils	212	100
Low oven	250	120
	300	150
Normal baking temp	350	175
	400	200
Very hot	450	230

Postage

When you send a letter within the United States the rates (as of 2000) are:

Letters up to one ounce in weight	33¢
Additional ounces	22¢
Postcards	20¢

If you send a letter internationally the rates are:

Letters up to 1/2 ounce in weight	60¢
Additional half ounces	40¢
Postcards	55¢

Telephones

Your phone number will be 10 digits and usually written in the following format:

*You must dial
all 10 digits
to place any
local
telephone call.*

503-640-0000

Area Code   Telephone Number

If you are calling anywhere within the United States that is outside of your area code you must first dial "1" and then the 10 digit number. If you are placing a call outside of the United States, you must first dial "011", then the country code, then the number.

American telphones have groups of three letters associated with each of the numbers on the keypad (except 1). These letters are often used by businesses to make their telephone number into a word, so that you will more easily remember it. When you are given a telephone number such as 1-800 Call ATT, you dial 1-800-225-5288.

Toll Free Telephone Numbers

When you call a telephone number with an 800 or 888 area code, there is no charge to you. Remember to dial 1 first.

900 Numbers

Certain numbers, designated by the 900 area code, have an additional charge associated with them. You are charged for the long distance call, and then charged for the service provided at that number. This service charge should be revealed at the time of the call. Technical Support for computer software may use this process.

Directory Assistance

You can get the telephone number of a business or a person in any city in the United States by calling:

ATT directory assistance	00
Qwest and GTE directory assistance	411

Telephone Book

A telephone book is divided into several sections.

Phone service pages (red) explain how to make Long Distance calls, How to use various phone services, where to call for repairs, and lists U.S. and international area codes and other similar information.

Government pages (blue) list government resources, first by city, then county, state, and the U.S. Government. Public schools are listed separately by school district, after the U.S. Government section.

Community Pages (green) have maps, zipcode information, and listings of local interests, including area attractions, sporting events, colleges, and some resources such as animal control and libraries.

Residential pages (white) give telephone numbers for all non-government, non-business listings.

Business Pages (grey) give telephone numbers for businesses listed alphabetically.

Business (yellow) is a listing of all businesses by type of service or business. These are known as the Yellow Pages (find further information in the Portland Basics section of this chapter).

Using a Pay Telephone

There are several styles of pay telephones. Some use coins (local telephone calls are 35¢), some will accept credit cards, some will accept telephone cards. Each one has the card that it will accept clearly written on the front. You will always pay more for a telephone call made at a pay telephone than you will for a call from home or a cellular telephone.

Telephone Cards

When you arrange for your home telephone, you may be given a calling card that will allow you to make calls and have them charged to your home telephone account. Alternatively you can purchase cash telephone cards at gas stations, supermarkets, etc. in various amounts ($10, $20). All telephone cards will have the instructions for use on the back. Most of them require you to dial a toll free number (beginning with 800, or 888) before you dial the telephone number you need to reach.

Time

The United States uses a 12-hour clock. Times are given with the designation of a.m. (an abbreviation of the Latin *ante meridiem*, meaning before noon) or p.m. (an abbreviation of the Latin *post meridiem*, meaning after noon).

Portland is eight hours earlier than the time at the Greenwich meridian 0° in England (-8 GMT).

There are four time-zones in the continental United States (referred to as Eastern, Central, Mountain, and Pacific). Portland is in the Pacific Time Zone. If you call Paris, the time will be nine hours later than in Portland. If you call New York, it will be three hours later than in Portland. If you call Tokyo it will be 17 hours later than in Portland. If you call Hawaii, it will be two hours earlier. There is a map in the front of your telephone book white pages that gives the exact range of each of the zones.

Often television programs that are broadcast nationally, will advertise future programs by announcing Eastern Time in addition to our local time. These programs may be listed as "8 P.M. ET/ 7 P.M. CT". If you have questions you can check the TV listing in the daily newspaper or weekly TV Guide for accuracy.

Most of the United States utilizes Day Light Savings (clocks are advanced one hour) for six months of the year. The United States is on Daylight Savings from the first Sunday in April to the last Sunday of October. Day Light Savings change dates are NOT standard throughout the world. Note that the states of Arizona, Hawaii, and Eastern Indiana do not use Daylight Savings Time. Local newspapers, TV, and radio always announce the time changes.

Tipping

Tipping is a very American institution. It is a way for rewarding good service (by giving a fair tip) and expressing displeasure for poor service (by leaving a small tip).

Tips can be a large part of a worker's wages. Waiters, bartenders, hairdressers, taxi drivers, hotel maids, and others, work in service industries with low basic wage levels. Both employer and employee expect tip money to add enough to their basic wages to result in a moderate standard of living.

Situation	Tip
Waiter or waitress	15-20% of bill, added to credit card receipt or left in cash at table.
Bartender/bar maid	50 ¢ per drink.
Hotel maid	$1/day, left each day rather than a lump sum at the end of the stay (as the maids work irregular shifts).
Airport skycaps, hotel bellboys	$1 or $2 per bag (depending on the weight).
Hotel porter	Tip of $1 each time they get you a taxi.

Valet parking	$2, paid when you get your car back.
Taxi	10% of the total trip.
Hairdresser	Round up to the next multiple of $5.
Newspaper delivery	$5 at Christmas.

Oregon Basics

Oregon is known as the Beaver State.

The capital of Oregon is Salem, which is about 40 miles south of Portland.

Oregon joined the United States in 1859.

The population of Oregon in 1992 was 2.97 million. This makes it 29th in rank in population density compared to other states.

It is tenth in rank in terms of area. The state is 395 miles across and 295 miles wide.

Oregon residents are known for being some of the most environmentally aware citizens in the country, taking great pride in the lakes, forest and coast areas.

By car, from Portland you can get to San Francisco in twelve hours or to Seattle in three.

The Pacific Northwest is a geologically active area. Mt. Hood and Mt. St. Helens are examples of local active volcanos. Crater Lake, and the other mountains in the Cascade range tell the stories of geologic turbulence. This area was inhabited by native people long before the explorers arrived from the eastern United States The settlement by non-native people began when Lewis and Clark spent the winter of 1805 on the Columbia River, near the modern day Astoria, during their exploration of the territory. By 1810 the fur trade was established. 53,000 immigrants traveled over the Oregon Trail from the 1840 to the 1860. The territory was granted statehood in 1859. There are many historic sites that you can visit to find out about the history and geology of the area. A good place to start is the Oregon Historical Center in Portland.

Portland Area Basics

Portland is a city that is shaped by two rivers. To the north, the Columbia River is the border between the state of Oregon and the state of Washington (and the city of Portland and the city of Vancouver). Portland was built at the junction of the Columbia and the Willamette Rivers. The Willamette River flows through the center of downtown Portland.

In downtown Portland, the east and west banks of the river are places full of shops, businesses, restaurants, and industrial zones. Social events happen along the west bank of the river throughout the summer, at McCall Waterfront Park. The east bank of the river is crowded by I-5, but there is a linear park (long and narrow green space) that runs along the river bank from the Rose Quarter, south to just below OMSI. To the east of Portland, the land gradually rises to the Cascade Mountains. Mt. Hood is the closest mountain to Portland in the Cascades. To the west of Portland there is an immediate ridge and next a long wide valley heading west to the coastal mountain range and the Pacific Ocean.

Portland is a city of 500,000 people, within a larger metropolitan area that is home to a total of 1.5 million people. Portland does not have the smog and industrial feel of some other United States cities. The economy is based on high technology, tourism, commercial fishing, lumber and wood products. Portland is the largest city in Oregon, although it is not the state capital.

Portland is 30 miles north of the 45th parallel. It is equivalent to Milan, Bordeaux, and the northern coast of Hokkaido in latitude. Portland is 40 miles east of the 122nd meridian (w).

The average temperature is 33.5 degrees F in January and 79.5 degrees F in July.

It is 78 miles to the Pacific Ocean and 65 miles to Mt. Hood.

Portland Metropolitan Area

By most definitions, the Portland Metropolitan Area covers Multnomah, Clackamas, and Washington Counties. The map on the next page shows the basic boundaries of these three counties as well as two others in Oregon and one in Washington.

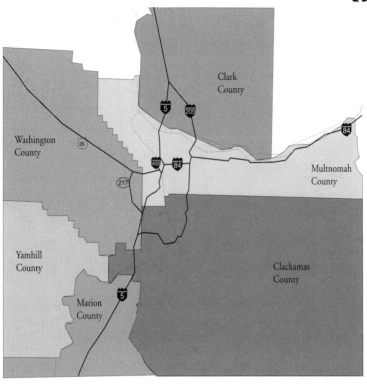

Metropolitan Counties

Metropolitan Area Addresses

The Willamette River divides the city into East and West. Burnside Street divides the city into North and South. This creates four quadrants - Northwest (also written at NW), Southwest (SW) Northeast (NE) and Southeast (SE).   Where the Willamette River turns northwest, Williams Street becomes a divider between NE and N sections of Portland.

(Refer to map on the next page).

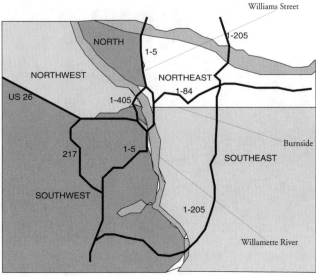

Address Locations in the Portland Area

Portland City Streets

In Portland, numbered streets run north and south, parallel to the river. If you think of the river as 0 Ave., the numbered streets go out on both sides of the river. Hence NW 185th is by Hillsboro and NE 102nd is by the airport. Exceptions to this system are found in the single numbered streets on either side of the river. On the east side, NE/SE 4th Ave. is called Martin Luther King, Jr. Blvd. (also referred to as MLK), a major one-way street running south. NE/SE 5th Ave. is called Grand Ave. and is one-way running north. On the west side SW 7th is called Broadway and SW 8th is called Park.

Another notable feature of Downtown Portland is the order of the streets in the NW area. Starting with Ankeney, one block south of Burnside and heading north, the named streets are in alphabetical order; Ankeney, Burnside, Couch, Davis, etc. to Thurman, Upshur, Vaughn and Wilson.

Older neighborhoods laid out in a grid make it easy to find your way around, especially when the cross streets have alphabetical names and the through streets are consecutively numbered.

Portland Area Resources

Yellow Pages

This is an invaluable resource for finding products and services that you need. The advertisements in the Yellow Pages can be helpful since they often list the types of services provided by a business as well as business hours, credit card acceptance, and even a map to their location. Remember that these are advertisements, and not endorsements of business by the telephone company.

You will also find the index at the back of the Yellow Pages itself to be useful. It helps when you are not certain of the exact word to use. For example, if you are looking for a microwave oven do you look under microwaves, ovens, electrical, cooking, kitchen appliances, or simply appliances? (The answer is appliances.)

A last note, throughout the Yellow Pages, there are sections labeled Fast Guides. This indicates that the same listings are given in a second section, arranged by location or by specialty (for example, restaurants).

Telephone Book Publishers

Three different publishers provide the telephone books in the Portland Metropolitan Area: GTE, Qwest, and Pacific Coast Publishing. The communities and counties included in the book will be printed on the front cover. Some books may combine all the colored page sections listed above into one book, but there may be more than one. For example the Qwest Portland telephone book, covering Multnomah, Washington and Clackamas counties, is actually three big books. Phone service pages, government pages, residential white pages, and business grey pages are found in one book. Community pages, phone service pages (again), government pages (again), business grey pages (again) and Yellow Pages A-L are in a second book. Yellow Pages M-Z and the index make up the third volume. Yellow Page headings are referenced in *this* book, but be advised that headings may differ between publishers.

You can order additional telephone books by calling:

Qwest	800-422-8793
GTE	800-888-8448
World Pages	800-826-4089

Classified Ads

Classified Ads is the section of the newspaper that contains numerous small advertisements for anything to be bought, sold or traded, including real estate. It also includes

employment opportunities and those seeking employment. **The Oregonian** has classified ads every day. On Saturday there are a greater number of automobile and truck classified ads, on Sunday there is a larger number of employment and real estate classified ads. An index at the front of the classified section will help you locate the topic that interests you.

Information Guide by Telephone

Several sources provide information via tape recorded messages that can be accessed 24 hours a day. The Inside Line can be found in the TV Click section of **The Sunday Oregonian**. Each Yellow Pages publisher also offers a guide of recorded messages.

Each service is independent but works in the same way. There is a list of topics including world news headlines, how to buy a house, weather forecasts, and horoscopes. (You can even get an update on your favorite television soap opera and get schedules of movies!) Each topic is assigned a four-digit code. To access the information, dial the ten-digit telephone number listed and, when prompted, key in the appropriate four-digit code to hear the information on the topic you have selected.

Culture Shock

Chapter 2

Culture Shock

The other chapters in this book will help you deal with the details of settling into a new city, but this one addresses the difficult emotions of moving to a new place. The first part of the chapter will help you interpret feelings, and reassure you that this emotional roller coaster is perfectly normal. The second section offers some observations about American culture and habits.

"One of the hardest lessons in life is that your circumstances do not make you happy, you make yourself happy." - an Indian Expat in Amsterdam

While you are establishing a new home in Portland, there will be times when you will feel that everything is beyond your control. It may be the first time in a long while that you feel so incompetent. It is a stressful and frustrating time. As you cope with the moving company's schedule or the way that the education system works in the United States, you will find certain things that cannot be influenced, regardless of how hard you try.

After the first few weeks of excitement and awe about this new city and country, you might find yourself feeling as though you have suffered a loss. Certain aspects of American culture may irritate you:

- the way people drive,
- you cannot buy bread that your family likes,
- the peanut butter tastes odd,
- restaurants rush you through your meal,
- no one speaks your language, only English, or
- the school is not doing enough to help your child adjust.

There are many things that can cause stress in your new life. Your reaction to the stress is within your control. The best way to survive stressful experiences is to understand your feelings. The process of growing accustomed to living in a new place is called Culture Shock. It can include the feelings of confusion over behavior, homesickness, a sense of not being accepted by members of the new home country, loss of self-esteem, and the sense of having no control.

Culture Shock Adjustment

There are usually four stages to the feelings of culture shock. You may find that these stages repeat at various points in time during your life in Portland.

You have the choice of how you will manage the process, and how you will respond to the stress of adapting to this new place as your home. The fact that you are here shows that you are willing to try.

Stages of Adjustment

In the first stage of moving to a new place, people usually have a positive attitude. As they are establishing themselves and their families, they find it really exciting to be here. This new country is full of adventure. It is a time when the similarities between one's home culture and the United States are obvious.

The next stage is a more critical one. Small problems may seem to be obstacles that can not be overcome. Things in American culture will be annoying and frustrating. The recognition that this is a long-term stay, not a short vacation can be depressing. At this stage the differences between cultures are obvious. It is easy to find fault with everything.

The third stage appears gradually. Cultural clues as to how to act are easier to interpret. Patterns in daily life are established. Problems of everyday living are manageable. Being able to laugh at yourself is a great sign that you are making the adjustments necessary to live here.

The final stage in the adjustment process is when it is easy to appreciate things from both your own culture and things from American culture, when it is possible to happily live in both environments. You might even include some American traditions in your own life.

And when you return to your home country, keep in mind that you will face culture shock again. You may go through these four stages of adjustment as you settle back into your home country. Going home may not be as easy as you think. You will find yourself missing the very things that made you so frustrated about the United States and Portland.

What Can You Do?

1) Keep an open mind. As you grow more familiar with the way things are done, you will find them less strange. Quick negative judgements can influence your impressions and make it more difficult to accept things as they are. Accepting the fact that there are no clear-cut answers will help alleviate the sense of frustration you can feel. Being flexible and patient will go a long way to helping you develop a sense of balance. Showing respect for this new place and having a sense of humor can defuse the tension you may be feeling from stress.

2) Recognize that the culture shock process effects your entire family. Your children will go through the same levels of adjustment as you and your partner. Have empathy for their feelings. Keep in mind that a lot of the problems you will hear expressed are a reflection of the adjustment process, as well as the normal problems of growing up; not necessarily the fault of Portland, Oregon.

3) Develop a sense of adventure. Learn a little history of the United States and of Portland itself. The Pacific Northwest is a fascinating place. How many cities have volcanoes so close by? This is a young place, having been settled by immigrant's only 150 years ago. There is a lot to learn about the native populations as well as the history of the settling of the American West. There are some fascinating monuments and parks that tell the story of the establishment of the West all within a day's drive of Portland.

4) Develop a routine. Even if it is simply going for a walk each morning or visiting a special shop that will help you buy ingredients for dinner, a routine will make it easier for you to make a life for yourself. Everyone periodically experiences the unsettling feeling of having nothing to do. A routine creates time in your life where you know exactly what you are doing.

5) Expect and explore differences. Pay attention to local events, festivals, and holidays. Join in the fun! Get tickets to attend local sports events, maybe a basketball (Trailblazers), hockey (Winterhawks), or baseball (Beavers) game. If you learn about the heroes (historic, scientific, athletic, and Hollywood) of the country, you will begin to understand how the modern American mentality has been formed. The more you read about American culture, the more you will be prepared for the many ways that it differs from your own.

6) Exercise. Join a fitness center, walk around your neighborhood, or take up a new sport. Oregon is a sport-person's paradise, abounding with opportunities for rock climbing, biking, wind surfing, running, kayaking, or playing American team sports such as soccer, American football, and baseball. There are lots of ways to stay fit and meet new people who share an interest with you.

7) Get enough daylight. Amazing as it sounds it is really important to get outside. Even in a place with as many gray days as Portland, being out in the fresh air will make an enormous difference in your attitude. Portland is lucky enough to have many beautiful parks, so use them! Go for a walk, have a picnic, or attend an outdoor concert or festival.

8) Get involved in your community. What do you want to do? Whether you volunteer, take a class, or join an interest group, finding people who share your interests is easy in Portland. The critical part of the process is not being afraid to ask for help!

9) Be patient with yourself. Give yourself time to adjust to your new home. It will take time to make new friends, to find a routine that works, and to learn your way around.

10) Be patient with your new culture. You cannot change it, but remember that you bring something special to it. When you leave you will be a different person. Your American friends will also be different for having met you. It is one of the treasures of international living.

11) Keep in touch with your family and friends. Call them. Telephone rates in the United States are inexpensive. Write to them. Regular mail takes less than a week to travel to any mid-sized international city. E-mail is instantaneous.

12) Write a journal. Regularly record your impressions of this new life in a book or on a computer. It is a great way to see how your thoughts evolve, as you grow more comfortable with the United States as a home. You might even send your journal writings to your family to give them a sense of what you are doing.

13) Help others. After you have had a little experience, share your newfound knowledge with newcomers. You will not only make it easier for someone else, but you will also gain confidence in your own survival skills.

14) Make new friends. If you have children, you will meet other parents through the school. Refer to Chapter 7, 'Making Portland your Home' for a list of resources to find international social and business clubs. There you can meet others who can share the experience of living in Portland from a non-American point of view.

Cultural Idiosyncrasies

Alcohol

The legal age for drinking in the United States is 21. No one under 21 may purchase or consume any alcoholic beverage, including beer or wine. No one under age 21 may be present in a pub or bar. If the facility has a dining area, children under 21 may sit with an adult in the dining room only. Children may not assist in carrying alcohol items to a check out stand at a market.

It is forbidden to carry alcohol in public places without having the bottle fully covered. In some states, alcohol can only be transported in the trunk of your car, because it is illegal to carry it in the car seating area. It is never legal to drink alcohol while driving.

In Oregon, you can purchase beer and wine in specialty shops and supermarkets. To purchase liquor you must go to a licensed liquor store (liquor is defined as having more than 14% alcohol). Liquor stores in Oregon are state-run and must be open eight hours a day (except Sunday and legal holidays) including the hours between 12 noon and 6 p.m. It is not possible to purchase beer or wine in a 24-hour supermarket between the hours of 2 a.m. and 7 a.m.

Many restaurants have their own wine lists. If you want to bring your own wine bottle with you it is a good idea to call ahead. You may be charged a service fee (called a 'corking fee') for opening the bottle, providing the glassware and serving.

If you are serving alcohol to guests in your home, as a host you are responsible to ensure that your guests do not drink excessively and then operate a car. There are severe penalties for this. Many Americans have adopted the rule of the 'designated driver' for social occasions. The designated driver does not drink and ensures that people arrive home safely. Another option is to arrange for a taxi service to escort someone home if s/he has drunk too much to safely drive. The Blood Alcohol limit for legal driving in Oregon is .08. In most states it is .10. This is the equivalent of a person weighing 160 lbs. having five drinks in one hour on an empty stomach.

Business Etiquette

As you have probably learned from your work colleagues, there is a difference in the way Americans conduct business. The dress code in your new office may be more casual than in your home country. Americans do not take personal offence if someone disagrees with them in a business setting. Instead, such a disagreement is often seen as a sign of thoughtful analysis, strength of character, and self-belief. However, the way that one chooses to express disagreement is important. Americans do not like to be told they are wrong. So, rather than saying, "The problem with that decision is…" put your opinion in a more cooperative form: " A difficulty I see with that decision is…."

Americans are competitive, which breeds pride in their company, country, and self. The American attitude is to make things happen, to take the initiative to act, rather than talk. All of these traits may be in contrast to the work and social environment with which you are familiar.

If you are learning to work within a U.S. company, some things to remember are:

A firm handshake is an important part of greeting people in business and in social occasions. Otherwise, physical contact is not a part of the U.S. business culture. In terms of personal space, Americans are most comfortable in conversation if they stand about an arm's length from the other person. If you get closer than that you will see your acquaintance back away.

People expect you to look them in the eyes while talking. It convinces them that you are sincere. If you do not make eye contact, it makes them feel as if you are untrustworthy.

It is always wise to arrange appointments to see people in advance, but because of the casual nature of American business you may be able to see people with very short notice.

In most conversations people will use your first name. If you are in doubt, listen to your co-workers or host. This casualness also extends to children and adults.

Gifts are rarely given in the United States between business people except during the December holiday seasons. When you are invited to someone's home, you can bring your host or hostess a gift, but it is not expected.

Customer Service

Americans have a fascination with customer service, which is the process of making the customers feel like their business is valued and that they are important. If you buy something expensive (like a mattress, appliance, car, stereo, or jewelry, etc.) do not be surprised if you get a thank you note from the salesperson.

When you go through the checkout line at the store, the clerk may ask, "Did you find everything you wanted?". The clerk is only making conversation and expecting you to say "Yes" (even if you did not find what you were looking for). Every cashier or clerk makes some sort of statement because it is important to say something to acknowledge your presence.

When you walk into a store you may be approached immediately by a salesperson whose job is to help you purchase something. The best thing you can say is "I am just looking" if you want some time to make decisions without assistance. However, if you have a question there is usually someone there to assist you.

As you leave a shop, the library, a restaurant, etc. you will be told to "have a nice day" (or some similar statement) as a way to say goodbye. Answers you can give, in that case, are "you too" or "thank you".

One of the advantages of a customer service emphasis is that it is easy to return something you have purchased, as long as it is still in good condition. You must have the original sales receipt. The store's returns policy will state (1) within what period you may return something, and (2) whether they will give you in-store credit or cash for the return. If you pay with a credit card, the purchase usually will be credited back to that same card.

Driving in Portland

Americans are impatient and undisciplined as drivers. When opinion surveys are taken, the results show that most people believe they are excellent drivers and all other drivers are careless. It may seem to you, as you observe drivers on U.S. roads, that paying attention to the law is done only when it benefits the driver. This lack of attention to the law shows up in many ways on Oregon highways and roads.

Some people will tend to select the left lane and stay in it, regardless of their speed, the law, or the number of cars lining up behind them. Sometimes this is because a driver is not paying attention to traffic flow, but often drivers keep in the left lane to avoid the merging traffic that is entering or exiting from the road on the right.

Some people ignore the solid yellow light at a stop signal, and end up driving through the red light. This traffic issue is so serious in Beaverton that the police actually installed signs stating "Red means Stop in Beaverton".

Some impatient drivers will change lanes erratically and pass on the right when traffic seems to be moving too slowly for them.

Our best advice to you is to drive defensively.

The Oregon Driving Manual is available from the Oregon Department of Motor Vehicles. Learn how the traffic laws differ from your home country. While the laws for driving in Portland are the same as anywhere in the United States, the drivers of this area do have a style that is all of their own. Refer to Chapter 11, 'Local Transportation' for more details on automobiles and driving.

Dual Income Families

A majority of American women work outside of the home. Many work full time, which is why your neighborhood may seem vacant during daylight hours. The dual income family (both husband and wife working full time) is common in the urban areas of the United States.

This lifestyle choice is extremely stressful. Every minute is scheduled, especially if there are children who also have active lives. Because of this lifestyle, your new friends may have less time to devote to establishing a friendship than friends in your home country. It also explains the need for the 24 hour a day, 7 days a week shopping options (also known as 24/7). There is no time during the week to manage a household.

Eating on the Run

One aspect of American culture that can be difficult to understand is the way Americans eat.

'Take away' means the same as 'take out'.

Americans have become a nation of people who eat more food away from home than in their homes. Many families do not have the chance to sit down together for dinner. Fast food is more often the choice over eating a sit-down meal in a restaurant. Drive-through windows at fast food restaurants encourage people to eat in their cars. Considering the high fat, empty calories of typical fast food fare, it is easy to see why more than 30% of the United States population is considered obese.

Convenience stores are another source of take-away food. Coffee-to-go with a prepackaged pastry is a common morning habit for many Americans on their commute to work.

A morning or afternoon coffee break may not be a time to actually stop working and relax; it may simply be drinking a cup of coffee at one's desk. Some people will eat their lunch at their desks as well.

Greeting People

"How are you?" is a common greeting for anyone with whom you have a casual friendship such as business associates, neighbors, parents at school, familiar faces at the gym, or the gas station attendant where you purchase gas regularly. This is not a question about your health but a form of greeting. The response is to just say "Fine, and how are you?". You will know when someone is asking particularly about your health by the tone of his or her voice.

Americans use idle conversation (also known as small talk) as a way to establish a short-term relationship with another person. Subjects like weather, sports, children, work, and family are often covered when you first meet someone. In social situations, people will introduce themselves with an explanation about the company for which they work and their position there.

If you speak English with an accent, people will ask you where you are from. This question is one of sincere curiosity, but at times it may feel more personal than you would like to answer. Americans often ask questions about the health of your family members. This is not to be nosy or rude but instead as a way of creating a common ground between you.

Being Politically Correct (PC)

Litigation

Americans believe foremost in their own individual rights. They also attach a great deal of importance to legal documents (contracts, rules of behavior, etc.) and the enforcement of such agreements. You have probably read in the newspapers in your home country about the litigious nature of the American culture. There is a tendency for people in the United States to sue in order to assert their rights. This may be of concern to you, but if you follow basic rules of courtesy and respect for individuals you will not run into any problems.

For all of the talk about individual freedoms and individual rights, there is a need in American society to have people conform to certain norms. For example, there are various groups of people who attempt to influence everything from books used in the public schools, to the dress code which is appropriate at a beach; even nude swimming for very small children is discouraged. It can be confusing to know what is appropriate and what is not. Pay attention to how others are acting and follow their lead.

Sexual Harassment

Sexual harassment in the United States is a very sensitive issue. A friendly advance towards another person may not be understood as humorous or positive. If you treat everyone with courtesy and respect regardless of company position or gender, you will protect yourself from cultural misinterpretation of your actions. Your company should have a written policy that can help you understand the nuances of the issue of sexual harassment.

Unattended Children

Never leave your children unattended in a car (even in your driveway) or on the side-walk (in a stroller) while you go in to shop, even if the child is asleep and you do not wish to wake him/her. The Child Protection laws in the United States have a great deal of latitude in interpretation. In some cases an action such as leaving a child unat-tended is considered abuse, and you may be cited for it.

Restaurants

Restaurant Etiquette

Finding a Restaurant

There are restaurants to satisfy most palates in Portland. With some research and ex-perimentation, you will surely find a few that you love. Each year there are reviews published in various newspapers on the best restaurants in Portland. Save your copy and use it as a reference throughout the year. You can also find weekly reviews in the **Oregonian's** 'A & E' section and the **Willamette Week**. These reviews will give a sense of the cuisine, the quality of the food, the ambiance of the restaurant itself, and a price guideline. The Yellow Pages listings are sorted according to types of restaurant, alphabetically, and by area. These listings are advertisements; they provide no evalua-tion of quality.

Turn Over

Most American restaurants are managed on the concept of 'table turn over'. This refers to the number of times a table will have guests in an evening. More expensive restau-rants may expect you to spend the evening eating dinner, but the norm in the United States is that you will eat quickly and leave. The table is then prepared for another set of guests.

You will experience this when the bill for the meal is brought to your table before you have finished eating, when coffee is served with dessert, or when the waiter clears the plates of people who have finished although others are still eating. Even restaurants that are more expensive might subtly hurry you through your meal so that they may seat a later party.

Reservations

It is best to call ahead to make a reservation for the time when you would like to be seated. For reservations at some popular restaurants you may need to call several weeks in advance of the date. You can usually get a table at a favorite restaurant if you can be flexible with the time of your seating.

Pets in Restaurants

In the United States, because of concerns for hygiene, animals are not allowed inside of a restaurant, unless it is a medical-assistance dog. Some cafes with sidewalk seating will allow you to have your pet sit with you outside.

Supermarket Shopping

As you have probably noticed, U.S. supermarkets sell a huge variety of products, from foods to car maintenance supplies. It can be overwhelming. One strategy for food shopping is to create a list of what you want to buy before you go shopping. Then, when you become distracted by the chocolate covered mint sandwich cookies, you can be reminded of what you actually need to purchase: yogurt for your two year old.

When you get to the check out stand (where you pay for your groceries) you will be asked by the cashier "Paper or plastic?" This is not a question about how you will pay for your groceries. It is a question about the type of bag to be used in packing your groceries. If you bring bags or boxes from home for your groceries, you will be given a small cash credit against your total bill. Most stores do not encourage you to pack your own groceries.

You have the choice of using cash, check, credit, or debit cards to pay for your groceries. When you use a debit card you may be asked if you want cash back. This refers to putting a higher charge on your debit card than the value of the groceries and giving you the difference in cash.

When a clerk at a supermarket takes your groceries to the car, you are not expected to tip.

Retail Stores

Many stores pay their sales people a wage based on the sales for which they are directly responsible, particularly in stores for cars, appliances, computers, and audio/video equipment. This wage system is an incentive for the salesperson to provide excellent customer service to a potential buyer, but for you, the customer, it can make a decision awkward. You may feel pressure from a sales person to purchase immediately. If you visit a store several times to get information before you make a final purchase, you may speak with several sales people. When you purchase, there may be a question of which one gets credit for the sale. You can help ease the situation by asking for the business card of the first person who helps you, always asking for the same sales person when you return, and mentioning that person's name when you make your purchase.

Smoking

The legal smoking age is 18. This means that no one under age 18 may purchase or use cigarettes, cigars, or pipe tobacco. You can purchase cigarettes, cigars, and pipe tobacco in supermarkets and convenience stores. Premium cigars can be found in specialty smoking shops.

In the United States, smoking is a sensitive issue. If you would like to smoke in a restaurant you should request to be seated in the smoking section, but be advised that some restaurants are smoke-free. If you are out with friends, you should inquire if it is acceptable to them before you light your cigar, cigarette, or pipe.

Telephone Etiquette

Americans answer the telephone at home with "Hello". There is no identification offered and as a result you may not know with whom you are speaking. At the office, people usually answer with their name "Jane Brown speaking," or simply "Jane Brown," or, in some cases, with only their last name, "Brown." In all cases, when you place a call it is best to say who you are, and continue with the purpose of your call.

Language

Chapter 3

Language

One of the hardest parts of living in a country other than your own is mastery of the language. You may have been speaking English since you were a child, or you may have only studied it for a few years in secondary school. If you are reading this book, you already have a good command of written English.

Regardless of how well prepared you are, it will be a challenge to speak English in the Portland area. English that is taught outside the United States is classic British English. English as it is spoken here has its own unique pronunciations, idioms, and word uses. As you travel throughout the United States you will hear a great range of regional variations. In some places it may feel as if you are hearing a language that is not English! These unique regional dialects can even be difficult for Americans to understand.

English as a Second Language

More people in the world speak English as a second language than speak English as their native tongue. The work you put into learning English while you are in Portland will be a good investment for your future travel to other parts of the world. Unfortunately, many Americans do not speak a second language, so English is necessary to feel truly comfortable living here. In Portland the most commonly spoken languages other than English are Spanish, Korean, and Japanese.

If you have children, they will also be facing the challenge of learning English. At both public (state supported) or private (tuition based) schools there are classes in English as a Second Language (known as ESL). There are also schools that offer education in languages other than English. Refer to Chapter 9, 'Education' for school options for yourself or your children.

The Stress of Learning a Language

Being in a new place with a different language (or perhaps with the same language but a foreign accent) can be intimidating. It is especially difficult when:

- answering the telephone,
- a doctor explains to you about your sick child,
- you have a car accident,
- you become lost,
- people are laughing at your pronunciation,
- you are frustrated with not being able to say what you are thinking, or
- your children come home from school with homework using vocabulary you do not understand.

It can be very discouraging.

Take a deep breath, laugh at yourself, and look for ways to improve. Watching TV and listening to the radio can help you learn the sounds of the language. You will find that you understand more English than you can speak. Eventually you will find yourself thinking in English. But that takes time, practice, and patience.

It also can be very tiring. People will immediately recognize that you are not from the United States and will ask you "where are you from?" This is friendly curiosity, but you grow weary of answering!

At the end of this chapter there is a list of resources for learning English (or any other language you may care to learn).

Learning to Listen to American English

The rich history of immigration to the United States is reflected in the way Americans speak English. American English is characterized by an ever-changing vocabulary. Sentence structure is based on classic British English, but words are used differently. There are many words in American English that have their source in the other languages brought to this country by immigrants. There are also words which have their source in the native languages originally spoken here. Your vocabulary will grow every day as you listen and read. You will find American English to be a very creative language.

English is a difficult language to learn. Pronunciations are not standard for the same sets of letters. An example is the 'ough' in the words 'though,' 'through,' 'thought,' and even 'enough.' To make it even more confusing, Americans are creative in their use of language. The same sentence might have different meanings for people from different societal groups.

American versus British English

Although Americans are taught 'proper English' in schools, many of the language rules are ignored when speaking. Some of the language difficulties you will encounter will have to do with the actual structure (usually shortening) of sentences and different meanings for known words. Others will have to do with the cultural use of language.

Americans, like native speakers of any language, speak quickly. It is also a common assumption amongst native English speakers that if you can speak a small amount of English then you are fluent. You will need to learn to ask people to speak more slowly and clearly. If you find yourself listening and nodding your head 'yes', hoping that you will understand, you are conveying the wrong message. You need to ask the speaker to

repeat what was just said. Do not be embarrassed. It is important that you get what you need; most people will gladly repeat themselves. Be forewarned, most people speak much more loudly when they repeat themselves. Remember that it is not because they are angry, rather they think it will help you to hear them.

Pronunciation and Usage of Words

Contractions

The use of contractions is common in American English. If it is new to you to hear contractions here is a list of some common ones, although it is not a complete list:

don't	do not
isn't	is not
it'll	it will
won't	will not
I'll	I will
can't	can not
doesn't	does not
there's	there is
I'm	I am
who's	who is
ain't	is not

Adverbs

Most adverbs are recognized by the 'ly' at the end as they describe a verb in a sentence such as quickly, excitedly, and really. In the Northwest many people use a shortened version of an adverb, dropping the 'ly' from the word. For example, you will hear 'we had a real good time,' as opposed to 'we had a really good time.'

Regional Pronunciation

The same word may be pronounced differently in the Northwest than in other parts of the United States. An example is the word 'Willamette.' In Portland it is pronounced with the emphasis on the second syllable. On the East Coast of the United States, it is pronounced with the emphasis on the last syllable.

Not all words are pronounced the same way within the region. An example of this is the word 'often.' Some people say all of the letters, others ignore the 'T.'

Native-American Words

Most Native-American languages were spoken and had no alphabet for written language. When words were written for the first time, it was with the English alphabet. Therefore many words in the Northwest, and the United States, are spelled in ways that make them difficult to pronounce. For examples, Sequim, WA; Yaquina, OR.; and Yachats, OR. Native-American words are pronounced, in many cases, with no emphasis on any syllable.

Don't be worried. Maintain a sense of humor as you travel and learn how the locals pronounce things. Of course some people will laugh at your speech, but just laugh along with them.

Idioms and Colorful Conversation

Americans frequently incorporate sports analogies in their daily conversation. These analogies are usually based in American sports such as American football, baseball, and basketball. You will hear such references in radio and TV programs, at work, or as your children play.

In the work environment people use words such as 'team' (meaning the people you work with), 'coaching' (a way of giving advice), or phrases such as 'ballpark figure' (an estimation of cost).

In daily conversation, someone who is not thinking clearly is 'out in left field.' Someone who paid a low price on a purchase really 'scored.'

Americans also make up words using references to well-known historical events or people. As many of these events have not been broadcast outside the United States, you will rightfully find them confusing. Sometimes these references are drawn from political experience. For example, any presidential crisis is a '(something)-gate' (an example is the phrase 'Monica-gate' in 1998). The reference to 'gate' is from the 1970's, when the Watergate Hotel was part of a scandal that resulted in President Nixon resigning from office.

Acronyms

Americans like to shorten terms. An acronym means that only the first letter of each word in a phrase is used. Some examples are words such as OK (meaning everything is fine), or OJ (meaning orange juice). The word snafu has become a real word (meaning a problematic situation), but it was an acronym for the phrase 'Situation Normal, All Fouled Up' (first used in World War II). NATO, IQ, MPH, LASER, and FBI all are acronyms.

You will see the phrase ASAP (meaning as soon as possible) or COD (cash on delivery). Some businesses have made their names into acronyms instead of using the entire title. This can be confusing if competitors have similar acronyms. The U.S.P.S. (United

States Postal Service) or UPS (United Parcel Service) could be easily confused.

There is a list at the end of this chapter that contains some commonly used acronyms and abbreviations. It is by no means complete. If you find an acronym that you can not translate easily, go to the website www.acronymfinder.com for help.

Abbreviations

Americans also use abbreviations (which are short forms of words). In some cases there are several ways to abbreviate!

Monday	M, or Mon.
Tuesday	T, or Tues.
Wednesday	W, or Wed.
Thursday	Th, Thu., or Thurs.
Friday	F, or Fri.
Saturday	S, or Sat.
Sunday	S, or Sun.

Slang

Americans have a tendency to shorten the words for many popular things. They also give new meanings and connotations to common words. At a coffee shop, an order for a simple cup of decaffeinated coffee with low-fat milk can involve words not normally associated with coffee: 'short, skinny, decaf, latte.' Do not be afraid to explain to the clerk that you do not understand.

Global Influence

English is an evolving language. The combination of immigration and international travel bring new words to the United States that become a part of everyday usage. In some cases, words are pronounced the same in English as they are in another language, but because of different alphabets, they are spelled differently. A few common examples of this are sushi, baklava, and chai. In some cases words are spelled the same as in a foreign language but pronounced with a definite American twist. An example of this is croissant.

Places to Go for English Classes

Adults

The universities and colleges in Portland offer many programs to assist adults in mastering English. Regardless of your native language, it is possible to take classes to improve your command of English.

Portland State University has a program called 'Intensive English Language Program' (IELP). This program offers a variety of courses to prepare students for academic classes at United States universities and colleges. Full time and part time students may attend classes given at five levels of instruction, ranging from entry level to advanced. Each level has core classes in grammar, reading, writing, and speaking/listening. The advanced level will prepare you to take the TOEFL test, which is required of non-native English speakers, for admission into universities and colleges. Contact IELP at Portland State University locally at 503-725-4088 (or elsewhere in the United States 800-547-8887 extension 4088). Or you can explore the process on the internet at www.pdx.edu.

Language Schools

Portland Community College offers free classes at its area campuses for persons whose native language is not English; these classes are part of its Basic Skills Program. Call the program at 503-788-6111 to find out about this option or visit www.pcc.edu.

There are private English tutors with whom you can work. There are also schools with language as their only focus.

[For more information on the TOEFL and the TSE examinations visit the website at www.toefl.org. Refer to Chapter 9, 'Education', for a discussion of these two examinations and local resources for them.]

Children

The public schools in Oregon and Washington offer special language training classes for children who are not native English speakers. Not all school districts offer ESL classes in every school. In some cases, students travel outside of their neighborhood to attend ESL classes. In all cases the ESL assistance in provided free of charge.

Some school departments will offer classes in a second language (Hillsboro offers science and math classes in Spanish). Some school departments have special educators who are trained to teach science and math in English as a second language. Some departments separate the ESL students into special classes for half-day and then have them be a part of regular classes for the rest of the day. It depends on the age of the child, the school system, and the numbers of ESL students within the school. Because each school department handles the ESL classes in a different way you will need to ask about the ESL program which is offered specifically for your child's age group. You should anticipate that your child will be evaluated for language skills and placed in a class which is appropriate to his/her skills.

The Beaverton School District has an ESL Welcome Center at 11375 SW Center Street. It is open from 8 a.m. to 4 p.m. weekdays. The phone number there is 503-672-3715. This center is a place where people with ESL needs are matched with interpreters who can assist in enrolling children in the local schools. Beaverton offers ESL classes in all of its schools. It also offers ESL training for adults.

Beaverton Public Schools Welcome Center	503-672-3715
Gresham Public Schools ESL Program	503-618-2462
Hillsboro Public Schools ESL Program	503-647-3827
Portland Public Schools ESL Program	503-916-5840
Tigard Public Schools ESL Program	503-431-4029
Vancouver Public Schools ESL Program	360-696-5224

Translation Services

There are at least 30 translation services within the Portland area.

You can get assistance in personal, legal, and medical matters, as well as arrange for business based projects. In most cases you will be charged by the hour.

Translators

*

Interpreters

Acronyms - Abbreviations

Abbreviation / Acronym	Meaning
ACT	American College Test
A.M.	ante meridiem (before noon)
AM	Amplitude modulation (radio frequency)
ad	advertisement
Aka	Also known as
ASAP	As soon as possible
ATM	Automated Teller Machine
Ave.	Avenue
BLT	Bacon Lettuce and Tomato (favorite adult sandwich)
Blvd.	Boulevard
C.	Cups
CD	Certificate of Deposit (banking)
CD	Compact Disk (music)
CD	Civil Defense (government)
CIA	Central Intelligence Agency
COD	Cash on delivery
Copy	Photocopy
D.C.	District of Columbia
Dept.	Department
DEQ	Department of Environmental Quality (Oregon)
DMV	Division of Motor Vehicles (Oregon)
Dr.	Doctor
Dr.	Drive (as in street name)
DSL / ADSL	Digital signal line / asynchronous digital signal line
DST	Daylight saving time
EAD	Employment Authorization Document
Enc.	Enclosure (used in a business letter)
ESL	English as a second language
F, Fri.	Friday
F.	Fahrenheit
FAA.	Federal Aviation Administration
Fax	Facsimile
FBI	Federal Bureau of Investigation
FedEx	Federal Express
FM	Frequency modulation (radio)

Ft.	Feet
FYI	For your information
GED	General Education Development
GMT	Greenwich Mean Time
Hwy	Highway
I	Interstate freeway (as in I-84)
ID	Identification (card)
In.	Inches
Info	Information
INS	Immigration and Naturalizations Service
IQ	Intelligence Quotient
IRS	Internal Revenue Service
ISP	Internet service provider
ITIN	Individual Taxpayer Identification Number
L.	Liters
LASER	Light Amplification by Stimulated Emission Radiation
Lb.	Pounds
M, Mon.	Monday
M.	Miles
MAX	Metropolitan Access (the name of the Portland light-rail sytem)
M-F	Monday Through Friday
Mo.	Month
Mph	Miles per hour
Mt.	Mountain, Mount
NATO	North Atlantic Treaty Organization
NE	Northeast (section of the city)
NW	Northwest (section of the city)
OJ	Orange Juice
OK	Oll Korrect (a misspelling of All Correct)
OR	The state of Oregon
Oz.	Ounces
P.M.	Post meridiem (after noon)
PB and J	Peanut Butter and Jelly (favorite children's sandwich)
PC	Politically Correct
PDT	Pacific Daylight Time
PDX	Portland International Airport
Phone	Telephone
Photo	Photograph, picture
PIN	Personal Identification Number
PST	Pacific standard time

Pt.	Pints
Qt.	Quarts
SAT	Scholastic Assessment Test
S, Sat.	Saturday
SE	Southeast (section of the city)
SFO	San Francisco
Snafu	Situation normal all fouled up
SSA	Social Security Administration
SSN	Social Security Number
St.	Street
St.	Saint (as in Mt. St. Helens)
Sun.	Sunday
SW	Southwest (section of the city)
T, Th, Thurs.	Thursday
T, Tues.	Tuesday
Tbsp., Tb.	Tablespoon (recipe measurement)
TOEFL	Test of English as a Foreign Language
TSE	Test of Spoken English
Tsp.	Teaspoon (recipe measurement)
TV	Television
U.S.	United States
UPS	United Parcel Service
U.S.P.S.	United States Postal Service
W, Wed.	Wednesday
WA	The state of Washington
www	World wide web
Yd.	Yards
Yr.	Year

Financial Matters

Chapter 4

Financial Matters

The U.S. financial system is based on the dollar and its economy is based on credit. Many people have developed a reliance on using borrowed money for which they pay a fee, called interest. The view in your home country may be to spend only what you have. But, strange as it may seem, borrowing is encouraged in the United States.

In this chapter we will present information about managing your finances with a new form of currency, in a different culture. In order to participate in this credit economy, you will need to thoroughly understand the types of financial institutions, credit, loans, interest rates, and other financial matters.

Types of Financial Institutions

There are two types of financial institutions in the United States. The first type provides banking services to both individuals and businesses and is called a bank. The second type provides banking services only to individuals. This second type is called a credit union. Both offer a wide range of banking services, but they differ in how and to whom these services are provided.

Banks offer the largest number of services. They also have the strictest rules such as how much money is needed to open an account or the criteria to be met to qualify for a loan.

Credit unions generally offer lower rates and are more lenient with certain types of loans. Credit unions are organized for a group of people who have a common interest, such as teachers, technology workers, or members of a particular organization. If you fit the criteria, you may join that particular credit union and use its services. For example, the Portland Teachers Credit Union serves employees (and their spouses and children) of the Portland Public Schools. Some people can meet the membership criteria for several credit unions. Check with your company's human resources department or your school administration to see if you qualify for any credit unions. Often the name of the credit union will indicate the group being served. You can also call and directly ask a credit union about membership.

Banks
•
Credit Unions

The following is a list of area banks and credit unions, many having several branch locations. This is not a complete list. You can find a complete list in the yellow pages. Call the main telephone numbers to ask about their services and fees.

Banks

Bank of America	800-873-2632
Bank of the Northwest	503-417-8800
Bank of the West	800-488-2265
Centennial Bank	503-968-2121
Clackamas County Bank	503-668-5501
Continental Savings Bank	503-636-5013
Key Bank of Oregon	503-790-7690
Sterling Savings Bank	800-305-0078
U S Bank	800-875-6267
Washington Federal Savings	503-226-1300
Washington Mutual	800-756-8000
Wells Fargo	800-688-9100
West Coast Bank	503-224-4245
Western Bank	503-526-6631

Credit Unions

Columbia Community Credit Union	503-285-5110
Consolidated Federal Credit Union	503-323-8070
Oregon Central Credit Union	503-239-5338
Oregon Telco Credit Union	503-227-5571
Portland Teachers Credit Union	503-228-7077

Branches

Financial institutions usually have a headquarters and one or more branch banks. Branch banks should offer any transaction that the main headquarters can do, including opening accounts. You can bank at any bank branch location, regardless of where you originally opened your account.

Banking Services

Both banks and credit unions offer a wide variety of financial services such as savings accounts, checking accounts, loans, mortgages, lines of credit, currency conversion, travelers checks, and investment accounts.

Types of Accounts

The most common account to have is a checking account. This type of account allows you to use your money easily through a form of payment called a check. You can use checks to pay bills and make purchases in place of cash, provided there is money in your account.

A second type of account is a savings account. A savings account usually earns interest. You do not write checks against a savings account. You withdraw money by going to the bank and completing a withdrawal slip or writing a check to the bank. You can also withdraw money using an ATM. You can also transfer money between savings and checking accounts. This can be arranged to happen automatically if you overdraw your checking account. Credit unions require you to have a savings account (called your member account) in order to open a checking account.

Each financial institution may call accounts by different names and each type of account may have different rules regarding minimum balance requirements, rate of interest earned, federal insurance, etc. Most banks and credit unions offer a wide variety of savings programs. Shop around for the type of account that suits you. There are many hidden charges (such as fees for withdrawing your money or making inquiries about your account over the phone), so be sure you understand all the fees and rules before you apply for any account. It is easy to close an account and take your money to another bank if you are not satisfied.

Opening an Account

When you go to a bank to open an account, look for a sign that says 'New Accounts' or 'Information.' Do not stand in line waiting to speak to someone behind the large counter. These are the bank tellers and they can help you with transactions once your account is established, but will direct you to someone else to open your account. To open an account you complete an application (at a credit union you pay a one-time membership fee, usually around $5), and show two pieces of identification (I.D.). One form must have a photo, such as a passport or driver's license. The second form can be a major credit card, resident alien card, or a piece of mail with your address on it, such as a utility bill. You will also need to deposit some amount of money in your account.

Checking Accounts

Checking accounts allow you easy access to cash and simplify bill paying. A check is a piece of paper that can be used like cash. Your checks will have your name and address printed on them, along with your financial institution and account information. When you wish to pay for a product or service, you write the name of the person or company you are paying (the payee), the amount, and the date on the check, sign it, and give it to the payee. This is the most common method of paying bills by mail since it is not acceptable to send cash. Checks will be ordered for you when you open your checking account.

Bank number   Check Number

Your name	**1002**
Your address	24-450
Your telephone number	1234
Your driver's license number	

DATE _____ (Month / Day / Year)

PAY TO THE ORDER OF   (To whom the check is being written) $ | Amount of the check written in numbers |

(Amount of the check written in words)   DOLLARS

MEMO   (Note to yourself about the expenditure)

Bank name
Bank address   (Your Signature)

⑆123404500 ⑆ 1234567890 ⑈ 1002

Bank Number   Check Number

Your Account Number

Sample Check

When you pay by check at a store or restaurant, they will commonly ask for identification, such as a driver's license or check guarantee card. If they ask for a second form of I.D. you can use a credit card or your passport. The clerk will also ask if the address on the check is your current address and will ask for your phone number. Some people chose to have their phone number and/or driver's license number printed on the checks for convenience.

A 'bad check' is also called a bounced or returned check.

A bad check is one for which there is no money in the account. When a bad check is written, the account is said to be overdrawn. Some stores and restaurants do not accept checks because of the risk of bad checks. These businesses will generally have a sign posted stating they do not accept checks.

Check Guarantee Cards

When you open your account, some banks will give you an identification card. This is known as a check guarantee card. It does not have your picture on it, but its purpose is to be used as a form of I.D. to guarantee that your check is good. Some banks do not offer a check guarantee card but your debit card can serve this purpose.

Depositing or Cashing Checks

A two-party check is a check payable to one person, who then endorses the back of the check, payable to someone else.

When you receive a check as payment you can cash the check or deposit it in an account at your bank. Either way you will need to endorse the check by signing the back of it in the space indicated for check endorsements. Endorsing a check means to make a check payable to a bank or someone else. A check must always be endorsed before it can be exchanged for cash, deposited to an account, or used as payment. As a precaution, you may wish to write, "Pay to the order of [your bank]" along with your signature, or better yet, wait until you are at the bank before endorsing it. An endorsed check is almost as good as cash.

Before bringing your endorsed check to the teller or ATM, you will need to fill out a deposit slip. These can be found behind the checks in your checkbook, or in the lobby of the bank. They are simply a form that the bank uses to record how much is being deposited, and to which account. With an endorsed check and a completed deposit slip, your bank will cash or deposit the check. If you try to cash a 'two-party check' at a place other than your bank, you will be denied or charged a fee.

Sample Deposit Slip

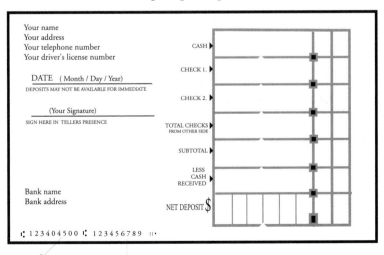

49

Overdraft Protection

Your bank may offer a service called overdraft protection. With overdraft protection, if you write a check when there is not enough money in your checking account, the bank will still honor the check. You will automatically be given a short-term loan. This is called a line of credit. This is a nice feature and particularly helpful if you are waiting for funds to arrive from overseas, but there is a charge for this service. Check with your financial institution on interest rates and service fees.

Debit cards are also called PIN cards, ATM cards, check cards, or some other name. PIN stands for Personal Identification Number.

Without overdraft protection, if you write a bad check (one that the bank will not pay due to your lack of funds), it will be returned to the store. A business will charge you around $25 for the bad (also called bounced) check and you will still owe the business for the amount of the check. Your bank will add returned check charges as well. **Do not write checks without sufficient funds.**

Debit Cards

A popular feature of U.S. banking is the debit card. You may arrange to get a card when you open your account, at which time you will also be asked to choose a four-digit PIN code. Many businesses, particularly grocery stores and discount department stores, have PIN machines available. You use the machine by swiping the card yourself and keying in your PIN code. The amount of your purchase is automatically deducted from your checking account. The card can also be used like a credit card if it is marked with a Visa or MasterCard symbol, in which case it is accepted in most businesses and restaurants. The important difference between a debit card and a credit card is that when a debit card is used, the money is taken out of your account immediately.

A check is said to be cleared when the bank has received the check and takes the money out of your account.

Account Statements

Account statements are usually mailed on a monthly basis. They list all the transactions (arranged by date), bank charges, interest earned, and the balance of each of your accounts. These are free. If you want to receive them more frequently, there will be an extra charge.

Banking by Telephone

Most financial institutions allow you to inquire about your account balance, checks that have been paid (cleared), and other transactions over the telephone. You can also transfer money between accounts and pay bills by telephone. Banking by telephone is usually an automated service controlled by your telephone keypad. It will require your PIN or other secure access code for security reasons.

Banking by ATM

(See discussion below on Automatic Teller Machines.)

Banking by Internet

Many financial institutions offer the option of maintaining your accounts online. You can access your accounts directly from your bank's website, view the latest balances and transactions, transfer funds between accounts, and download account information into your personal accounting software.

You can also authorize the payment of bills, either directly at the bank's website, or with your own software. After your bank receives your authorization, they will print a check to the payee and mail it to the address you specify. The average cost per transaction is $0.25. The advantage of banking by Internet is that you can pay bills and manage your accounts from anywhere in the world.

Automatic Bill Payment through the Payee

Many financial institutions support automatic payment of bills to some businesses. Utilities (telephone, gas, electric, cable, water), credit card companies, schools, and fitness centers are a few of the types of businesses which offer the service of billing your bank directly. You make arrangements with, for example, the telephone company. At a specific date each month, the amount of your telephone bill is withdrawn from your bank account. To set this up, you complete a form supplied by the telephone company and send it to them with a deposit slip, which gives them the necessary bank information. You receive a copy of the bill each month, prior to payment. You can stop a particular payment or cancel the service completely at any time. This is a useful service, particularly if you travel and want the assurance that your regular monthly bills are paid.

Bank by Mail

Any financial institution will allow you to bank by mail. This service is most commonly used for mailing deposits and paying loans.

Other Services

Banks and credit unions offer a variety of services including currency conversion, traveler's checks, a range of savings services, safe deposit boxes, money market accounts, investment counseling, and retirement planning. These services are not provided at all branches.

Banking Hours and Holidays

In general, financial institutions are open 9:00 a.m. to 5:00 p.m. Monday through Friday. A few branch banks may be open Saturday mornings. They are closed on all Federal Holidays (refer to Chapter 15, 'Holidays').

Automatic Teller Machines (ATMs)

ATMs are everywhere. You can find them in (or just outside of) banks, grocery stores, convenience stores, restaurants, shopping malls; anywhere you might need cash. These machines allow you to do a variety of transactions including withdrawing cash, making deposits, transferring funds between accounts, and inquiring on account balances.

You access the ATM with your debit card. Your bank is part of one or more banking systems, which allows you to access your account information through an ATM. To know if a particular ATM is part of a system that your bank uses, you can compare the bank system symbols displayed on or around the ATM machine with those symbols appearing on your Debit card. ATM symbols include but are in no way limited to: Pulse®, Pulse Pay®, Instant Cash®, The Exchange®, Accel®, Interlink®, MasterCard®, Star®, Cirrus®, Global Access®, and Maestro®. One Portland area ATM suggests trying any card. In addition to the proper ATM card, you will need to know your four-digit PIN code.

Bank Specific ATMs

If your bank (determined by the large sign prominently displayed above the ATM stating the bank affiliation) provides a machine, then you can use the ATM at no charge. In addition, you can make deposits.

If a machine is not managed by your bank and the machine accepts your card, you can use the ATM to make withdrawals, but not deposits. You will probably be charged a fee by the ATM and possibly by your bank. Any ATM fees will be deducted from your account and will appear on your next bank statement. ATMs are required by law to inform you of the fee you will be charged, although this does not include any fees your bank may charge. Ask your bank to clearly explain their fees.

ATM Instructions

Most Portland ATMs offer instructions in English and Spanish. Each ATM is slightly different. Read the instructions carefully to know which buttons are for which responses.

You will be given the following instructions or questions:

Enter your PIN code.

Are you making a deposit, withdrawal, fund transfer, or account inquiry?

Which account would you like to use: checking, savings, or other?

Do you want another transaction?

Safety tips for using the ATM.

Protect the secrecy of your pin code. Do not give anyone your pin code. Do not write your pin code down or keep it in your wallet; memorize it. If you forget your pin code, call your bank. Do not use an obvious code like your birthday, street address, or telephone number. Change your pin code from time to time. Above all, do not write your pin code on your debit card.

Keep your debit card in a safe place such as your wallet or purse, as you would cash. Do not lend your card to anyone.

Be aware of your surroundings when approaching or using an ATM. Shield the keypad when you enter your PIN code to prevent others from seeing it.

Do not accept offers of help with your ATM transaction.

Take your receipt with you or tear it up and throw it away.

(ATM instructions continued)

Be careful using an ATM at night or in an isolated area. Park your car near the ATM in a well-lit area. If the ATM is dark or you feel uneasy, choose another ATM. Have your debit card ready before you reach the ATM so you do not have to reach into your purse or wallet.

If someone threatens you and demands your cash and card, do what they ask. Then report the theft to the police. Robberies rarely occur at ATMs in Portland.

If your card is lost or stolen, report it immediately to the police and your financial institution. The telephone number to call is written on the back of your card Therefore, write this telephone number down in a safe place since you will not have it when the card is missing. When you delay in reporting a lost or stolen card, you will continue to be liable for expenditures. Reporting it as early as possible will save you money.

ATMs for International Residents

ATMs can be particularly useful for you if your home country bank is part of an international system recognized here, such as Cirrus. It allows you to withdraw funds and check balances with your own bank whether it is in another part of the United States or in your home country. In addition, it may be one of the easiest and least expensive ways to convert your home currency to U.S. dollars. It is fast and you are usually not charged a conversion fee. The ATM fee for international transactions is slightly higher, but is still, by far, the least expensive way to bank. Some experts say that the currency conversion rates offered through an ATM are the most favorable.

Credit Cards

A credit card is a banking service that allows you to receive a single monthly bill for all purchases and services you pay with the card. You then must pay at least the minimum amount due and are charged interest on the remainder of your balance. Fiscally responsible individuals will pay the entire amount owed each month, thereby never paying any finance charges.

The major commercial credit cards recognized in the United States are MasterCard, Visa, American Express, and Discover Card. Banks offer Visa or MasterCard. Ask your financial institution which one it offers, and be sure to compare the interest rate and annual fee with cards offered by other financial institutions. Your bank may have a special offer on one of these cards for non-U.S. customers. In selecting a financial institution, one of your criteria may need to be that they will approve you for a major credit card.

Credit card application forms can be found where ever that credit card is accepted. This applies to Master Card and Visa as well; your bank is not the only source for these two cards. Financial institutions throughout the United States market their cards across the country. Many offer no annual fee, airline miles, or low interest rates. The difficulty may be in finding one that accepts non-Americans. Look on the Internet, ask international friends for the name of their credit card company, call different banks to ask about their approval policies, or pick up an application at a bank or store and submit it. It is possible you will need to establish an U.S. credit rating before you will be granted a credit card in the United States

One other option, if you are having difficulty getting approved for a credit card, is ONE CREDIT (888-339-7818). This credit card company advertises aggressively and offers a secured line of credit. You pay a specified amount, which is then held on deposit for you. They will give you a MasterCard or Visa with a matching line of credit. After a period of time, as you demonstrate your ability to make timely payments, your line of credit will be increased. You can then qualify for other credit cards that have more favorable terms.

Many stores offer their own credit cards and may have more lenient approval guidelines. Target, Nordstrom's, Meier & Frank, and Sears all offer credit cards. Although we do not encourage you to get yourself heavily indebted, a history of timely credit card payments can boost your U.S. credit rating.

A line of credit is a specified amount of money that a bank is willing to lend to you. You are not given the money outright. Instead you draw on the money as you need it, through a credit card or by check.

Transferring Money

Wiring Funds

Money Orders

You can have money wired to your U.S. bank account from your home country account through your home country bank. You can also do it through a money order service. For any wire transfer, you will need to provide the name of your bank, the amount to be wired, and your signature. The cost ranges from about $20 to $50.

American Express no longer wires money from inside the United States, although American Express offices outside the United States offer this service. Moneygram was the service previously used by American Express. They can be reached at 800-926-9400 (for service in Spanish the number is 800-955-7777) to find a local office.

Western Union also serves this area. Call 800-325-6000 or 800-325-4045 (Spanish) to find a local office.

Cashing Checks on a Foreign Bank

Many banks will cash checks drawn on overseas banks. Some may charge a fee. If you are a new customer, your account may not be credited with the check amount until after the check has cleared.

Cash Advance on Your Credit Card

Banks and some hotels will give you a cash advance on your credit card. There is a fee for this and you will be charged interest daily on the amount borrowed beginning immediately.

ATM Withdrawals

You can use the debit card from your home country bank to withdraw cash as discussed above under ATMs.

Loans

Interest rates on loans vary with the type of loan. Car loans, home mortgages, and home improvement loans have varying rates. To apply for a loan you will need to fill out an application, state the reasons for the loan, and be able to demonstrate a good credit history. Credit unions tend to be more flexible when approving loans. You may be able to get a loan from a credit union, simply based on the security of funds in a savings account deposited with them. You may be able to get a loan if a friend or family member with a good U.S. credit rating will co-sign the loan. Putting a large sum down on a purchase is also helpful when asking to borrow the remainder. Co-signing and large down payments are particularly useful for obtaining car loans and home mortgages. Credit unions also may be generous with approving car loans. Some car dealerships are also quite lenient (for more information on buying a car, refer to Chapter 11, 'Local Transportation').

Your Credit Rating

The biggest problem to overcome as a non-American trying to participate in this credit-oriented economy is not having a credit rating. Generally lenders do not consider your credit history (savings accounts, loans, mortgages, or credit card payment history) from another country. Therefore it is necessary that you establish one in the United States. The simplest way to do this is to get a credit card and use it, being sure to always make your payments on time. Any credit card will do. The key is to show your ability to make timely payments.

If you are anxious to establish a credit rating in the shortest time possible and can qualify for membership at two different credit unions, here is an acceptable method of accelerating the process. Open an account with a credit union, placing $1000-$2000 (as much as you can afford to set aside) in a savings account. Then apply for a loan at this credit union, using the money in your savings account as collateral. (Usually a bank will not do this because it would need more than just the savings account collateral as the basis for the loan, but you can always ask.) The credit union will lend you something less than the full amount in your savings account. Take this money to a second credit union and place it in a savings account. Then take out a loan at this second credit union and deposit the proceeds in your checking account. Start paying off these loans from your checking account and be sure your payments are on time. Also, be sure that the credit unions will be reporting your payment history to a credit bureau. It will cost you some money in interest and membership fees at the two credit unions, but within 90 days you will have created a good credit history showing you have made timely payments on two different loans.

Credit Reports

There are nationwide credit reporting companies which maintain records on everyone in the United States who has ever had a bank account, made a purchase with a credit card, or taken out a loan. When you apply for a loan, the lender will order a credit report from one or more of these companies. Your records are referenced by social security number. If you do not have a social security number (refer to Chapter 13,

'Legal Concerns'), you cannot apply for a loan. The credit report will list any outstanding loans, late payments, defaulted loans, outstanding taxes, or any bankruptcy filings.

Maintaining a Bank Account in Your Home Country

It is a good idea to maintain a bank account in your home country. You may have ongoing expenses or a major credit card that will be paid out of your home bank. If your home country financial institution offers online or telephone banking services similar to those described above, these bills can be paid easily and in a timely manner.

Finding Your Home

Chapter 5

Finding Your Home

The Portland Metropolitan Area consists of numerous small communities. Each one has its own personality and caters to different lifestyles. Where you choose to live will make the difference between enjoying your new home or feeling isolated by it. If you have the option of living in temporary housing before you choose a new home, we recommend it. This will give you an opportunity to discover which areas of Portland you like. Finding the area that best suits you will be worth the time and effort, especially if you will be living here for a while.

Understanding Portland

Portland alone has over ninety official neighborhoods. The locals residents may call their neighborhood, or group of neighborhoods, by a different name than what you see on a map. It is often unclear where one neighborhood ends and another begins. When you overlay this with the variety of housing, shopping, and entertainment opportunities found within neighborhoods, it becomes impossible to describe any area completely and accurately. Real estate companies have excellent resources for this. In addition, we have listed area guidebooks in Chapter 16, 'More Information.'

This chapter begins with some basic geography, defines a few terms, and points out some features so that you can begin to find the area that best suits you and your family. Of course, nothing will replace taking a tour with a knowledgeable Portland resident or realtor.

Close-In and Further-Out

Some people like to live close to the city center in Portland. The neighborhoods that are close to the city center (under a ten minute drive) are known as close-in. These neighborhoods have many of the advantages of living downtown, yet have the charm of tree-lined streets, well-maintained, older homes with a yard, and often have a park close by.

You will hear the term 'suburbs' used to describe areas that are further-out from the downtown area. These residential neighborhoods on the edge of a city are also called bedroom communities, planned communities, or developments. They have the feeling of being both rural and urban. They are usually set apart from shopping and other services, and the roads tend to bend and form cul de sacs. This is in contrast to the grid pattern found in the older neighborhoods. In this chapter we will distinguish between neighborhoods close-in and those further-out.

Close-in means an area is within a ten minute drive to downtown Portland. Further-out means an area is greater than a ten-minute drive.

General Layout of the City

The Portland Metropolitan Area includes Multnomah, Washington, and Clackamas Counties and extends into the state of Washington to include the city of Vancouver in Clark County.

Portland itself is divided into east and west sections by the Willamette River. Burnside St., which runs east and west, divides the city further into north and south sections. This creates four sections or quadrants: Northwest (NW), Northeast (NE), Southeast (SE), and Southwest (SW). The NE quadrant is divided further. The Willamette River does not run perfectly straight north and south but bends toward the west at the north end of Portland. On the east bank and extending to Williams St. is a section known as North Portland. Some Portland resources include North Portland with NE; others consider North Portland separately.

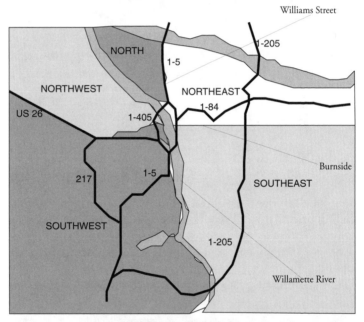

Address Locations in the Portland Area

In Portland, numbered streets stretch from the north to the south, parallel to the river. If you think of the river as 0 Ave., the numbered streets extend out on both sides of the river. Hence, NW 185th Ave. is near Hillsboro and NE 102nd Ave. is near the airport. Exceptions are close-in on either side of the river. On the east side, NE/SE 4th Ave. is called Martin Luther King, Jr. Blvd. (more easily referred to as MLK), a main one-way street running south. NE/SE 5th Ave. is called Grand Ave. and is a main one-way street running north. The other exception is in downtown where SW 7th Ave. is named Broadway and SW 8th Ave. is named Park.

Another notable feature is the order of the streets in the close-in NW area. Starting with Ankeney, one block south of Burnside, and heading north, the named streets are in alphabetical order; from Ankeney, Burnside, Couch, and Davis to Thurman, Upshur, Vaughn, and Wilson. The older neighborhoods laid out in a grid, such as this NW area, make it easy to get around in, especially when you know the named and numbered streets.

Finding a Home

What Are You Looking For?

As you explore the Portland area and what it has to offer, you need to think about your own needs and desires. What makes a place feel like home to you? Do you prefer old or new architecture, an apartment or a house? Do you want to live near work, near your child's school, near recreational areas, near shopping, or near a park? Do you like living in the city center with its easy access to restaurants and cultural activities, or out in the country? After you have answered these questions, drive around the residential areas you think fit your needs. If you would like more assistance in finding an area, ask a realtor or your relocation agent to take you on a tour of the city. Or ask colleagues at work, fellow students, acquaintances, or parents and teachers at your child's school where they chose to live and why. You may also find a Portland guidebook or other relocation literature helpful.

Matching Portland Neighborhoods and Your Lifestyle

In this section we make some generalizations regarding how your lifestyle might fit with the various types of communities found in Portland. Our comments may reflect our own biases or may represent generally accepted attitudes. We are not sure. Regardless, we hope you find it useful if it at least gets you started asking the right questions.

Home During the Day?

If you or your partner are planning to be home during the day and are hoping to meet other people who are doing the same, you may want to choose a neighborhood with older homes near an eclectic shopping district. These tend to attract residents with a mix of ages and the nearby shopping encourages residents to interact. The NW 23rd area has desirable living spaces with many old Victorian homes converted to apartments and condominiums. It also has one of the most popular and unique shopping areas in Portland, including a great selection of restaurants. NE Portland (particularly around Lloyd, the NE Broadway shopping district, and Hollywood areas) and SE Portland (notably, Sellwood, Hawthorne, and Belmont areas) have coffee shops where people tend to gather and a variety of shops for browsing.

Eclectic means a wide range of styles.

☞ **A condominium (or condo) is an apartment, or portion of a converted home, which you own. You share in the ownership of the common areas of the building and pay a monthly fee for upkeep. Duplexes are two, single-family dwellings under one roof.**

Single or Couple?

If you are in the United States alone or as a couple with no children, you may not want the added responsibility of a home and yard. Condominiums allow home ownership without the hassle of maintaining the property, which frees up your time to enjoy Oregon's recreational offerings or pursue other interests. Condominiums, particularly in the downtown area, tend to attract working couples or individuals who are not likely to be at home during the day. Condominiums and apartments can be found just about anywhere in the city. Apartment complexes, many with pools and fitness facilities are common. Note that the ones further-out in NE are closer to Mt. Hood and the Columbia River Gorge, while those on the west side are closer to the coast.

A yard refers to the whole property surrounding the home (broken down further into front yard, back yard, and side yard). A garden refers to any area that has flowers or bushes.

Rowhouses or duplexes are a compromise between an apartment or condominium and a single family home. Maintenance is limited, yet a small garden may be available for you to work or relax in. Rowhouses are becoming more common, as more are being built throughout the city. For now, they are most commonly found in John's Landing, and the NW 23rd area. You can find a duplex just about anywhere.

Family?

Families tend to locate near schools. Goose Hollow is the closest single family home neighborhood to downtown. It is also close to the International School. Newer homes, such as those found in the newer neighborhoods of NW and SW tend to attract families with dual incomes. More modest homes, usually found in older neighborhoods may find the mother or father home during the day and children home after school.

Other Considerations?

Older Neighborhoods

The character of a neighborhood is also determined by the layout of the streets. Some people feel the grid pattern, smaller blocks, and narrow streets of so many older Portland neighborhoods make it easier to meet people. Homes are closer together, kids are playing basketball in the street, and people are walking their dogs, working in their front yards, or sitting on their front porches. Irvington (NE), Alameda (NE), Laurelhurst (NE), Mt. Tabor (SE) are examples of this. Ladd's Addition, a planned community in SE built between 1910 and 1925 has a unique spoked-wheel layout with a park at its center and four other parks strategically placed around it. Residents there like the cozy feel of this neighborhood and tend to remain there. One other point to consider, if you are thinking of moving into an older neighborhood, is that older homes often have the disadvantage of needing more maintenance than newer homes.

A cul de sac is a residential street that is closed at one end and widened to fit several houses that sit in a semi-circle. This forms a cluster of homes and restricts traffic.

Newer Neighborhoods

Newer neighborhoods generally have wider streets and cul de sacs forming pockets of four or five homes. The houses are designed with outdoor living spaces in the back yard and little or no front porch area, which can limit the cozy, intimate feeling of a neighborhood. This does not mean these residents are any less friendly, only the opportunity for meeting neighbors may be less obvious. However, if the neighborhood is planned correctly, a nearby park can replace the front yard as the meeting place for neighbors. Forest Park, Bauer Woods, Hartung Farms, Bethany Estates, and Rock Creek are examples in NW. Neighborhoods around the communities of Happy Valley and Clackamas in SE, and Gladstone and West Linn to the south are seeing new growth. Developments in the SW communities of Tualatin, Tigard, and Beaverton continue to expand.

Walking to Shopping

Newcomers to the United States often remark on how large the houses are and how spread out the real estate is from town centers. You may be accustomed to walking or riding your bike to do shopping and other errands. Some areas of Portland can accommodate this, while other areas are too far away from shopping, or roads are too busy for walking or biking safely. Downtown, NW 23rd area, and areas immediately surrounding the smaller, eclectic shopping districts in NE and SE, are best suited for walking to shopping.

Downtown

Downtown is especially suited for people who like everything close by and enjoy walking to get there. Cultural events, art galleries, movie theatres, corporate offices, government buildings, diverse shopping, a wide variety of restaurants, nightlife, Chinatown, Saturday Market, Waterfront Park, the Central Library, Portland State University, and easy access to mass transit are all available in Portland's thriving downtown. The Pearl District area has condominiums, apartments, and lofts (warehouses converted to apartments). River Place is an area with condominiums near shops, hotels, an athletic club, and a marina. Goose Hollow has single-family homes and is near the International School. Easy access to public transportation options makes this the most convenient area if you do not have a car.

Public Transportation

If you will be relying on public transportation but want to live further out, you will need to determine the location of access points for the bus and light rail. You can not assume every residence is close to a bus or MAX stop (refer to Chapter 11, 'Local Transportation,' for route information).

Housing Styles

The architecture of Portland homes is a mix of Victorian, Tudor, Craftsman Bungalow, Portland Four-Square, Colonial, Contemporary, and Ranch, to name a few. They are mostly wood construction, with some brick and stucco. Foundations are made of stone, brick, poured concrete or cement block. Full or partial basements, houses built on

Victorian Style Home

Tudor Style Home

slabs of concrete, or concrete footings are all common. Roofs are most often made with composition shingles.

Portland is only 150 years old, so the oldest homes may not seem old compared to other parts of the world. The Victorian style homes were built between 1875 and 1910. Craftsman Bungalows, Portland Four-Square, Tudor, and Colonials appeared around 1900. Common (and costly) problems seen in these homes include the need to up-

Portland Four-Square Style Home

Colonial Style Home

Craftsman Bungalow Style Home

grade the plumbing, heating, and electrical systems, water damage due to leaking foundations, repairing sash windows, and dry-rot of exterior wood trim and siding. Exposed asbestos must be removed or contained and requires careful handling. Many people choose to remodel older homes, trying to keep within the original style of the home and neighborhood. They enjoy living in an older neighborhood but want the modern conveniences of an updated house.

Ranch style homes were built in the 1950's and 60's and the Contemporary style homes followed in the 1970's.

Most new construction in close-in areas consists of the renovation of commercial buildings for mixed use (shops, services, and living spaces in one building), apartments, or condominiums. New homes are built in neighborhoods found further-out.

Ranch Style Home

Contemporary Style Home

Surrounding Cities and Townships

Portland Metropolitan Area

Portland itself is located in Multnomah County. By most definitions, the Portland Metropolitan area encompasses Multnomah, Washington and Clackamas Counties. The map below shows the boundaries of these three counties, as well as others in Oregon and Washington that are within easy traveling distance of downtown Portland.

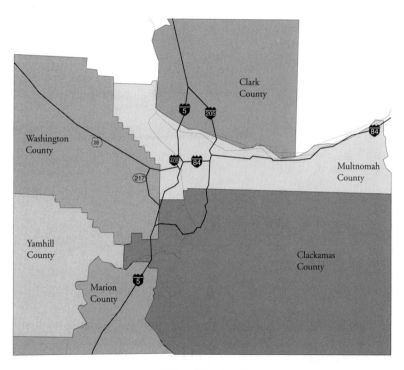

Metropolitan Counties

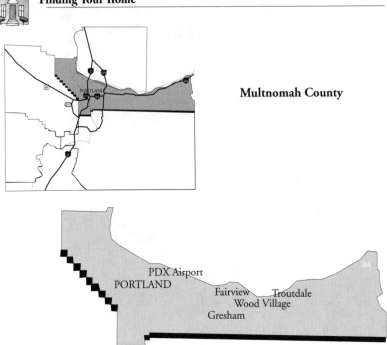

Multnomah County

Multnomah County

Gresham is the eastern end of the MAX line and is the fastest growing area in Multnomah County. It is home to Mt. Hood Community College. Troutdale, Fairview, and Wood Village are just to the north.

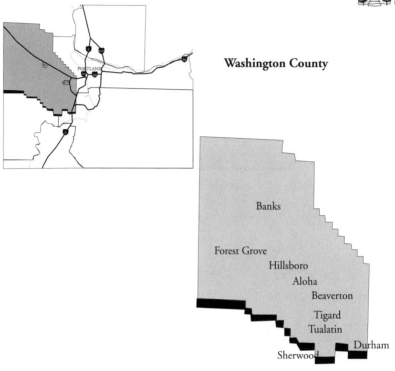

Washington County

Beaverton is a fast-growing area with an abundance of new construction, shopping, and businesses spread throughout, and a wide range of housing options. Hillsboro is the site of many hi-tech corporations and less expensive housing. Aloha, Forest Grove, Banks, Sherwood, Durham, Tualatin, and Tigard (with Washington Square Mall) are all communities found in Washington County.

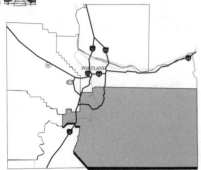

Clackamas County

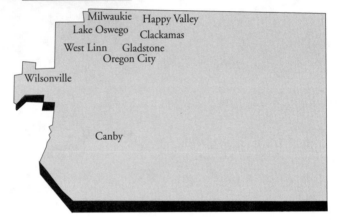

Milwaukie Happy Valley
Lake Oswego Clackamas
West Linn Gladstone
Oregon City
Wilsonville

Canby

Clackamas County

Milwaukie is a mix of residential, commercial, and industrial areas just south of the eclectic neighborhoods in SE Portland, yet close to the suburban shopping and growth of the Clackamas area. Lake Oswego is a very popular location offering lake front properties, moderate to very high priced homes, parks, golf courses, hiking trails, and water sports. Further south are West Linn, Gladstone, and Oregon City. Lake Oswego is home to Marylhurst College. These communities are fast growing and have good schools. Happy Valley and Clackamas are near the Clackamas Town Center shopping mall.

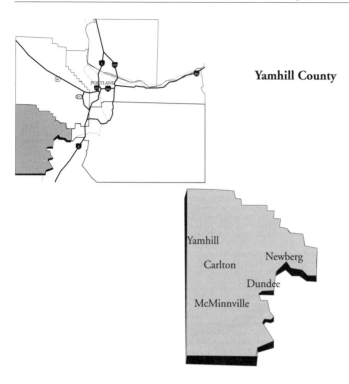

Yamhill County

Yamhill County

Yamhill County to the southwest of Portland is where you will find Newberg, Dundee, Yamhill, Lafayette, Carlton and McMinnville.

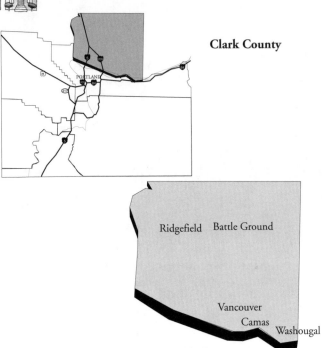

Clark County

Ridgefield   Battle Ground

Vancouver
Camas
Washougal

Clark County, Washington

Vancouver is about a 20-minute drive from downtown Portland (except during rush hour). Neighborhoods include Arnada, Lincoln, and Cascade Park. The ages of houses ranges from over one hundred years old in Arnada, to those built in the 1960's and 1970's in Lincoln, to Cascade Park, a development popular with families looking for newer homes. There is no state income tax in Washington, and property taxes are lower than in Portland. However, residents must have a Washington driver's license, which is considerably more expensive than Oregon, and there is state sales tax in Washington. If you work in Oregon and live in Washington you must pay Oregon state income tax.

Renting versus Buying

The single most important factor in deciding whether you will be renting or buying is how long you plan on living in the United States. If you are planning to stay less than three years, it is often better to rent. A home is a large investment and cannot always be sold easily, if the need arises.

Renting gives you flexibility. It is relatively easy to move out of an apartment or rental house and you do not have the responsibility of repairs and capital maintenance.

Renting is also called leasing.

The advantages of owning a home are that you are not having to deal with a landlord and you may realize tax benefits. You are free to make choices about how to make the house more livable and there is a feeling of comfort when living in your own home. If you are paying U.S. income tax, the mortgage interest is deductible.

Renting

Newspaper want ads. Ads for houses and apartments for rent appear in the real estate section of the newspaper everyday, listed by location.

Rent amount per month   *Features*

> FOR RENT. 1 BD. $495. frplc. off str prk. bkyd. W&D avail. no pets, no smoking. nr park. NE. 777-7777

Contact Information   *Restrictions*   *Describes location or gives address*

1 Bedroom Apartment For Rent
777-7777

Basic information on the rental

Contact this phone number for more information

For Rent signs posted on property. Drive around the neighborhoods you are interested in and write down phone numbers. Large apartment buildings may have an office where you can stop in to inquire of vacancies. For houses for rent, it is best to call the telephone number on the sign and make an appointment.

Ad: abbreviation for advertisement.

Real estate magazines. Listings of properties for rent in a magazine format can be found in the front of grocery stores and other shops. These publications come out once a week or twice a month and are free.

Property Management Companies. These companies are hired by owners of properties that are being rented. They handle all areas of renting, from finding rentors to collecting rent and doing repairs. Each property management company has their own list of rental properties to offer you.

Property Managment

Relocation Service

Relocation Services. Your employer may provide you with a relocation service to help you in all areas of your move to Portland; you can also hire one privately. Some services are part of a larger real estate firm; others will introduce you to a real estate company.

Human Resources Department. Your employer may recommend a property management company or relocation service to help you find rental housing.

Rental Application

The owner or manager of a rental property is called a landlord.

After you have looked at a house or apartment and say you are interested, the landlord will ask you to complete an application form. There is often a fee of approximately $30 to process the application. The landlord will use the information you supply on this form to verify your financial standing with your bank, and verify your income and employment with your employer. They will also request a credit report to review your credit history (refer to Chapter 4, 'Financial Matters').

Upfront Payments

If your application is approved, you will be asked to pay a security deposit and the first month's rent. Some landlords may ask for the last month's rent as well. A security deposit can range from $0 to more than one month's rent. It is refundable at the time you move out, provided the apartment is in good condition.

Apartment versus a House

When deciding whether to rent an apartment or a house, you may want to consider how much time you will be spending at home. A house will require more maintenance on your part. You may be required to take care of the lawn or may be responsible for a larger share of the utilities. If you enjoy being at home, appreciate your own yard, and generally like your privacy, renting a home may be a good option for you.

Furnished versus Unfurnished

Apartments and homes will come either furnished or unfurnished. Furnished apartments come with furniture, kitchen items, and maybe even bed linens and towels. These are more expensive than similar unfurnished apartments.

Other Costs

Landlords may or may not allow pets. Some will charge an extra fee or increase your security deposit if you have pets. Parking may be available adjacent to the building, on the street, or in a covered parking garage. This may cost extra. It is common to be required to pay for monthly gas, electricity, telephone, and cable television expenses while the owner will pay for garbage service, sewer, and water costs. Arrangements vary regarding who is responsible for which utilities.

Leases

You may be asked to sign a lease (a contract that says you agree to rent the apartment or home for a specified period of time). You may be allowed to go month-to-month, which simply means you are not bound by a contract, but usually required to give a month or two notice in advance of when you will move out. Be sure you understand all of the terms before you sign anything. Be particularly mindful of how much notice you need to give when you want to move, or if you can get out of a lease under certain circumstances (for example, if you are suddenly called back to your home country).

Renter's Insurance

It is recommended you have renter's insurance, which you can purchase through an insurance agent. This will protect your personal property in case of fire, theft, vandalism, or damage caused by certain types of weather.

Insurance

Inspection with the Landlord

Before you move in, take a tour of the apartment or home with the landlord. Note any existing damage so that everyone agrees on its condition when you move in. This will insure that any previous damage is not blamed on you when you move out, thus protecting the return of your security deposit.

Buying a Home

How to Find Homes for Sale or Rent

Real Estate

Realtor. These professionals know the real estate market, neighborhoods, and school districts and have access to all properties for sale. Realtors are affiliated with real estate companies. Some real estate companies are large, nation-wide organizations. Others are small, local firms. The most important thing is that you are comfortable working with your realtor.

Most people find a realtor through a friend or co-worker. You can find realtors listed in the Yellow Pages. They also advertise in the housing section of the Oregonian. Yellow pages and newspaper advertisements will list the real estate companies' web site addresses, which allows you to look at properties for sale by area and price range at your leisure. You can also learn about the real estate companies' services and office locations on these web sites. You may find a realtor you like at an open house or one that is listed on a For Sale sign. If you are working with a relocation company, they can also connect you with a realtor.

Most people use a realtor to find a home because they are a great resource. There is usually no cost to using a realtor. They know the rules of buying and selling real estate, can help with writing offers of sale, negotiating the sale, and finding financing. Although someone selling his home will chose a particular realtor to work with, all realtors have the same list of homes for sale.

Newspaper want ads. Ads for homes, condos, apartments, land, etc., for sale or rent appear in the real estate section of the newspaper everyday, listed by location. A special Housing section of the Sunday newspaper features neighborhoods and the real estate companies include special listings of their homes. 'Open Houses' will also be advertised. An open house is an opportunity to walk through a home for sale without having an appointment or having to go with a realtor. The listing realtor will be there to answer questions. Open houses are usually held on Sundays. You can drive around in your favorite neighborhoods looking for open house signs.

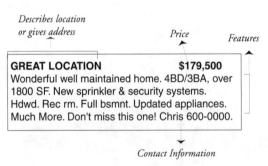

Describes location or gives address

Price

Features

> **GREAT LOCATION**   **$179,500**
> Wonderful well maintained home. 4BD/3BA, over
> 1800 SF. New sprinkler & security systems.
> Hdwd. Rec rm. Full bsmnt. Updated appliances.
> Much More. Don't miss this one! Chris 600-0000.

Contact Information

For Sale or For Rent signs posted on property. Drive around the neighborhoods you are interested in and write down phone numbers. As a courtesy, you should call first to make an appointment to see the inside of the house or apartment unless it is during an open house.

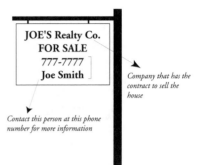

JOE'S Realty Co.
FOR SALE
777-7777
Joe Smith

Company that has the contract to sell the house

Contact this person at this phone number for more information

Real estate magazines. Listings of properties for sale or rent in a magazine format can be found in the front of grocery stores and other shops. These publications come out once a week or twice a month and are free.

Relocation services. Your employer may connect you with a relocation service to help you in all areas of your move. You may also hire one privately. Some relocation services will introduce you to an independent real estate company, other relocation services are part of a larger real estate firm.

Relocation Service

Human resources department. Your employer may recommend a property management company, relocation service, or real estate agent.

Working with a Realtor

Most people use a realtor to find a home. If you are not familiar with Portland, a good realtor can be helpful in showing you the various neighborhoods and explaining the complexities of what can be an overwhelming process. As you look at properties, in addition to pointing out the physical features of the house, the realtor can also tell you what public schools your children would be attending and the property taxes of the home.

A realtor is also called real-estate agent or simply agent. A real-estate broker can also work as an agent, but has had further certification. The listing agent is the realtor who is representing the seller.

Obviously, you need to have a good working relationship with your realtor. If your realtor does not take the time to find out what you are looking for, is showing you properties that do not fit your criteria, is not calling to show you properties, or if you are simply uncomfortable working with this particular realtor, find another one. Since realtors earn their money from the sale of a home, you, as a buyer, receive their service for no additional cost.

Multiple Listing Service (MLS)

A realtor has access to the multiple listing service, known as MLS. MLS lists all homes and condominiums for sale. This is the most complete list, since most homes for sale are not advertised in the newspaper. In addition the realtor can give you the addresses of homes listed so you can drive by to see if you like the neighborhood and the look of the house from the outside before making an appointment. The realtor will be able to arrange to see the inside of the house.

Qualifying the Buyer

The realtor will first ask you questions about what you want or do not want in a house and your price range. The realtor will use this information to show you only those properties that meet your criteria. The realtor may also discuss financing options with you, recommend a mortgage company or broker, and discuss the advantages of pre-qualifying or pre-approval for financing. This process is called qualifying the buyer. Your realtor wants to understand exactly what you are looking for, how serious you are about buying, and when you hope to buy.

Buyer/Broker Agreements

When you agree to work with a realtor, the realtor will ask you to sign a buyer/agency disclosure. This simply allows the realty company to represent you, but does not legally bind you to work with that realtor. You may wish to enter into an agreement called a buyer/broker agreement, which allows the realtor to protect your rights as your representative. If you feel at a disadvantage because you are making a large financial commitment in a country with which you are not completely familiar, this could be a very good option. Most realty companies offer buyer/broker agreements, although they will probably feel confident that they can, in good faith, keep your interests foremost even if the seller is paying the commissions. Note, however, that it appears real estate companies are moving toward requiring all buyers to sign buyer/broker agreements.

Making the Offer

After you have decided on a home, your realtor will help you write the offer that will be presented to the seller. An offer, also called an earnest money agreement, is a written document that lists all the terms of the purchase, which include the purchase price, items included with the home, repairs the seller needs to make, financing arrangements, etc. It will also list the dates when various things need to happen before the sale is complete. It is of utmost importance that this offer is written carefully since it becomes a legally binding contract if accepted by the seller.

Contingencies

A well written offer will include contingencies that will protect you financially in case the sale is not proceeding as you would like. A contingency is a condition that needs to be met before the transaction can continue. If the conditions you outline in the offer are not met, you are not obligated to buy the house. The two most common contingencies included in almost all offers are (1) the home passing inspection by you and/or a licensed inspector (usually seven days is allowed for this), and (2) that you, the buyer, obtain financing. The realtor will arrange the inspection.

The realtor can advise you, taking into consideration the market, the economy in the Portland area, and even the time of year, whether you should make a full price offer or something different than the asking price. The realtor should be able to show you recent selling prices of other comparable properties in the area. Other things to consider are zoning restrictions, easements, and/or restrictive covenants. Your realtor can explain these terms.

Finally, the offer should list any items you want to stay with the house so that there is no confusion. You need to be specific regarding appliances, window coverings, carpets, light fixtures, fireplace tools and screens, gas-grills, security systems, water conditioners, etc. The offer will also state how long the offer is good for, the anticipated closing date, and the date the house changes possession.

Earnest Money

The offer will also specify the amount of earnest money you wish to pay. Earnest money is the amount you will pay after all the contingencies in the offer have been met. This financially binds you to the agreement and shows the seller that you are sincerely interested in completing the transaction. The seller may take the house off the market (stop showing the house to other potentail buyers) at this time. After paying the earnest money, if you change your mind and no longer want to buy the house, the seller can keep the earnest money.

Escrow Account

The earnest money is placed in an account called an escrow account. This account is held by a third party, usually a title insurance company, until the closing so that there are no misunderstandings by either party regarding any part of this transaction. You will hear the term escrow used in other ways too, and those will be explained below.

Closing

The closing is a process in which all the papers are signed (and there are a lot of them), you will pay for the property, and the seller hands over the keys. It is very common for a third party to handle this transaction. This third party can be a real estate attorney, but more commonly is a representative of a title insurance company. The seller's real estate agent (called the listing agent) specifies which title insurance company will handle the closing, although both parties need to agree. You will probably go to the title insurance company to sign the papers. You will do this at a different time than the seller, so you may never meet. Closing usually occurs three to six weeks after making an offer on a house.

Title Insurance Companies

The title insurance company representative understands the financing arrangements and prepares and reviews the paper work to make sure everything is in order. Title insurance companies (also called escrow companies) do background checks on the property to make sure there are no problems (called liens and encumbrances) with the property that would prevent ownership changing hands.

Closing Costs

At the close of the sale, the seller pays the commissions of both his own and the buyer's realtor.

There are many closing costs. Here is a list of a few of them:

Loan origination fee	Title examination fee
Appraisal fee	Recording fee
Credit report fee	Flood certification
Property taxes	Environmental inspection fee
Inspection fee	Pest and dry rot inspection fee
Assumption fee	Hazard insurance
Closing or escrow fee	Flood insurance
Mortgage broker fee	Mortgage insurance
Processing fee	Title insurance

The title insurance representative will explain all these closing costs to you. They should also have been explained to you at the time you wrote the offer, along with an estimate of the dollar amount of these costs, either by your realtor or your lender.

Closing Costs Placed in Escrow

As mentioned before, an escrow account is used by a third party (in this case, the title insurance company) to hold money paid by the buyer before it is time to pay it to the seller. Two common payments made to escrow accounts are for property taxes and homeowner's insurance. These costs should have been explained to you as they are often lumped together and considered part of your mortgage payment.

Property Taxes

Once you own property you will receive a property tax bill annually. You have the option of paying the whole amount at one time or paying in installments. There is a discount offered to you if you pay the full amount by the due date. If you do not pay your property taxes, you will be fined.

Since the closing will rarely be on the date the taxes are due, taxes paid by the owner will be pro-rated for the portion of the year from the time of closing to the next tax due date. You will pay this amount at closing and it will be placed in an escrow account and paid to the county at the appropriate time. Your lender may also require that you pay a portion of your property taxes each month as part of your mortgage payment. This too, will be placed in the escrow account.

Homeowner's Insurance

Your mortgage lender will need proof from your insurance company that you will have homeowner's insurance at the time of closing. Your realtor can recommend an insurance agent. An insurance agent can explain the various features of a homeowner's insurance policy. The basics include: insurance on the home itself (referred to as the dwelling on an insurance policy) in case of theft, vandalism, fire, or other circumstances, your furnishings, clothes, etc. (referred to as personal property), and personal liability. The cost of insurance (paid annually) will depend on the value of these items mentioned above and the amount of the deductible. A deductible is the amount you pay before insurance will start paying on a claim.

Financing a Home Purchase

Buying a home is a large financial investment. Most Americans wish to fulfill 'The American Dream' of owning their own home, although it is increasingly difficult as housing costs increase. This purchase is generally done by taking out a home loan called a mortgage. The most important single factor in this process is being able to find someone who will lend you the money. Banks, mortgage companies, and mortgage brokers are most commonly used to finance home purchases. However, if you have your own source of funds in your home country, the only issue would be getting the money over to the United States. No seller will turn down cash but you must prove you have it. A bank account statement is acceptable during the beginning phases of the home buying process.

**Real Estate
Loans &
Contracts**

Finding a Lender

Your real estate agent may be able to suggest a lender. If you are working with a relocation company, they will be able to recommend lenders they have had experience with. Ask neighbors or colleagues if they can recommend a lender. Try the financial institution with which you bank. Look in the real estate section of the newspaper that lists lenders and the interest rates they offer on their loans. This may be a good place to start, however, just because they are in the newspaper does not mean they are reputable. The advertised interest rates may be different than what you are offered once you are in their office.

Types of Lenders

Banks. You do not have to have an account with a bank to get a mortgage, so you can apply for a loan at several different banks. However, a bank has many rules to follow regarding the financial and personal status of the people it lends to. Banks cannot be very flexible and if you do not fit well into the criteria imposed by them, you will not likely be approved for a loan. Banks can be more flexible with larger down payments.

Mortgage Companies. A mortgage company is a financial institution that is in the business of lending money for real estate transactions. Mortgage companies may have more flexibility than banks in approving loans because they get their money from a wider variety of sources. They will also have rules to follow which limit what they can do for a customer.

Mortgage Brokers. A mortgage broker is an independent person or company who specializes in finding lenders. They will have the largest variety of loans to chose from. Since they are not restricted by bank or mortgage company rules, they can find financing for almost anyone. However, they may charge higher fees.

What to Ask When Looking for a Lender

When looking for a lender, you can pick several and ask the same questions and compare their responses. Ask for a good faith estimate and a quote of their APR (annual percentage rate). A good lender will, in turn, ask you a few questions:

- What is the amount of the loan you are looking for?
- How much is the down payment?
- How long do you plan on being in the home?
- How many years do you want the loan for?

The lender can then give you a good faith estimate. This is an estimate of how much you will have to pay at closing. The lender will also quote the APR (the percentage interest rate that you will be paying after it is adjusted for closing costs).

After you have spoken with several lenders you will know approximately what it will cost you to get a loan and the amount of a down payment you will need at a particular interest rate. You can also make a determination as to which lender(s) you like working with and who is willing to work with you.

Credit Rating & Credit Reports

Refer to Chapter 4, 'Financial Matters.'

Mortgage Application

A lender will have you complete a loan application and pay an application fee (around $25). You will need to provide them with:

- your current or most recent payroll stub,
- the addresses you have lived at for the last two years,
- your employer's name for last two years and your gross pay,
- bank statements for the last three months from each bank account,
- open credit card balances, account numbers, and monthly payments,
- loan balances,
- addresses of any property you own, and names and addresses of any lenders for these properties, and
- your social security number (refer to Chapter 13, 'Legal Concerns').

A lender will also want to see that you are reliable and not likely to leave the country. A green card is very helpful (refer to Chapter 13, 'Legal Concerns'), since it conveys a certain level of permanence in the country. Assurances from your employer, such as intent to sponsor you for a green card, or an employment contract covering more than one or two years may also be useful to prove reliability.

Lenders will look at your gross monthly income, review your employment history, calculate assets including checking, savings, stocks, bonds, etc. Lenders recommend that your monthly mortgage payments (including principal, interest, taxes, and insurance) should not exceed approximately 30% of your monthly gross income. Loan amounts do not exceed 100% of the appraised value of the home.

Pre-Qualifying and Pre-Approval for Loans

Many realtors and lenders recommend pre-qualifying or getting pre-approval for a home loan, before or while you are looking at properties. This gives you more information to help with selecting the right home since it gives you an idea of the price range you can afford.

Pre-qualifying is an informal estimate of the amount of money the lender would be willing to lend you, given the personal financial data you provide. The lender does not verify any of your information, and is not bound to this quick approximation.

Pre-approval requires you actually go through the loan application process. The lender will process the application, verifying the information you have provided. The lender can then tell you how much money s/he will loan to you. Pre-approval may give you an advantage when it comes time to making an offer on a house. The seller is assured the transaction will go through without delay.

Down Payment

The down payment is the amount you pay (or put down) at the time you buy the home. It is generally 10-20% of the sales price. The difference between the purchase price and the down payment is your mortgage. The more money you can put towards your down payment, the lower your mortgage will be, which could save you a considerable amount of money in interest costs over the life of the loan. Some lenders may offer special features on their loans when you put down 25% or more. Lenders also advise that non-Americans will have a better chance of being approved for a loan if they can put down a large down payment.

Components of the Mortgage

The components of a mortgage calculation are the interest rate and the length of the loan (called the loan period). Typically, the shorter the length of the mortgage, the lower the interest rate. Interest rates fluctuate daily, so you should pay attention to the rate of your mortgage on the day it becomes final. Mortgages are usually paid over a period of 15-30 years.

Another loan term to know is the pre-payment penalty, which is an additional amount to be paid if you want to make additional loan payments or pay the loan off early. This feature limits your flexibility, but may offer a lower interest rate.

Your mortgage payment is made of two parts: principal and interest. The interest is paying the lender for the service of using its money. The principal is actually going towards paying for the home. The shorter the loan period, the faster you build equity in your home.

Fixed Rate or Adjustable Rate Mortgages

There are many types of mortgages with a variety of terms or features. The two most common loans are the fixed rate and adjustable rate loans.

The fixed rate loan simply means the stated interest rate will not change over the life of the loan. The adjustable rate mortgage (know as an ARM) allows for the interest rate to be adjusted by the lender. There is usually a limit to how often and by how much the interest rate can increase. Other types of loans include convertible ARMS and balloon loans that can be explained to you by your lender.

Other Ways to Finance Your Purchase

Land Contract

The seller may offer financing. Sellers will have a variety of reasons for doing this, but a common reason would be that the seller is an older person with no mortgage on the home. The seller may prefer to receive regular monthly payments, rather than the entire proceeds of the sale in a lump sum. This type of loan is called a land contract.

Assumable Mortgages

The seller may have an assumable mortgage, meaning you can take over making the payments on the seller's mortgage. Lenders do not write assumable mortgages very often now, but it was a common practice a few years ago.

A low interest loan that might be available to you if you are a Permanent Resident Alien (hold a green card) is a Federal Housing Authority (FHA) loan. These loans are provided by the U.S. government to help people buy homes. There are several restrictions, but a lender will be able to determine if you are eligible.

People buy and sell homes and take out loans everyday. The process may seem overwhelming, but when you work with knowledgeable, respected professionals, they can make the home buying process much easier.

Real Estate Advertisement Abbreviations

App fee	application fee
Avail	available
Ba, bth	bathroom
Bd, bdrm	bedroom
Bkyd	backyard
Blks	blocks
Brkfst rm	breakfast room
Bsmnt	basement
Cond	condition
Dwntwn	downtown
Elec svc	electric service
Ext	exterior
Fac	facility
Famrm	family room
Fncd	fenced
Frml ent	formal entrance
Frnt	front
Frplc, fplc	fireplace
Furn	furnace
Immac	immaculate
Include	includes, included
Int	interior
Kit, kitch	kitchen
Lrg	large
Lvl	level
Mstr bth	master bath
Mtn	mountain
Nghbrhd	neighborhood
Offstr prk	off street parking
Pd	paid
Priv, prvt	private
Rec rm	recreation room
Refin hdwd flrs	refinished hardwood floors
Refurb	refurbished
Sf, sqft	square feet
Strcs	staircase
Strg	storage
Updtd	updated
W&D hkup	washer & dryer hookup
W/	with
Wdwk	woodwork
Wndws	windows

Making Your
House a Home

Chapter 6

Making Your House a Home

This chapter will discuss the services and products you want and need to make your home more comfortable and your life more enjoyable. Topics covered are arranged in alphabetical order.

When you move into your house, apartment or condominium, you will need to contact the water, gas and electric and telephone companies. In most cases you will simply be changing over the charges to your name without interrupting service or requiring a service person to come to your home. Other services, such as cable television and special Internet access will require that you set up a new account and arrange for a service person to come to your residence to install equipment.

Utilities include water and sewer, gas and electric, telephone, cable television, garbage pickup and Internet connections.

☞ **There are several ways to pay for certain basic household services. Your various utility bills will be mailed to you monthly, with the exception of water and sewer, which is billed quarterly. You can pay by check (never send cash in the mail), electronically or set up automatic payment (refer to Chapter 4, 'Financial Matters'). If you pay by check you can drop off your payment at certain mail stores or some drug stores, to save postage.**

Appliances

American kitchens will usually have a refrigerator (you may be surprised by the capacity), a microwave oven, a dishwasher, and a range (stovetop and oven). Some homes also have a garbage disposal (a machine, sitting below the sink, that purees garbage so that it can flow down the drain), a trash compactor (a machine that compresses the air from paper and other items in the trashcan to make a more easily handled unit), and an icemaker (which automatically produces ice cubes and will be part of the refrigerator). Most houses have a washing machine and a dryer. You may think dryers are unnecessary, but in the United States, drying clothes on a line is an exception, not the rule. Your new home may come equipped with these appliances, or you may have to arrange for them.

Purchasing or Rental

Appliances

Electrical appliances can be found in a variety of retail stores. Look in the Yellow Pages for large items such as refrigerators, stoves, microwave ovens, washing machines, clothes dryers, televisions, VCRs and some audio equipment.

If you purchase a large appliance, you can arrange to have it delivered. You may have to pay extra for this service. The delivery person may also install it, but this may also cost extra and should be arranged in advance. Many appliance stores offer financing or payment plans, if you qualify.

**Vacuum
Cleaners**
*
Audio
*
Rental

You can also find used appliances. Some appliance stores have used items for sale; just ask. You can also look in the classified ads.

Smaller items such as bathroom or kitchen appliances, vacuum cleaners, air conditioners, and space heaters can be found at any discount department store. There are also specialty vacuum cleaner stores and audio stores. Specialty kitchen stores may offer more unusual styles of kitchen appliances. Espresso machines can be found at coffee shops or department stores. All of these products can also be purchased on the Internet.

If you will be in the United States for a short period of time, it is possible to arrange to rent major appliances

Repair

**Appliances-
Major-
Service
& Repair**

**Appliances-
Small**
*
**Stereo & Hi Fi-
Repair &
Parts**

For repair of these appliances, call the store from which you purchased them. In the telephone book you will find independent repair people who service many types of appliances, and repair divisions of major manufacturers who repair one brand exclusively.

If you need a large appliance repaired, a repairperson will come to your home. Most service companies will give you an estimate of the time of day when you can expect the technician to arrive. This is usually a two-hour period. You will need to be home, or arrange with someone else to be there to let the technician enter. You will be charged a minimum standard fee whether or not the technician is able to fix the appliance. In addition, you will be charged for parts used and the time it took the technician to make the repair. In most cases you will be asked to pay the amount due at the time of the repair. Most companies accept credit card, check or cash. Ask about the payment policy at the time you call for an appointment.

For repair of audio equipment and other smaller appliances, you will be expected to deliver this type of equipment to a repair location yourself.

Maintenance

Furnaces

Some appliances require yearly maintenance, for example, the heating system in your home. **Furnaces** in the Northwest are usually forced hot air (recognized by vents in the floor and walls), or forced hot water (with piped radiators along the walls). Furnaces can be fueled with natural gas or oil. The technician will want to know both of these characteristics when you make the appointment for service. If your home has a natural gas or oil furnace, a professional should do yearly maintenance. If your home is heated electrically (with individual radiators in each room) you can vacuum the dust from the radiators yourself.

The **washing machine** will need to have the filters cleaned periodically. **Dryers** also need to have the lint cleared from the filter and vent pipes on a regular basis. **Refrigerator** coils need to be cleaned annually. **Smoke detectors** need dusting monthly.

The water in the Portland area is considered very soft (low levels of calcium and magnesium). For this reason you do not have to add salt of any kind to your **dishwasher** to enhance performance.

Automobiles

Purchase

Please refer to Chapter 11, 'Local Transportation' for information on buying a car.

Repair

Dealerships, Service Chains and Independent Garages

You can get your car serviced at an automobile dealership or at an independent repair shop. You can also go to a national chain repair center such as PepBoys or Sears. These automotive repair shops charge separately for parts and labor. The work will be itemized on your bill. Labor is the amount of time the mechanic used to diagnose and repair the problem and to install any parts. Parts will be billed separately. Labor is billed at a standard hourly rate, which should be posted on the wall of the shop. If you do not see it, ask. All repair centers will charge you an environmental fee (usually 5-10% percent of the total bill) for disposing of chemicals they use on your car. Most automotive repair shops require an appointment.

A repair center is called a garage, service center or service department of a dealership.

Specific Service Chains (Mieneke, Jiffy Lube, Midas, Les Schwab, etc.)

Auto Repair & Service

*

Tires

Some repair centers offer specialized service on common maintenance or repair problems. For example, Jiffy Lube will do oil and filter changes and lubrications. Midas and Mieneke both replace mufflers, brakes and shocks. Les Schwab sells tires. These places generally charge a single rate that includes parts and labor. The work is usually less expensive than going to a regular automotive repair shop (but not always). You can call for an appointment or just drive in and wait for the next available time.

Use the Yellow Pages to find listings sorted by location.

Child Care and Babysitting

Finding child care is always difficult when you move to a new city.

For babysitting (short term, occasional care) many local residents like to use the neighborhood teenagers. Youths from about age 12 are commonly hired for about $2/hour and up. The Red Cross offers a babysitting class which focuses on safety for those 12 years and older. You can check with the local schools or churches to find teens interested in babysitting.

For professional child care on a regular basis, contact the Metro Child Care Resource and Referral, which has a list of child care providers. The Auntie Fay Agency at 503-293-6252 or Northwest Nannies Institute at 503-245-5288 provide nannies starting at $7-$9/hour. Nannies are age 18 and older and have been trained or have experience and their references and background have been thoroughly checked.

Contractors, Handymen, Tradesmen

Contractors

If you do not want to do home improvement or repair work yourself, you can hire someone to do it for you. As in your home country, the hardest part is finding someone who is capable and honest. Referrals from friends, neighbors, or co-workers are always best. You can also go to a lumberyard where professionals get their materials and ask for referrals. You can look in the Yellow Pages for a list of builders/contractors who can oversee the whole project from design to completion. If you need a specific job done, you can look in the Yellow Pages under that particular trade (for example, Electrician, Plumber, Painter, Carpenter, Tile-Ceramic-Contractors & Dealers). The Oregonian publishes a "services" guide, daily, within the Classified Ads.

Plumbers repair and install the water system in your house. **Electricians** will install and repair the wiring. If you are doing renovations and have walls that need to be plastered you would call a **dry wall specialist**. If you want wallpaper hung or have walls painted, you would call on a **paperhanger** or **painter**. You can usually get recommendations for these skills at a store that sells wallpaper and paint. If you need to have your roof repaired, a **roofer** is the person to call. If you want to have furniture built for you, contact a **cabinetmaker**.

If you have small jobs such as picture hanging or small repairs, you could enlist the help of a 'handy man'. Get a referral from a local hardware store or find one advertised in the classified ads.

Copy Centers

Copy centers, also called instant printers or duplicating services, are places where you can go to make a large number of copies in a variety of formats, from business cards to blueprints to T-shirts. They also offer computer time rental, Internet access and printing services. Copy centers can be open 24 hours a day. They will give you the choice of making the copies yourself or leaving it for them to do within 24 hours (for a slightly higher cost). Some names of copy centers are Kinko's, Sir Speedy, Lazerquick, Copies Plus, Kopy World and Pip. In December, these stores also offer custom Christmas card printing.

Copy & Duplicating Services

Dry Cleaners and Laundry

Cleaners
*
Tailors

Dry cleaners are common and found in every part of the city. These businesses usually offer both dry cleaning and laundering services. Often dry cleaners offer tailoring or alterations. Alterations are minor repairs and adjustments such as hemming, replacing buttons, linings or zippers or adjusting waistbands. Tailoring is more extensive changes to garments and making garments from original designs.

**Laundries-
Self-Service**

If you do not have a washing machine in your home, you will find Laundromats (coin operated laundry) throughout Portland. At these places you use the washing machine and dryers for a fee. You can bring your own detergent (or purchase individual packages there). Some laundromats offer laundry-folding services (for a small fee).

Electricity

Two electric companies provide service to the Portland Metropolitan area. If you are uncertain about how to establish service, you can call to determine which provides service to your home address.

Portland General Electric (PGE)   503- 228-6322
Pacific Power & Light (PP&L)   888- 221-7070

Electronics and Computers

The standard for electrical power in the United States is 110 volts (written 110V) and 60 cycles (or Hertz). This differs from most other countries including those in Europe, Asia, Africa and Australia, which use 220V/50 Hz.

The three types of United States 110 V plug ends look like this:

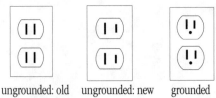

ungrounded: old   ungrounded: new   grounded

The 220V dryer plug looks like this:

Transformers

To make your non-U.S. appliance usable, the devices described below are available at electronics stores. We found Norvac Electronics Inc., 7940 SW Nimbus Ave., Beaverton, 503-644-1025 and Radar Inc., 704 SE Washington, Portland 503-232-3404 particularly helpful. Some of the larger electronic stores in the area are Best Buy, Good Guys, Sears and Fry's.

Electronic Equipment & Supplies

Transformers A transformer is a device that 'transforms' or changes one type of electrical current into another. In the United States you would plug your 220V appliance into an appropriate transformer and then plug the transformer into the 110V wall outlet. Transformers are most often used for medium sized electronic equipment such as computers, printers, television's, VCR's, sewing machines, audio equipment, blenders, coffee makers, toasters and food processors. Transformers are not appropriate for large appliances such as washing machines, refrigerators, microwave ovens and air conditioners. Also, transformers do not convert cycles, therefore they are not useful for clocks or appliances with timers. Appliances with motors, such as food processors and sewing machines will wear out more quickly when used with a transformer. Transformers come in a variety of sizes depending on the load (number of watts) they can carry. They may also indicate the types of appliances they are suited for. Transformers can range in price (based on capacity) from $15 to several hundred dollars. Some transformers even have the feature of being able to 'step up' to 220V or 'step down' to 110V with a flip of a switch. These are called reverse transformers.

Electrical Plug Adapters These little adapters are equipped with the U.S. standard flat pins on one end and accepts your country's plug on the other end. This allows you to plug your device directly into the wall or into an U.S. extension cord, power strip or transformer. The current is not converted, so this is not appropriate for 220V appliances being plugged into 110V outlets. It is perfect, though, for 110V appliances or computers and other devices which can switch between 110V and 220V, which do not have the standard U.S. prongs.

☞ **Although transformers are available, they have disadvantages. They are cumbersome to use. Small transformers such as one used for an electric razor can easily fall out of the wall outlet due to weight. A hairdryer, a relatively lightweight appliance, will require a very large transformer due to the high wattage it requires to work. In addition, it is risky to have extraneous electrical cords around water, such as with bathroom and kitchen appliances. Finally, if you use the wrong size of transformer or it is not plugged in properly,**

97

the motor can burn out. This is a costly mistake with large appliances such as computers, printers, television or stereo equipment.

We recommend avoiding using transformers when you can. Buying a new U.S. item may be less expensive than buying the transformer to make your old one work. Small appliances such as irons, hair dryers, coffee makers, etc. are inexpensive and available in all discount department stores. If you have brought your computer equipment or television or stereo with you, be sure to chose the correct transformer carefully and be sure you are using it properly before turning on your equipment.

Computers

If you are interested in buying a computer in the United States, you can find one locally or on the Internet.

Computers

If you have brought your computer from your home country, the single most important thing you can do when attempting to plug in your computer system is to carefully read both the manual that came with the equipment and the label on the back of the equipment.

Of all the devices that make up your non-U.S. computer system, the computer itself may be the easiest device to plug in. Most new computers are self-adapting from 220V/50 to 110V/60. Older models are equipped with a switch, which allows you to change from 220V/50 to 110V/60. This switch is usually red and located near the power supply.

If this label is on your machine, look for a switch to make the change. You can call the manufacturer (or read the manual) to determine if switching is done internally. If the label on your machine only lists one voltage, it can not be switched.

Power Specification Label

115/230V, 2A/1A, 60/50 Hz

This device can be plugged into a 110V/60 Hz outlet or 220V/50 Hz outlet.

New printers are also coming out with this toggle switch or internal voltage adaptation. However, the older models will require a transformer. Other computer peripherals (printers, speakers, modems, fax machines, scanners) do not have this switch (although technology is always changing). You will need transformers for them as well.

Surge Suppressors

Your computer peripherals should be plugged into a surge suppressor. A surge suppressor is a device that checks the electricity coming through the wall outlet. If there is an unusually large amount of voltage coming into the surge suppressor at one time (for example, during a lightening storm), the suppressor turns the power off rather than sending that power on to (and perhaps damaging) your computer and peripherals. A transformer does not act like a surge suppressor, therefore even if you use a transformer, you will still need to use a surge suppressor.

A surge suppressor is also called a voltage regulator, stabilizer or surge protector.

Power Strips and Extension Cords

A power strip is an extension cord with multiple ports for several appliances. Most people use power strips to plug in their computer and peripherals since a single wall outlet is not enough to accommodate several pieces of equipment. Power strips can come equipped with a surge suppressor.

☞ **Do not mix 110V and 220V power cords on the same power strip. Use grounded plugs on your power cords. Be careful to not overload a circuit by placing too many items on a power strip. Add up the amps listed on the appliances you will plug into the extension cord and compare to the maximum load recommended for the cord or power strip.**

Putting it all together

If you have brought your computer equipment, including a power strip/surge suppressor from a country whose power is different than 110V, you will need at least one transformer. All the devices are plugged into the power strip/surge suppressor, without flipping any red switches to 110V. A plug adapter is used to connect the power strip/surge suppressor to the transformer. The transformer is plugged into the wall. The total number of watts used by all the computer devices determines the size of transformer you will need.

If you have a mix of equipment using 110V and 220V, or are using a power strip/surge suppressor purchased in the United States, you will need a plug adapter for each device that has an incompatible plug. In addition you will need to put the devices on separate power strips/surge suppressors and use a transformer for the 220V dedicated power strip/surge suppressor as described in the previous paragraph.

☞ **The devices for which it is most critical to be surge protected are the computer, monitor and printer.**

Computer Repair

You can check with a computer repair store for additional information. However, in researching this topic, we found many shops that were not familiar with having to modify the voltage. Keep asking until you find some one who is knowledgeable in this area. If you use a Macintosh computer, you will find that most computer stores do not work on Macs. However, The Computer Store (both N.E. and Tigard locations) services Macs.

Connecting to the Internet

When it comes time to setting up your computer for Internet service, you have several options. You will need to weigh the factors of cost, speed and ease of use.

Dial up Connections

Internet Access Providers

The most common and oldest method of connecting your computer to the Internet is through a phone line. This requires a standard modem and a contract with an Internet Service Provider (known as an ISP) who can provide you with a local-access telephone number that gets you into the Internet. The cost for this type of service with unlimited access time is about $20/month (note this cost does not include any telephone service costs). You will need to install the software provided by the ISP to their specifications. The ISP will provide telephone support, but will not come to your house to install the software for you.

Your connection speed will be limited by your modem's capacity. One problem with using this method of Internet connection is that when you are connected to the Internet, you can not use your phone. You may want to install an additional telephone line dedicated to the Internet.

There are national and local ISPs in the United States. Local ISPs will provide you with better customer service, but when you travel, you will need to arrange for a means of calling in from out of state. National ISPs can give you a local number for most areas of the United States and, in some cases, many parts of the world. You will need to have software for browsing and e-mail.

DSL and T1 Lines

DSL (digital subscriber line) and T1 lines are a type of telephone service that gives extremely fast Internet connections through your existing telephone line. Availability of this service is dependent on how close your home is to the telephone company. When you arrange for your home telephone service, ask about the availability of DSL. Or find an ISP that supports DSL connections and they can help you with arranging to have DSL cable installed. There are several DSL service providers in the Portland area.

T1 lines were originally meant for business use, however they are available in some exclusive residential neighborhoods. It is usually more expensive, but extremely fast service. The other options mentioned are more appropriate for home use.

Cable Modems

Television-Cable & CATV

With this option, which is not available in all areas, your computer is connected to the same cable that brings cable television into your home. The cable modem company (AT&T in the Portland Metropolitan Area) will loan you a special translator and install unique interface software (Excite@home). The cost of this type of service is around $50/month for unlimited hours of access. The cable company will come to your home, install the cable, translator and software onto your computer and ensure it is working. There is an installation fee of up to $150 that is usually discounted or waived if you sign a one-year contract.

The advantage of this method is you can talk on the telephone and be on the Internet at the same time. Two disadvantages are:

Your computer is always connected to the Internet, and therefore susceptible to hackers (this is also a disadvantage with DSL lines), and

The number of people on line at one time limits your connection speed. At times connecting is extremely fast, and at other times, the speed is the same as a dial up modem.

WebTV

With this option you use your television set and your telephone line, but **not your** computer. This service, like cable modem, is not available in every neighborhood. The cost is about $50 a month and three levels of service are available. In addition, you must purchase a WebTV translator, which allows you to have access to the television, the Internet, and e-mail through your television. You can find WebTV translators at local electronics stores.

Other Options

The technology surrounding Internet access is rapidly evolving. The options discussed above, commonly used in 2000, may be obsolete in the near future. Use of cellular telephones, hand held devices such as Palm and wireless Internet laptops are already available. Other options will undoubtedly appear to take their place.

Exterminators

Houses of wood construction, in a damp environment are prone to carpenter ants and termite damage. If you see insects in your house, chances are there is a problem. There is a selection of products found at department stores or garden centers, which can help, get rid of the insect problem. Or call an exterminator.

Pest Control Services

In addition to house insect pests, another common problem is moles in your yard. Some pest control services can handle mole problems as well.

Film Developing

Photo Finishing

There are many options for having your camera film developed. Discount stores, grocery stores, film developing businesses, and camera shops offer film developing. Some of these stores offer one-hour service. These stores usually use less expensive paper, reducing the cost of the prints. In many cases, you can get two prints of each photo for about the same price as one set if you order them at the same time. The standard size for photo prints is 4x6 inches. If you prefer the smaller 3x5 inch print you may have to wait a day or two. You will also have the choice of glossy or matte finish. Most black and white film developing will take a few days. Other services include digital photo developing, enlargements, and photo Christmas Cards.

Furniture

Furniture-Rent & Lease

You can find just about every kind of furniture including expensive, trendy, unfinished (meaning you paint or stain it yourself), and new or used. Many furniture stores offer payment plans to qualified buyers.

You may wish to rent or lease furniture. This is a good option if you are only planning to stay in Portland a short time.

You can also find used furniture in the classified ads. Small neighborhood newspapers also have classified ad sections. Garage sales are also good places to find used furniture at low prices.

Garage Sales

Many Portlanders occasionally sell personal items out of their home. These 'events', called garage sales, yard sales, estate sales or tag sales are very popular. Spring, summer and fall is the garage sale season. They are held on weekends, usually starting on Friday. Look in the classified ads under garage sales. Or just look around your neighborhood for hand made signs nailed to the telephone poles announcing the time and address of the sale. It is a great way to find miscellaneous furniture, household items, and clothes and sporting equipment at a bargain.

Garbage and Recycling

Garbage and recycling is collected once a week on the same day and lawn and garden debris is collected once or twice a month. Private companies do garbage removal. Call one of these numbers to find out which hauler serves your area:

Clackamas County Information	503-655-8521
City of Portland Information	503-823-7202
Washington County Information	503-648-8609

Recycling containers are provided by the garbage hauler at no charge. The Pacific Northwest prides itself on its recycling efforts. Each hauler may have slightly different requirements about what and how to recycle your garbage, but the most common items recycled, which will be collected each week at your curb, are:

Newspapers	Plastic bottles
Magazines and catalogs	Milk jugs
Telephone books	Aluminum
Brown paper bags	Tin cans
Corrugated cardboard	Aerosol cans
Scrap paper and junk mail	Scrap metal
Milk cartons and other gable-top cartons	Glass jars and bottles
Drink boxes	Motor oil

You can contact your hauler if you have any questions on recycling. You can also call the recycling hotline (Metro Recycling Information) at 503-234-3000.

☞ **Aluminum cans and many types of plastic bottles can be returned to any grocery store for a refund of the deposit that was paid when the bottled product was purchased. The label will indicate which states handle deposits and the amount of the deposit (5 or 10 cents). The abbreviation for Oregon is OR. Many stores have placed bottle return machines outside that allow you to return your bottles and cans yourself. The machine will print out a receipt that you can redeem in the store. At other stores, which do not have these machines, someone can assist you with your returns.**

Gardening and Landscaping

Gardners

*

Landscapers

Many people use a lawn service to mow, fertilize and edge their lawns, remove leaves in the fall and prune shrubs. Ask your neighbors, look for flyers that local gardeners leave at your door advertising their services, or look in the classified ads. Landscape companies can also handle more extensive landscaping projects such as installing retaining walls, paths or outdoor lighting.

Hair Care

Beauty Salons & Services

*

Barbers

There are three main types of shops that cut and style hair: barber shops, salons, and low cost haircut chains. If you are a man, you can go to a barbershop (no appointment necessary, just walk in and wait). You usually must schedule an appointment at a salon (serves both men and women), although some places have a sign that says 'walk-ins welcome'. This means you are welcome to wait for the next available stylist. The last option for both men and women is to go to a national haircut chain where cuts are given on a first come-first served basis. The cost of a haircut will be approximately $15 at this last option. The price of a haircut, styling or other services at a salon will depend on the reputation of the stylist and the number of added services you request. As in your home country, you can get recommendations from friends as to where they go, or you can try different places until you find one that works for you.

Heating Oil

Oil

Many older homes use oil furnaces. The oil tank (usually buried) on your property will need to be filled periodically. You are not restricted to a particular company, so shop for the best price.

104

Home Improvement Stores

It has become more popular to do home renovations by yourself. Home improvement stores such as Home Depot and Home Base can be found in all parts of the Portland Metropolitan Area. These stores sell the tools and materials needed to do just about any home improvement project. They offer classes on such topics as sponge painting, tiling, plumbing, and projects for children.

**Home
Improvement**
*
Hardware

Home Security Systems and Smoke Alarms

There are a wide variety of residential security systems. Features can vary between companies so it is best to look at several systems to see what suits you or what you are familiar with from your home country. Although this type of business is visible and growing, most homes currently do not have security systems. Refer to Chapter 10, 'Safety' for more information on home security.

Smoke detectors can be found in hardware stores and department stores (such as Fred Meyer). Detectors should have batteries replaced every six months.

**Security Equip,
Systems &
Monitoring**

House Cleaning

House cleaning services will come to your home as often as you wish. Most people who use house cleaning services have their home cleaned on a regular schedule. You can also ask your neighbors for referrals. A reputable house cleaning service will be bonded and insured to protect you and them against damage that can accidentally occur.

**House
Cleaning**

Interior Decorating

Interior Decorators & Designers

Interior Decorators can be very helpful. These professionals can help you with all the details of decorating your home: coordinating paint, furniture, carpet, wallpaper, and window coverings. Furniture stores, paint stores, carpet and drapery stores employ someone who is trained in this area. If you bring samples of fabric or paint colors to the decorator, their advice may be free. If a decorator comes to your home, you will be charged by the hour. This fee may be credited against your account if you buy their products. Ask about the cost of service before you agree to anything. A professional will be happy to explain their policy.

Mail

Mail Delivery and the U.S. Postal Service

Mail is delivered everyday except Sundays and federal holidays (refer to Chapter 15, 'Holidays') by a U.S. Postal Service (U.S.P.S.) mail carrier. Post offices, marked by a red, white and blue sign with an eagle on it and displaying the American flag, are located in every city and town. Smaller satellite post office branches can be found in neighborhoods and sometimes inside supermarkets. Most supermarkets also sell postage stamps at the checkout counter or information desk. The post office is a place for you to buy postage stamps, mail packages, pick up mail from a post office box, and purchase postal money orders. In some, but not all, larger post offices you can get passport applications, and talk with INS inspectors. It has no other government functions or services.

Sending Mail

Street Mail Boxes

A public, on-street mailbox is a large blue chest with a rounded top and clearly marked U.S. Postal Service. On it is a label giving the days of the week and times of day when mail is collected. When you mail a letter in an on-street mailbox you will need to have the correct postage (refer to Chapter 1, 'Basics'). The post office will not deliver mail that does not have postage. Writing a return address on an envelope allows the post office to return it to you if the letter is undeliverable. Delivery of any letter not having a return address will be delayed because of the perceived risk of letter bombs.

Home Mailboxes

You can place outgoing mail, with correct postage, in your home mailbox. Your mail carrier will pick it up when s/he delivers your mail. If you do this, you should raise the red flag on the side of the box to let the carrier know that you have mail to be taken away. If you have a mail slot, you can clip your outgoing mail to the outside of the slot. It is a good idea to take important pieces of mail to a public mailbox or to the post office, since occasionally thieves will steal mail from home mailboxes.

Zip Codes

Mail is delivered more quickly if your letters include the zip code. Zip codes for the state of Oregon are listed near the front of the telephone book. You can call the Portland Main Post Office (800-275-8777) for zip code information for other parts of the United States. You can also visit the U.S.P.S. website www.new.usps.com for zip code information.

Mailing Packages

If you send a package internationally, you will be required to complete a customs form declaring its contents and value. Each country has a duty free level. You must pay a tax for items valued above this level, just as when you travel and must declare items going through customs. If you ship an item which has a declared value above this level, the receiving party may also have to pay a duty on it before it is delivered. The customs agents of the country to which it is being sent may open the package, but it will not be opened by the U.S.P.S.

Mailing Centers

Many shopping centers have mailing centers. Names of some of these businesses are Mailboxes and More, Mailboxes Etc., Postal Annex, and Mailbox Plus. These stores offer a range of services, including copy services (usually do-it-yourself), sending and receiving faxes, receiving mail in private mailboxes, notary service, making of keys and rubber stamps, sending packages, and sales of shipping materials. You can take an item that is already wrapped or something to be wrapped by them for shipping. The store will give you several options for shipping the package. Usually the decision between these shipping options is based on the value (for insurance purposes), the weight of the item, and its destination, all influencing the cost of shipping. Options will in-

Mail Boxes

*

**Mailboxes-
Rental &
Receiving**

clude the U.S. Postal Service, UPS (United Parcel Service) and FedEx (Federal Express). The U.S.P.S. rates will be at a higher cost than sending the same package at a regular post office since these mailing services are private companies, not a part of the U.S. Postal Service. Each of these services offers international overnight delivery.

Natural Gas

Furnaces, stoves, and water heaters are the most common uses of natural gas. The only gas company in the Portland area is:

Northwest Natural Gas (NW Natural Gas)   503-226-4210

Newspapers

Portland Area Newspapers

For Portland Metropolitan Area local news, sports, and weather, and some international coverage, there are several daily and weekly newspapers.

The Oregonian is published seven days a week. The paper can be delivered to your home in the early morning. You can also purchase copies at most coffee stores, supermarkets, and gas station mini-markets. There are also newspaper dispensers on street corners in parts of the Portland area. Call 503-221-8240 or 360-896-5701 to arrange for home delivery. The cost for home delivery is less than $5 a week. Access their website at www.oregonian.com.

The Columbian is the Vancouver daily newspaper. You can get a home delivery of the paper by calling 360-694-2312 or 503-224-1654. Access their website at www.columbian.com. The home delivery of the Columbian is less than $15 a week.

Willamette Week is published each Wednesday. It is a free newspaper that you can pick up at coffee stores, street corners, supermarkets, and other newspaper delivery sites within Portland. You can also read the paper on their website www.wweek.com.

The Business Journal is a weekly paper devoted to local business news. You can subscribe by calling 503-274-8733.

The Skanner provides local and national news with an African-American perspective. Call 503-285-5555.

Smaller town papers report town news only. The paper will cover school and sports events, theater and music performances, and special events within the town.

Hillsboro Argus is published each Tuesday and Thursday. Call 503-648-1131.

Tigard Times / Tualatin Times is published each Thursday. Call 503-684-0360.

The Gresham Outlook is published each Wednesday and Saturday. Call 503-665-2181.

Lake Oswego Review is published each Thursday. Call 503-635-8811.

Beaverton Valley Times is published each Thursday. Call 503-684-0360.

U.S. Newspapers

There are several daily newspapers distributed across the United States. Most of these can be purchased in the same places that sell The Oregonian and The Columbian.

The New York Times can be delivered to your home (in the morning) throughout Portland, 7 days a week. Call 800-698-4637 or visit their website at www.homedelivery.nytimes.com. The cost of a seven-day subscription is approximately $40/ month.

The Washington Post can be delivered by mail six to eight days after its publication date. You can subscribe by calling 202-334-6100 or visiting their website at www.washington.post.com. The cost is $60/week for seven-day delivery.

USA Today is published Monday through Friday. It has abbreviated reporting on top issues. A one-year subscription is less than $125. To subscribe you can call 800-9872-0001 and ask for key code 620. You can also access their website at www.usatoday.com.

Wall Street Journal has some international, general interest news but is primarily a business newspaper. Call 800-975-8609. The cost is approximately $175/ year for home delivery, Monday through Friday, but this service is only available in certain areas.

International News

American newspapers report international news, however it is not in-depth. International newspapers and the Internet are good resources for news covering world affairs.

Newspaper

The International Herald Tribune calls itself 'the worlds' daily newspaper'. It is a joint venture between The New York Times and The Washington Post. Like The Washington Post, it is delivered by mail, usually several days out of date. The cost of a one-year subscription is $360. To subscribe visit www.iht.com.

Internet

You can access your home country's newspapers from pppp.net/links/news/. This website links to 10,000 newspaper and magazine sites worldwide. You can read about your home country and world news in your own language. www.cnn.com will connect you to world news in English. Current news stories are sorted by region.

Pets

If you have come to the United States and brought your pet with you, you have already dealt with the customs regulations for bringing pets into the United States.

A pet can be a lifeline for you when you first arrive in this country. Walking your dog can be a great way to meet people. An animal gives you and a stranger a topic of conversation. Animals can provide affection and companionship in times when you are feeling the most homesick. A kitten playing with a ball of string can make you laugh when you are sad. Animals however have their own care issues. If you are planning to bring your pet with you when you move to the United States (or when you return to your home country) you must be certain that you follow the regulations that have been established by the customs office.

Importing a Pet

There is usually no quarantine period for bringing a cat or dog into the United States (exceptions to this rule are the Islands of Hawaii, and Guam). All birds and animals must be imported under healthy and humane conditions. This means the airline (or other carrier) must have made arrangements for a suitable cage, space on the flight, ventilation, and protection from the elements. Cleaning, feeding, watering, and other necessary services must be provided. Every imported container of pets must be labeled with your name, as well as an accurate invoice specifying the number and each species being imported. Your animals will be inspected; so you must arrange in advance with the carrier to have an inspector available when you arrive. If your animal does not pass the inspection it will be sent back or destroyed. Animals are examined at the Port of Entry, the place where you first arrive in the United States, even if it is not your final destination.

Airlines may refuse to carry pets on certain routes at certain times of the year. The heat in the summer, or cold of the winter can easily overcome an animal if it is left for several hours on a tarmac at an airport.

Dogs, cats, and turtles are imported with no duty charged. Other animals may be subject to a customs duty, which can be a part of your overall duty exemption if they are imported for your own personal use and not for resale.

If you are bringing in breeding stock, you will be required to complete special forms.

Dogs

All domestic dogs must be free of evidence of diseases when inspected at the Port of Entry. Dogs must receive a rabies vaccine at least 30 days before entering the United States. You must present the certificate of Rabies vaccination and it is recommended that the certificate be in English. The certificate must identify the animal, the date of vaccination, and its expiration, and be signed by a licensed veterinarian.

Cats

All domestic cats must be free of evidence of diseases when inspected at the Port of Entry.

Birds

If you are bringing birds into the country you will need to get a special permit from the U.S. Fish and Wildlife Service. Usually a bird must stay in quarantine for 30 days at a cost of $200/bird. Quarantine facilities are in five ports of entry: New York, New York; McAllen, Texas; San Francisco, California; Miami, Florida; and Los Angeles, California. This quarantine space must be pre-arranged (you can do this at American Consulates and embassies). The bird must have a certificate of health from a veterinarian of the country from which it has come.

Pet Training

If you are coming from Canada you are exempt from the quarantine period provided that the bird is in your possession for at least 90 days and found to be healthy at the border crossing when inspected by a veterinarian.

*

Dog and Cat Training

Pet Etiquette

There are several animal schools for teaching your pet to behave in public and at home. These schools offer group classes as well as individual appointments to work on specific behavior problems (barking, scratching, digging, etc).

There are several things you should know about pets in the United States, especially if you are accustomed to traveling with your pet. Many hotels will have a special set of rooms for people traveling with a pet, but you must arrange for this in advance. Animals are not allowed in restaurants in the United States, nor in other public spaces, such as shopping malls and airports (with the exception, of course, of guide and assistance dogs). Animals are also not allowed in National Parks.

Clean up after your pet

It is only fair that when you walk your dog, you clean up after him or her. There are special plastic bags and gloves available at pet stores to make this task less awkward. Some leashes have a plastic bag dispenser built into the handle. In any case, it is your responsibility as an owner to pick up after your dog. In some places there are fines for not doing so.

Leash Laws

Many communities in the United States have leash laws, which are designed to keep your pet at his home and out of the neighbors' yards. Pets should not be allowed to run loose. When you walk your dog on the street, you will be expected to keep it on a leash. Most dog walking parks in Portland require a leash. There are, however, three off-leash-areas in Portland where your dog can run with others. These are in West Delta Park, Chimney Park, and Gabriel Park in Portland. There are also off-leash parks in West Linn and Milwaukie.

When your dog is on a leash s/he is more likely to display aggressive behavior around other dogs. S/he is protecting you and will respond differently (more aggressively) than if it were not on a leash. If you encounter another dog, keep your dog on a short lead until you have passed. Be considerate of others who may be fearful of dogs or who may not know how to act around a dog. You are responsible for your dog's actions.

Licensing

Your dog must be licensed with the county in which you live. If you live in Multnomah County you must also license your cat. Call the Animal Control Department within your county (under Government Pages, by county, in the telephone book) for licensing forms. You will need to provide proof that your animal has a current rabies vaccination. If your pet is neutered and you can provide proof, you pay a reduced fee. You will be given a metal tag that identifies your animal. This must be renewed annually. Your rabies tag, which you receive from the Veterinarian when the dog gets a rabies vaccination, is NOT a dog license tag.

You must license your dog (and cat in Multnomah County) within 30 days of his/her arrival in Clackamas and Multnomah Counties. In Washington County you have six months to get a license for your dog.

Pet Health

You may find pests and health conditions in the United States that you do not encounter in your home country. Your veterinarian can assist you in understanding these problems and provide you with effective treatments and preventative vaccinations.

Heartworm is one of the most dangerous of all the internal parasites. Mosquitoes transmit Heartworm disease by biting an infected dog, then passing the infection to other dogs they bite. The Heartworm larvae migrate to the dog's heart and lungs where they mature into adults and can grow up to 14 inches in length. These adult worms can cause severe and potentially fatal damage to the heart, lungs, and other vital organs. Symptoms of Heartworm disease are essentially those of other cardiac diseases including coughing, fatigue, and loss of appetite. However, these warning signs do not typically appear until the disease is in its advanced stages, making treatment risky as well as costly. Heartworm infections are common along the Atlantic and Gulf Coasts, the Mississippi River Valley and its tributaries, and have now been reported in all 50 states and Canada. Your dog and cat can contract Heartworm disease anywhere there are mosquitoes, both indoors and outdoors, and at any time of the year. Ask your veterinarian about their preferred method of Heartworm prevention.

Veterinarians

Finding a Veterinarian

Look in your neighborhood, in the Yellow Pages, or ask a friend for the name of their veterinarian. Veterinary offices are also called animal hospitals. Pet Passports for keeping records of your pets' vaccinations are NOT used in the United States.

Vaccinations

When you board your pet you will need to present a paper from your veterinarian with the dates of current vaccinations and other health records. For dogs this will include:

- if the animal has been spayed or neutered,
- rabies vaccine,
- DHLPP vaccine (Canine Distemper, Canine Hepatitis, Leptospirosis),
- Parainfluenza and Parvo virus vaccine,
- Corona Virus vaccine,
- Corona vaccine,
- CRV vaccine, and
- Bordatella vaccine.

For a cat this will include:

- if the animal has been spayed or neutered,
- Rabies (FRV),
- FVRCP (a 3 in 1 vaccine that stands for Feline Viral Rhinotracheitis, Calici Virus, and Panleukopenia), and
- FeLV (Feline Leukemia Virus).

Emergency Assistance

If your pet has an accident during hours that your veterinarian is not available, it is possible to take it to the Dove Lewis Emergency Animal Hospital. Always call before you take your animal there to ensure that they are able to help. There are three locations:

Downtown at 1984 NW Pettygrove	503-228-7282
Westside at 18990 SW Shaw in Aloha	503-645-5800
Eastside at 10564 SE Washington	503-262-7194

Boarding Your Pet

Licensed kennels will be members of the American Boarding Kennels Association (ABKA). You will be told in advance the price of boarding, per day. This price is based on the size of your dog. Cats are boarded at a single rate regardless of age or breed. The rate is calculated for every day that the pet is on the premises. For example, if you are away from a Monday to a Monday you will be charged for eight days of boarding even if the pet is there for a short period of time on any one of the days. If you have a more exotic animal such as a ferret, ask the boarding facility regarding their policy on such an animal. Not all boarding facilities will accept exotic animals.

Any good kennel will encourage you to come and tour the facility before you agree to leave your animal there. In the United States, all animals are kept separately with no shared cages or play runs. You can request that your dog be given a bath before s/he is returned to you to remove the scent of disinfectant from his/her coat.

Care in your Home

These services will come to your home (usually once a day) and spend a set period of time with your animal while you are gone. They will ensure that there is food and water, as well as walking and playing with your pet. These services function within a limited travel distance from a central location.

You can use the pet care services through www.mylackey.com. These services provide dog exercise care ranging from 30-minute walks to 90 minutes of playtime.

Finding a Pet

If you decide to adopt a pet you have several places to turn. There are certified breeders who can give you the background and history of your new pet to ensure the genetic quality. You can purchase a dog, cat, ferret, gerbil, fish or bird at a pet shop. Some shops specialize in certain types of animals. Or you can adopt one from an Animal Shelter, where you will find animals that have been given up by their former owners. In some cases you can find puppies and kittens, but usually the animals are older. You will be asked to pay a fee to cover costs and given a discount if you agree to have the pet neutered.

Dog and Cat Kennels

*

Pet Boarding and Sitting

Pet Exercising, Feeding and Sitting

Animal Shelters

Radio Stations

Most radio stations are commercial. In the western part of the United States, call letters begin with 'K'. In the eastern part of the country the call letters begin with 'W'. The Portland radio stations are:

AM Radio Stations

Call Letters	Tune to	Programming
KBMS	1480	Urban Contemporary
KBNP	1410	Business/News/Talk
KBPS	1450	Classical
KEX	1190	Talk/Full Service
KFXX	1520	Sports/Talk
KISN	910	Nostalgia/Oldies
KKEY	1150	Talk
KMUZ	1230	Spanish
KPDQ	800	Inspirational
KOTK	620	Talk
KUIK	1360	News/Sports/Talk
KUPL	970	Country
KVAN	1550	Talk
KWJJ	1080	Country
KXL	750	News/Talk
KXYQ	1010	Talk

FM Radio Stations

Call Letters	Tune to:	Style
KBOO	90.7	Alternative
KBPS	89.9	Classical
KBVM	88.3	Inspirational
KGON	92.3	Classic Rock
KINK	102	Album Rock & Jazz
KISN	97.1	Classic Oldies
K103	103	Contemporary
KMHD	89.1	Jazz
KNRK	94.7	Modern Rock
KKJZ	106.7	Smooth Jazz
KOPB	91.5	News/Educational
KPDQ	93.7	Inspirational
KRRC	104.1	Alternative Rock
KUFO	101.1	Album Rock
KUPL	98.5	Country
KWJJ	99.5	Country
KXL	95.5	70's
KXYQ	105.1	Classic Rock
KKCQ	103	Adult Contemporary

Telephone

Local telephone service is provided by one of several telephone companies, depending on the area. Qwest (800-244-1111) provides service to most of the Portland area.

GTE Northwest (800-483-4100) serves the following communities outside Portland:

Aloha	Gaston	Sherwood
Banks	Gresham	Stafford
Beaverton	Hillsboro	Tigard
Boring	Sandy	Tualatin
Forest Grove	Scholls	Wilsonville

Telephone Company Services

Local telephone companies offer a variety of services, such as voice-mail services, call waiting, and caller I.D. The telephone company will also rent a handset to you, but most people own their own handset. Handsets can be purchased at any electronics store. The U.S. telephone jack is known as a RJ-11. This may or may not be similar to the telephone jack in your home country. Telephone cords can be purchased at electronics stores or Fred Meyer.

Telephone Directories

Three different publishers (GTE, Qwest and WorldPages.com) provide the telephone books in the Portland Metropolitan Area. GTE and Qwest provide their telephone directories to their customers with whom they provide telephone service. WorldPages.com delivers their books to everyone. You can have any of these telephone books delivered to your door, free by calling:

Qwest Dex	1-800-422-8793
GTE	1-800-888-8448
WorldPages.com	1-800-826-4089

The communities and counties included in each telephone book will be printed on the front cover. Some books may combine all sections into one book, or there may be more than one book. For example, the Qwest Portland telephone book, covering Multnomah, Washington, and Clackamas Counties is actually three books. The first includes phone service, government, residential, and business listings. Community, phone service, government, business and Yellow Pages A-L are included in the second book. Yellow Pages M-Z and the index make up the third.

*The word
telephone is
commonly
shortened to
phone.*

Do you need all three publishers' offerings of telephone books? No. Choose the book you think you would use the most and recycle the others. Qwest is the most comprehensive, encompassing all three counties. But if, for example, you do not plan to shop outside Washington County, you may only want GTE's single volume of Washington County listings.

Long Distance Telephone Services

At the time you set up local telephone service, you will be asked to choose a long distance telephone company. The largest companies are listed below or look in the Yellow Pages.

**Telecommuni-
cations
Companies**

AT&T	800-222-0300
MCI	800-950-5555
Sprint	800-877-7746
Qwest	888-452-6200
Verizon	888-483-4999

It is difficult to shop for long distance services since each company's fee schedule is slightly different and you probably do not know how many long distance calls you are going to be making. You can ask friends or colleagues, who make international calls, which company they use and why. Many of the companies offer packages for international calls and provide calling cards. You can change your long distance phone company if you are not satisfied with their service or cost. There may be a fee to make this change.

Your long distance phone charges will be included on your local phone company's bill so you only need to make one payment.

Cellular Phones

**Cellular &
Wireless Phones
& Service**

Cellular telephones are very common in the United States and cellular telephone companies have gotten quite competitive. Look for advertisements for the most competitive package of handset and services. Global Star and Voice Stream offer systems using GSM satellite technology to make it possible to use the same telephone service throughout the world. This is particularly useful for those who travel internationally.

Television

You do not have to contract with a cable television company to receive local Portland television stations. An antenna will improve the clarity of the picture. The stations you can receive without cable are:

The word television is commonly shortened to TV.

Portland Broadcast Stations

Call Letters	Channel	Affiliation
KATU	2	ABC
KOIN	6	CBS
KGW	8	NBC
KOPB	10	Public Broadcasting
KPTV	12	Local Independent
KPDX	49	Fox
KWBP	32	Warner Bros.

Cable Television

If you would like additional television stations, you will need to subscribe through a cable company. AT&T provides cable television service to the Portland area. If you choose to get cable, you will have a large decoder box installed by a technician. You can order cable service by calling:

AT&T serving Portland/Tualatin Valley	503-605-4800
AT&T serving Milwaukie	503-654-2266
AT&T serving Southern Washington	503-605-4721

There are three levels of cable television service:

Basic Service: local Portland broadcast channels, plus educational, shopping, inspirational and community channels.

Expanded Basic Service: basic service with movies and more programming channels.

Digital Cable: all the expanded cable channels, with digital movie and music channels.

AT&T can provide the details of the various stations available under the different levels of service.

**Television-
Cable & CATV**

☞ **If you want international news and sports, you will need to receive Digital Cable.**

Satellite Dishes

**Satellite
Equipment
and Systems**

*

**Television -
Cable and
Satellite
Systems &
Service**

There are several companies in the Portland area which offer satellite dish service as an alternative to cable for television. You must purchase the satellite dish, and have it programmed towards the appropriate position in the sky. There is a monthly access fee for the service. Each satellite system offers a different combination of programs.

VCRs

There are three television broadcast standards in the world:

NTSC (National Standards Committee)
PAL (Phase Alternating Line)
SECAM (Système Electonique Pour Couleur Avec Memoire)

NTSC is used in the United States. If you have brought videos from your home country which are in PAL or SECAM, you will need to ensure that any VCR you purchase here is capable of reading that format.

Water and Sewer

**Water-Bottled
& Bulk**

The Bull Run Watershed is considered one of the cleanest water supplies in the world and supplies much of Portland's water. Portland water is not hard; there is no need to add salt to your water heaters or dishwashers. Some water reservoirs have fluoride added to the water as a health measure (refer to Chapter 7, 'Health Care' for further information on fluoride). Your water utility can tell you what chemicals have been added to your water. Some people choose to use filters on their faucets or drink bottled water. Look in the Yellow Pages if you would like bottled water delivered to your home.

Portland is divided into a number of water districts. If you are uncertain as to where to establish your water and sewer services account, contact your city hall.

Making Portland Your Home

Chapter 7

Making Portland Your Home

We think you will find Portland to be a fun and friendly place. It hosts many cultural events and offers a variety of support services, clubs, and organizations. The Northwest is known for its natural beauty and varied recreational opportunities. As we mentioned in Chapter 2, 'Culture Shock,' a successful move means staying active and finding things to do that interest you. This chapter will help you do just that.

Business Associations

The following is a list of business organizations with international or cultural ties. This list is not complete. If you are looking for a particular business organization, the World Trade Center (503-464-8888), World Affairs Council of Oregon (503-274-7488), or the Portland Chamber of Commerce may be of assistance.

Chinese Chamber of Commerce	503-224-4082
Hispanic Chamber of Commerce	503-222-0280
Japan America Society of Oregon	503-228-9411
Korean Chamber of Commerce (Portland)	503-293-9036
(Beaverton)	503-646-4688
NW China Council	503-973-5451
Portland/Guadalajara Sister City Association	503-222-9807
Small Business International Trade Office	503-274-7482
Taiwan Commerce Assoc. of Portland	360-256-1092

Chambers of Commerce

A chamber of commerce is an association of businesses in a particular area. Their goal is to promote the economic health of the community. Businesses, not individuals, join the local chamber, but one of the chamber's services is to help visitors and new residents find the resources they need. Local chambers can answer questions about schools, events, utilities, banks, etc.

Portland Chamber of Commerce

The Portland Chamber of Commerce offers a relocation packet for about $25. This packet includes a Portland area street map and a relocation guide with information on what there is to see and do around Portland. There is also information on taxes, schools, housing, etc., and a video that takes you on a tour of the various neighborhoods in the area. The Portland Chamber is located at 221 NW 2nd in downtown Portland and the phone number is 503-228-9411. Their website, which also lists their services and resources, is www.pdxchamber.org.

Other Local Chambers of Commerce

Chambers of
Commerce

There are also smaller local Chambers of Commerce which provide information specific to that community. For example, Beaverton's Chamber of Commerce has a relocation packet filled with information relevant to the Beaverton area.

Beaverton Chamber of Commerce	503-644-0123
Gresham Chamber of Commerce	503-665-1131
Hillsboro Chamber of Commerce	503-648-1102
Lake Oswego Chamber of Commerce	503-636-3634
Milwaukie Chamber of Commerce	503-654-7777
Oregon City Chamber of Commerce	503-656-1619
Tigard Chamber of Commerce	503-639-1656
Tualatin Chamber of Commerce	503-692-0780
West Linn Chamber of Commerce	503-655-6744
Wilsonville Chamber of Commerce	503-682-0411

Cultural Events

There are many events in Portland throughout the year. There are several good tourist guidebooks for Portland that list year round museums and activities as well as events that make Portland special. You can find a short list of these in Chapter 16, 'More Information'.

The A & E Section included with the Friday issue of The Oregonian lists a variety of activities including movies, concerts, live/dance music, theatre, and art shows. It also lists family and children's events, fairs, museum exhibits, and more. The Willamette Week prints a full cultural calendar in each weekly issue.

The following section covers the locations for events, including how to find out about and obtain tickets to events at these locations, and how to get there by public transportation.

Event Locations

Portland and the surrounding area offers a wide variety of activities, concerts, festivals, and events to keep you busy throughout the year. From apples to zebras there is always something going on. The following are the major venues for many of the local events. Two of these locations are outside the Portland area. We include them because you often see them mentioned.

Civic Auditorium, also known as Keller Auditorium

Downtown Portland   503-247-6560
222 SW Clay
(SW Third between Clay and Market)
www.portland.citysearch.com
This location is home to touring theater companies, concerts and the Portland
    Opera.
Parking is available in local parking garages for a fee.
There is no close MAX stop. When the Central City streetcar starts to run regularly
    in 2001, there will be a connection to the Civic Auditorium from the Library/
    SW 9th and Galleria/SW 10th MAX stops.

Civic Stadium, also known as the PGE Stadium

Downtown Portland   503-248-4345
1776 SW Madison
www.civicstadium.com
This stadium is the home of Portland's minor league baseball team, the Rockies.
    It is the location of many outdoor sport competitions.
On-street parking is available.
MAX stop - Civic Stadium

McCall Waterfront Park

SW Naito Parkway between Clay and the Steel Bridge
www.parks.ci.portland.or.us/parks/waterfrontpark
This park is the site for the Rose Festival Fun Center in June, and food and music
    festivals throughout the summer.
Parking is available in local parking garages for a fee.
MAX stops - Yamhill District, Oak Street/SW1st, or Skidmore Fountain

Oregon Convention Center

777 NE Martin Luther King Blvd   800-791-2250
www.oregoncc.org
This site hosts large and small conventions, tradeshows and public shows.
Parking is available in local parking garages for a fee.
MAX stop - Convention Center

Portland Metropolitan Expo Center

2060 N Marine Drive   503-285-7756
www.expocenter.org
This exposition center hosts small and large expositions, sports events, and other
    public events, such as the Catlin Gable Rummage sale.
Parking is available in local parking garages for a fee.
No MAX access at this time.
Bus Route 6 - MLK

The Gorge Amphitheater

754 Silica Road NW
George, Washington 98848
www.barstop.com/gorge
This has been rated the best outdoor amphitheater for music concerts. It is about
    a six hour drive from Portland.
Parking is available for a fee.

126

Pioneer Courthouse Square

Downtown Portland Broadway and Yamhill
Main office phone   503-223-1613
Event Hotline   503-768-5634
www.portlandparks.org/parks/pioneercourthouse
Known as Portland's living room, Pioneer Courthouse Square is the pride of
    downtown Portland, hosting cultural and seasonal events and informal con-
    certs.
Parking is available in local parking garages for a fee.
MAX stop - Pioneer Courthouse Square

Portland Center for the Performing Arts

Downtown Portland   503-248-4335
www.pcpa.com   or 503-796-9293
This umbrella organization includes the following theaters:
    The Arlene Schnitzer Concert Hall, Keller Civic Auditorium (see separately,
    above), the Newmark Theater, and the Dolores Winningstad Theatre. This
    facility hosts 1,000 performances annually including music, dance, and the-
    atre for adults and children.
Parking is available in local parking garages for a fee, and some on-street park-
    ing.
MAX stop - Library/SW9[th] or Galleria /SW10[th], then walk three blocks south

Portland International Raceway

West Delta Park   503-823-7223
1940 N. Victory Blvd.
www.portlandraceway.com
This location hosts competitive events including bicycle, motorcycle, go-kart,
    sports car and drag races.
Parking is available in local parking garages for a fee.
No MAX access.
Bus Route 8 - NE 15th Street

Portland Meadows

1001 N Schmeer Road   503-285-9144
Portland 97217
www.PortlandMeadows.com

Horseracing is held here from October to April. It is also the Portland area's largest outdoor concert venue.

For concert schedules call Double Tee Productions at 503-227-4418 or www.doubletee.com.

Parking is available for a fee.

There is no MAX access.

Bus Route 13- Portland Meadows

Rose Quarter

One Center Court   503-321-3211
www.rosequarter.com

The Rose Garden, Memorial Coliseum and Exhibit Hall offer everything from NBA Basketball to concerts to family shows such as the circus and ice-skating productions.

Parking is available in local parking garages for a fee.

MAX stop - Rose Center TC

Purchasing Event Tickets

Tickets to Portland area events are easy to purchase. Advertising for these events usually lists the different options available to purchase tickets for the particular event. These options may include buying directly from the box office, a ticket outlet, telephone, or through the Internet. If the event is sold out, tickets are usually available in the classified ads.

Direct Purchase of Tickets

The box office of the site where the event will take place sells tickets during normal business hours. There are usually no service fees associated with this type of purchase.

Fred Meyer and GI Joe's stores have ticket outlets where you can purchase tickets to almost any event. A service fee is attached to these purchases and ranges from $1.50 to $3.00 per ticket.

Charge by Phone

You can also order tickets directly from the theater or event location by telephone. You will need to have a valid credit card. A service fee may be added. Usually you will be given the choice of having the tickets mailed to you, or held at the box office. If the tickets are held for you at the box office, you can pick them up at the window labeled 'Will Call'.

Several businesses sell event tickets by phone (with a credit card) for a fee. The two largest and most reputable independent ticket outlets are:

Ticketmaster	503-224-4400
Fastixx	503-224-8499

Purchase Online

You can also purchase some event tickets online. Both ticket outlets mentioned above offer this service and provide concert and event information through their websites:

Ticketmaster	www.ticketmaster.com
Fastixx	www.fastixx.com

You can also find information and purchase tickets through Portland's www.digitalcity.com. You will need a credit card for any online purchases and will be charged a service fee.

Classified Ads

If the event you want to attend is sold out, you may be able to find tickets in the classified advertising section of the local papers. However, remember to be cautious because these tickets can be much more expensive.

Fitness Centers

Health Clubs

Health clubs (including fitness centers and gyms) offer a wide range of fitness programs for their members. The types of services and activities vary greatly between clubs.

Some clubs are expensive, providing a wide range of activities and classes, pristine equipment, and deluxe amenities. Others have well-used equipment and few classes, but at a lower price.

Members pay a monthly fee that can range from $25 to over $200. You may also have to pay a one-time initiation fee that can be from $0 (during special promotions) to several hundred dollars. Some clubs offer special rates for families or for employees of certain companies. Considering all of these variables, shop around. Most clubs offer a free one-time use of the facilities or a trial period at a reduced rate to give you the chance to see if the facilities meet your needs.

Activities and services offered at a fitness center may include:

- aerobic activities (stationary bikes, rowing machines, treadmills, and stair climbing machines),
- weight training,
- aerobic, weight training, and spinning classes,
- yoga, stretching, Tai Chi, and similar classes,
- tennis, handball, squash, and racquetball,
- swimming,
- indoor wall rock climbing,
- basketball and volleyball,
- childcare, lessons, and activities for children,
- massage, physical therapy, and tanning beds, and
- amenities such as a snack bar, towel service, and toiletries.

Community Recreational Facilities

Each community offers public recreational facilities. These facilities are part of the local parks and recreation departments. You are not restricted to your own community's facilities. You can use any of the facilities listed below, although the cost may be slightly higher if you live out of the area. Your realtor can tell you which recreational facility is considered to be in your area.

These recreational facilities offer a wide range of services. Many offer classes ranging from crafts to drama to sports. The classes and activities are popular since they are inexpensive, convenient, and of good quality. Each facility may have a pool, weight lifting equipment, basketball and volleyball courts, gymnastics equipment, etc. They are a good resource for community events and club meetings.

The following is a list of the community recreational facilities in the Portland Metropolitan Area.

Clark County	360-696-8171	www.co.clark.wa.us/environ/parks
Forest Grove	503-359-3238	Not available
Gresham	503-618-2531	www.ci.gresham.or.us/departments/des/ parksandrec
Hillsboro	503-681-6120	www.ci.hillsboro.or.us/parksrec
North Clackamas	503-794-8002	www.co.clackamas.or.us/ncprd
Portland	503-823-7529	www.portlandparks.org
Tualatin	503-645-6433	www.thprd.org
Vancouver	360-696-8171	www.ci.vancouver.wa.us/parks-recreation

Visit the websites or phone for a free catalog. Catalogs come out four times a year, just prior to a new season of offerings. They are mailed to all residents that the facility serves and can also be found at the library.

Martial Arts Facilities

There are many gyms that offer training in the various martial arts disciplines.

Martial Arts

Internet Sites

You can browse the Internet for local information. www.portland.citysearch.com, www.cascadelink.com, and www.oregonlive.com are good websites for local and regional information.

Libraries

Multnomah, Washington, and Clackamas County

The Portland area has three different library systems. Multnomah County, Washington County, and Clackamas County libraries are separate systems. They offer their own programs and maintain separate book (and other materials) inventories. The three systems, however, have an agreement that makes the resources of the three library systems available to all residents. You can hold a library card for any (or all three) county library systems. This increases the resources and activities available to you.

Clark County, Washington

The library system in Clark County is the Fort Vancouver Regional Library District. This library system also provides a variety of services and offers a wealth of resources.

Branch Libraries

Each county has several branch libraries. To find the library nearest you, ask your relocation agent, realtor, neighbor, or someone at your child's school. You can also look in the blue government section in the front of the phone book under 'Libraries' in the section for your county.

Materials at one branch can be easily transferred to another branch. Materials may be exchanged between the three Oregon county systems, but may take longer. Ask a library employee for assistance.

The largest library within the three counties is Multnomah County's Central Library located at 810 SW 10th Ave. in downtown Portland. This library holds the largest selection of materials at one site and hosts a wide variety of activities.

How to Use Your Library

You will need a library card to be able to use any of the services offered or to check out any materials. You can get a library card (at no cost) by completing a form at any branch library. You will need to show a piece of identification: either a driver's license or a passport. This card will be good at any branch library within that particular library system.

Other materials that can be borrowed in addition to books include videos, CD's, audio-cassette tapes, and computer software. Libraries often have a variety of books in other languages.

You can place a hold on materials that are already checked out. The library will call you when the materials have been returned. Books can generally be checked out for three weeks, other materials for varying periods of time. Materials can be renewed up to 99 times, if someone else has not placed a hold on them. A fine is charged if materials are returned late.

Other Services

Libraries offer a wide variety of services and activities. They hold lectures, demonstrations, workshops, performances, and have computers for public use. Classes are offered including computer instruction on how to use the Internet. The library is a great place for kids, too. Along with the children's books, there are story-times (a great place for children to hear English), crafts, puppet shows, book discussions, and music concerts. These offerings are free, but using the Internet or taking a class will require a library card.

The library is often a center for community events. Community newsletters and newspapers are available for you to take. Posters are displayed announcing local clubs and group activities.

Library Hours

Library hours vary widely between branches. Many are open Sundays and evenings. Some are closed on Mondays. Check online or call the branch for their hours.

Library Computer Systems

Each library system has its own separate website and catalog database. Here is how you access them from home:

Region	Catalog of Resources	Website
Multnomah County	DYNA	www.multnomah.lib.or.us/lib
Washington County	WILI	www.wilinet.wccls.lib.or.us
Clackamas County	LINAS	www.lincc.lib.or.us
Fort Vancouver Regional Library District		www.fvrl.org

These websites can assist you with finding community support services and organizations, volunteer opportunities within and outside of the library, and resource materials. If, while using one of the online systems, you find a resource you would like to view, you can place the item on hold, have it sent to your local branch, or even have it mailed to you (you will have to pay the postage). Anyone can search for materials, but if you want to reserve them, you will need a library card.

Movies and Films

There is a variety of film choices in movie theaters in the Portland area. Large multiple screen theaters may have up to 14 first-run movies. Some cinemas show classic films, others show international films (usually with English subtitles), and some show only films from the independent film industry.

In addition you can choose the environment in which you watch a film. There are theaters at which you can sit in armchairs and have a beer. Others provide dinner at your table during the movie. Most theatres simply provide cushioned seating and snack foods.

Movie Theater is the same as Cinema. Film is the same as movie.

Most theaters do not allow you to bring your own food into the theater and encourage you to purchase food from concession stands. Movies in the United States do not usually include an intermission.

You can read the movie listings in the local newspapers, or call the theater directly.

Each day The Oregonian carries movie listings with times at which they are being shown. A complete listing of movies along with movie reviews is published in the A & E section included each Friday in The Oregonian. The Willamette Week also publishes movie listings.

Regal Cinemas is a dominant chain of cinemas in Portland. There are several movie houses under the name of the McMenamins Theater Pubs. There are also several smaller theaters. Newberg, Oregon has the only local drive-in movie theater, which is only open during the summer months.

Tickets

There are several options for purchasing movie tickets.

Telephone

Regal Cinemas allows you to purchase tickets by telephone (503-235-7469). Select a movie, the time you want to see it, and the theater. If seats are available, you are asked to give a credit card number. The tickets will be held at the theater for you. When you arrive at the theatre, go to the special desk for pre-reserved tickets. Slide the same credit card through the computer and the tickets will be released to you. You can reserve tickets up to three days in advance.

Century Theaters allow you to purchase tickets up to five days in advance (503-775-0000).

In Person

You can of course buy tickets at the movie theater at the time of the showing. However, if you go to a popular movie at a busy time (weekend nights, for example), the particular show time may be sold out. You can buy tickets in advance (up to 48 hours) at any box office.

Websites

Movie theater tickets can be purchased online. Rules and restrictions are similar to purchasing tickets by telephone. This can be done at the following websites:

Regal Cinemas	www.regalcinema.com
McMenamins	www.mcmenamins.com
Century Theaters	www.centurytheaters.com

Ticket Price Discounts

Movies shown during the day (matinees) are approximately half the cost of what it would be for an evening showing. These reduced price shows will be indicated in the newspaper listings with a parenthesis '( )' around the show times.

Discount Days

Some theaters have a policy that all shows on Monday are discounted. Any movies listed in the paper with a check or a star next to them do not qualify for the special Monday discounts. However, these movies will still qualify for the matinee discounts discussed above.

Bringing Babies

KOIN Theaters have a special viewing room for parents with small children. You can see the film without disturbing others in the theater if your child cries.

Movie Ratings

The movie industry voluntarily submits its films to a Rating Board before they are released. This Rating Board (a panel of parents) judges a film's appropriateness for children. The rating is based on the theme of the film, and the use of language, sex, nudity, and drugs. The rating does not give an indication of the quality of the film. The following code is used to rate films.

G - General Audiences, all ages

The G rating means that the film will contain nothing that is offensive for even the very youngest children to see and hear. Violence will be minimal; dialog will only use everyday language.

PG - Parental Guidance

The PG rating means that the film may contain subjects that a parent will need to explain to the child before or after seeing the film. There may be moderate horror and violence but no drug usage or sex scenes.

PG13 - Parents strongly cautioned

A PG13 rating signifies that the film is inappropriate for children under age 13. Harsh language, some drug usage, and suggestive sex scenes may be included.

R - Restricted

An R rating means that no one under age 17 may be admitted without a parent or adult guardian. The film has adult content, including strong language, a disquieting theme, and/or a harsh portrayal of violence, sex and drug usage.

NC-17 - No one aged 17 and under is admitted

The NC-17 rating signifies that the rating board feels the film is for adults only. This rating does not imply pornography, but rather that it may have excessive violence, sexually explicit language, and/or sex scenes.

Newspapers

Local newspapers are an excellent way to become connected with your new home. Not only can a newspaper inform you of local and regional news, but also it will report on issues of concern to the community. You can read interesting articles on a vast array of topics or find things you want to do in the area. For subscription information refer to Chapter 6, 'Making your House a Home'.

The Oregonian

The Oregonian offers a different weekly feature section each weekday:

Monday - Tech NW (local hi-tech business news)
Tuesday - Food Day (recipes, articles on seasonal foods)
Wednesday - Science (articles on current topics in the sciences)
Thursday - Home and Garden (outside living features), Local county news section
Friday - A&E (Arts and Entertainment)

Willamette Week

This free local news weekly is published every Wednesday. It offers an independent perspective on local news and events and publishes a full cultural calendar.

Portland Parent, Portland Family

Portland Parent and Portland Family are two free newspapers listing family activities, schools, day care centers, and camps.

Outdoor Recreation

The Pacific Northwest is a playground for the outdoor recreation enthusiast. Portland makes an ideal home base for anyone who enjoys the outdoors, with easy accessibility to a diverse range of environments. Within a few hours' drive are rivers, mountains, deserts, and beaches. Oregon's many State and National Parks, as well as the abundance of National Forests in the western states, offer countless opportunities for skiing, kayaking, canoeing, surfing, windsurfing, hiking, biking, rock climbing, mountaineering, camping, and fishing.

A good way to find out what there is to do and where to do it is to ask friends, coworkers, or neighbors what they like to do. Maybe you can join them. Or get a guidebook at the library or a bookstore. Health clubs and outdoor gear stores may have bulletin boards on which they post local activities or trips. As mentioned above, the A&E section of the Friday Oregonian lists local bike trips and hikes with the name of a contact person to call if you have questions.

Sno Park Permits, Trail Head Permits, State and National Park Permits

If you plan to spend time in the mountains or the National or State Parks and intend to use your own car to get there, you need to consider the parking requirements.

If you are planning to park your car in the areas subject to heavy snowfall in the mountains (to go skiing, for example) you must have a Sno Park permit. This annual permit costs less than $30. When you park your car, you place this permit on the inside of your windshield. The money collected from the sale of these permits is used to maintain the highways during the winter months. These permits are available (after October 1) from most outdoor sporting goods stores including GI Joe's, REI and Oregon Mountain Community.

In the summer there are special permits required at many of the hiking trails within the National Forests (Washington and Oregon share a single pass that is valid in both states). You can purchase annual passes from the same outdoor stores above or you can purchase a single day use pass when you arrive at the park or trail head.

State Parks and National Parks also require a use–permit. You can purchase a single day-use permit at the parks when you arrive. You can also purchase an annual State (or National) Park permit that will provide you access all year to any State (or National) Park. The state annual permit costs approximately $30 and with $5 more, you can get a second permit for your second car.

Social Clubs and Organizations

Portland has many things to see and do, but it is always more enjoyable to do them with other people. A great way to find people who have similar interests is to join a club or organization. Ask friends or colleagues if they are involved with any groups or activities, or know of any organizations that would be of particular interest to you.

Your local library is a good resource. Within each library, there will be a bulletin board posted with announcements of local community groups' meetings, as well as brochures and local newspapers for you to take with you.

The Multnomah County Library offers an outstanding resource for finding a group with your particular interests. This listing is not limited to Multnomah County. Within the www.multnomah.lib.or.us/lib website, select the library catalog. If you then select the web version, choose Organizations. If you choose the text version, select *18 Other Resources*, then *2 Community Organization Database*. (These instructions are as of fall 2000.) Most clubs, groups and organizations in the area are listed. It gives a brief description of each group and a contact person and phone number.

☞ **You can go to the library and use their computers or ask the library staff to assist you.**

Another excellent Internet resource to find local special interest groups is www.cascadelink.com.

Visitor's Association

For information on things to do in the area, including local events, attractions, and museums, contact the Portland Oregon Visitor's Association (POVA). They are located at Two World Trade Center, on the corner of Southwest Naito Parkway and Salmon Street in downtown Portland. Their phone number is 503-222-2223, or toll free 1-87-PORTLAND (1-877-678-5263). Information is available online at www.pova.com.

Volunteering

If you are looking for activities that will make a difference in the community or in someone's life, volunteering may be for you. Portland has a variety of non-profit organizations where you can volunteer your time. Whether you are snuggling sick babies in the hospital, building homes for low-income families, or picking up trash at the coast, your help will be greatly appreciated. Volunteering allows you to meet other people, develop life and career skills, and give you a sense of belonging in your community. This may be particularly valuable to partners who had been working in their home country but are not allowed to work in the United States.

Volunteering at School

If you have children, an obvious place to volunteer is at their school. Teachers may appreciate your help in the classroom. The Parent Teacher Association (PTA) needs people to help with school projects, events, or fundraising. The school library always needs assistance shelving books. Sports activities and other clubs need adults to drive and chaperone for trips. As your child brings home notices of these activities, call the contact person to offer your help.

One Time versus Ongoing Volunteering

Organizations may have a one-time need for help at a specific event. Other volunteer work can be ongoing. When looking for an ongoing opportunity, you will probably complete an application and go to an interview to discuss your goals as a volunteer and the skills you can offer. Often there will be a group orientation to familiarize you with the organization. Some organizations may only hold new volunteer orientations at certain times of the year. You may have to wait for the next orientation before you can start volunteering.

Local versus International Volunteering

You can choose to work with a local organization or to volunteer at a branch of an international organization. The advantage of working with an international organization is that you may have been involved with the organization in your home country or are hoping to continue your involvement when you return home.

Internet Resources

The following websites have lists of organizations that need volunteers:

Web address	Phone number
www.volunteermatch.org National directory, searchable by zip code.	415-241-6872
www.servenet.org National directory, searchable by zip code.	800-VOLUNTEER
www.idealist.org International directory, searchable by country, state, and zip code.	212-843-3973
www.cascadelink.org Portland/Vancouver specific directory.	None
www.volunteerworks.org Portland/Vancouver specific, matches your interests with available opportunities.	503-413-7855
www.handsonportland.org Portland specific directory of no commitment opportunities.	503-234-3581

Other Ways to Find Opportunities

Each Thursday under the heading 'Volunteers' in the Living Section of the Oregonian is a list of organizations needing volunteers.

If you would like to volunteer at a specific organization, call their main telephone number (in the white pages section of the yellow pages) and ask to speak to the volunteer coordinator.

Worship

Religious freedom is strongly protected in the U.S. A large variety of religions are practiced here, so you should be able to find a group similar to that which you are accustomed. In looking for a place of worship, you may want to try attending several different services, before you find the group that best meets your needs. A good way to find a place of worship is to contact a relevant cultural organization.

The Religion Section of the Saturday Oregonian lists worship services for Saturday evening and Sunday, but it is not complete. The Yellow Pages, under 'Churches,' lists religious groups by type of religion. Call the places of worship that look promising to you to find out when services are held and what languages the services are conducted in. Many of the smaller organizations will have answering machines on which you can leave a message. If the greeting on the machine is in your language, it is likely services will be conducted in that language as well.

Another option for finding a place of worship is to contact an organization from your culture and ask them about worship opportunities. As discussed above under Social Clubs and Organizations, the Multnomah County Library website can help in this search.

Another potential resource is the group of local organizations devoted to helping refugees. They may be able to help you in finding a similar cultural and religious group. These organizations are:

Lutheran Family Services	503-233-0042
Jewish Family and Child Services	503-226-7079
Catholic Charities	503-231-4866
Sponsors Organized to Assist Refugees (SPOAR)	503-284-3002
World Affairs Council of Oregon	503-274-7488

Health Care

Chapter 8

Health Care

Medical care in the United States will be different from what you are familiar with in your home country. The U.S. medical system is closely tied to the health insurance industry. Consequently, the type of health insurance you have will determine how and what kind of medical care you receive. There are almost limitless types of insurance programs and the many confusing details to understand. It is easy to become frustrated. It is neither possible nor practical to explain all of the insurance options here, but we can tell you where to go to find health insurance and medical care. To be comfortable with this health system you need to know how to find the care you need, and to understand your health insurance and its policies.

The U.S. is the largest country in the world that does not provide national health care to its citizens.

Health Care Providers

There are over 5000 physicians in 150 specialties and sub-specialties in the greater Portland metropolitan area. Simply choosing a doctor may seem overwhelming. In addition, there are over 15 hospitals, including two very fine children's hospitals. All are equipped with emergency rooms.

Your Physician

Physicians generally practice in office buildings called clinics. These medical clinics are not necessarily close to a hospital. An entire building may be devoted to health care practices and services, or it may be shared by a variety of businesses. You will not find a physician working out of his/her home and it is very rare that a physician will come to your home.

Types of Physicians

For general health problems and routine exams for you and your family, you will probably wish to find a family or general practitioner. Depending on your needs, there are a variety of specialists that you may choose to visit (a pediatrician for children, an obstetrician/gynecologist for women's health, a cardiac surgeon if you need heart surgery, etc.). Your health insurance may require you to select from a specific list of doctors (see 'Health Insurance' below). That aside, there are several steps you can take to find a doctor that is right for you.

All Physicians are addressed as Doctor and written with Dr. before their name or M.D. after their name.

How to Find the Right Physician

Ask friends, neighbors, co-workers, fellow students, parents of your child's friends, or your child's teachers to recommend a doctor. Call the physician referral services listed in the Yellow Pages. The website for the American Medical Association (www.ama-assn.org) allows you to select a physician by specialty, city, and even zip code.

145

What is Important to You?

Hospitals
*
Physicians

There are some choices to make as you think about your health care. Do you wish to see a doctor of the same sex, or one who performs a particular treatment? Do you need to have a doctor whose office is near your home, work, or school? Do you need a hospital with specific technology? Narrow your choices to three.

Interviewing the Doctor's Office Staff

After narrowing your choice, call each of the three physician's offices to see if they are accepting patients. If so, ask the following questions:

> How far in advance do you have to make an appointment?
>
> If you become ill, is it possible to see the doctor that same day?
>
> Is the doctor on time for the appointments or is there usually a long wait? (In other words, how easy is it to see your doctor? If s/he is too busy, find another doctor.)
>
> Does the doctor accept patient phone calls? Are they restricted to a particular time of day?
>
> Will the doctor return phone calls?
>
> Will the doctor prescribe medications without seeing the patient, for example, recurring problems such as ear infection or bronchitis?
>
> Is a nurse available to take calls?
>
> How long has the doctor been practicing medicine?
>
> Does s/he ever come to the home?
>
> Does the doctor offer interpreter services?
>
> How many doctors are in the practice and can you use one of these doctors if your physician is not available?
>
> Does the office accept your particular health insurance?
>
> Does the clinic require any payments at the time of the appointment?

It is important to know how to get medical help before you need it.

If you do not like the answers to any of these questions or if the receptionist is rude, call another doctor.

Interviewing the Doctor

Before selecting your physician, s/he may require you to set up a 'get acquainted' visit. You may wish to set one up even if the physician does not require it. Be sure to find out the cost and if your insurance will cover it. If you would like to meet the physician but feel uncomfortable with this initial visit, bring a friend.

If you do not have answers to the questions listed above, ask during this visit. In addition, ask the physician if s/he treats a particular condition and the preferred treatment options. Also, ask what to do when you need medical help after office hours (nights and weekends).

It is important to be able to communicate with your physician and understand your medical care. If this is not the case, call another doctor.

Hospitals

Some of the major hospitals in the area include:

Adventist Medical Center   503-257-2500
10123 SE Market St.
Portland, OR 97216
www.AdventisHealthNW.com

Eastmoreland Hospital   503-234-0411
2900 SE Steel St.
Portland, OR 97202
www.eastmoreland.nahc.net

Hospitals

Legacy Emanuel Hospital & Health Center   503-413-2200
2801 N. Gantenbein Ave.
Portland, OR 97227
www.legacyhealth.org

Legacy Good Samaritan Hospital & Medical Center   503-413-7711
1015 NW 22nd Ave.
Portland, OR 97210
www.legacyhealth.org

Legacy Meridian Park Hospital   503-692-1212
19300 SW 65th Ave.
Tualatin, OR 97062
www.legacyhealth.org

Legacy Mt. Hood Medical Center   503-674-1122
24800 SE Stark
Gresham, OR 97030
www.legacyhealth.org

Oregon Health Sciences University (OHSU)   503-494-8311
3181 SW Sam Jackson Park Road
Portland, OR 07201-3098
www.ohsu.edu

Providence Milwaukie Hospital   503-513-8300
10150 SE 32nd Ave.
Milwaukie, OR 97222
www.providence.org

Providence Portland Medical Center   503-215-1111
4805 NE Glisan St.
Portland, OR 97213
www.providence.org

Providence St. Vincent Medical Center   503-216-1234
9204 SW Barnes Rd.
Portland, OR 97225
www.providence.org

Southwest Washington Medical Center   503-972-3000
400 NE Mother Joseph Place
Vancouver, WA 98664
www.swmedctr.com

Tuality Community Hospital   503-681-1111
335 SE 8th
Hillsboro, OR 97123
www.tuality.com

Tuality Forest Grove Hospital   503-357-2173
1809 Maple St.
Forest Grove, OR 97116
www.tuality.com

Willamette Falls Hospital   503-656-1631
1500 Division St
Oregon City, OR 97045

Woodland Park Hospital   503-257-5500
10300 NE Hancock
Portland, OR

Emergency Rooms

Emergency Rooms are attached to hospitals and are used to treat patients with life-or-limb threatening conditions.

Urgent Care Facilities

Another type of medical facility is an urgent care facility (also called convenient care or immediate care). This type of facility treats non-life-threatening illnesses and injuries for people who may not have a physician or if their physician is unable to see them. An urgent care unit is less expensive than an emergency room and is usually open evenings and weekends. But be sure to ask your insurance company if this type of facility's services are covered by insurance. Some urgent care facilities in the area include:

Adventist Health Convenient Care   503-666-6717
18750 SE Stark
Portland, OR 97233
www.AdventistHealthNW.com

Legacy Good Samaritan Convenience Care Center   503-413-8090
1015 NW 22nd Ave.
Portland, OR 97219
www.legacyhealth.org

Tanasbourne Urgent Care   503-690-6818
1881 NW 185th Ave.
Aloha, OR

Tuality at Aloha Urgent Care   503-681-4223
17175 SW TV Hwy.
Aloha, OR 97006
www.tuality.com

Southwest Washington Emergency Care Clinic   360-696-5232
3400 Main St.
Vancouver, WA 98663
www.swmedctr.com

Willamette Falls Immediate Care   503-654-8417
9775 SE Sunnyside Rd. Suite 200
Clackamas, OR 97015

Other Health Clinics

If you are a student, there may be a health clinic on your college campus for minor illnesses or injuries. Schools have part-time or full-time nurses on staff. Some high schools have actual medical clinics.

The Department of Health has clinics for low-income people and offers free vaccinations at locations around the area periodically throughout the year.

Emergency Care versus Urgent Care

Urgent Care is less urgent than emergency care.

It is important to understand those times when you would use an emergency room and when you would use an urgent care facility. If you are prepared, you will not be intimidated by the health care system when you need it most.

You will probably experience more situations requiring urgent care than true emergency situations. If you seek urgent care at an emergency room you will be disappointed. You can wait a long time in an emergency room waiting area to see a doctor since the true emergencies will take priority. In addition, emergency room fees are very expensive and insurance will most likely not cover urgent care treatment in an emergency room. Conversely, if you seek emergency care in an urgent care center, you will most likely be transported to an emergency room. The time this takes could mean the difference between life, more complicated health problems or even death. In a true emergency, you need to go directly to the emergency room.

If after reading the descriptions below you still have questions about the differences between emergency and urgent care, ask the customer service representative of your insurance company, your company's human resources contact, or your physician. They can explain the distinctions more clearly.

Emergency Care

Emergency care is for life or limb threatening conditions. Serious injury, severe bleeding, heart attack, loss of consciousness, acute allergic reaction, ruptured aneurysm, acute appendicitis, stoppage or acute difficulty in breathing, convulsions, seizure, drug overdose, and acute abdominal pain are all examples of health conditions requiring emergency care.

In a medical emergency, call 911 from any phone. They will ask if you need an ambulance, the fire department, or the police. Know the address you are calling from, and do not hang up until you are told to or help arrives. The ambulance will take the patient to the hospital where the patient's physician practices, if known, or the nearest appropriate medical facility.

The 911 emergency telephone number is a free call from any phone, including payphones.

Urgent Care

Urgent care is for medical conditions that need immediate attention but are not as serious as emergencies. Usually the patient needs to see the doctor that same day to get treatment or a prescription. Ear infections, allergic reactions such as a rash, broken bones not causing excessive bleeding, cuts which may require stitches but bleeding is controlled are examples of health conditions requiring urgent care. In these situations you would call your doctor. If s/he is not able to see you in a timely manner, go to the nearest urgent care facility.

Poison Control

For poisoning, the Poison Control Center has a help phone that is staffed 24 hours a day. If you or someone you know has swallowed or been exposed to a poisonous substance, you can call the Poison Control Center, describe the problem and they can tell you what to do immediately. The phone number is 503-494-8968. It is listed on the inside front cover of every phone book.

☞ **In case of an emergency, carry your insurance card with you at all times. If you do not have insurance or cannot prove you have insurance, you may receive minimum treatment at an emergency room. If you cannot pay at the time of receiving care, treatment will not go beyond that minimum level.**

Interpreter/Translation Services

Translators and Interpreters

If you are having trouble understanding your doctor or other medical personnel, or if you feel you are having trouble being understood, ask to use an interpreter. Hospitals offer interpreter services; your doctor's office will probably be familiar with them too. If you need medical records translated either from or into your native language, translation services are available.

Having a Baby

Birth Centers

The customary method of delivering a baby in the United States is in a hospital by a physician specialist (obstetrician). Midwives are becoming more common and can be found as members of medical practices along side obstetricians, delivering babies in the hospital. If you prefer having your baby at home, or other alternative birthing method, ask a midwife or look in the yellow pages.

Birthing Classes

During the pregnancy, the mother is strongly encouraged to meet with her obstetrician or midwife on a regular basis (called pre-natal care and covered by most insurance) and attend birthing classes. Your obstetrician or midwife can recommend a birthing class which will instruct you and your partner in the birthing process. If you have given birth before, you may still find the class useful. Not only will it refresh your memory, but also introduce you to American-English terminology, United States customs and techiniques, and specific hospital policies. In addition, you will receive free samples and coupons of American baby products; products you may not be familiar with in your own country. Most importantly, the class can provide you with valuable resources such as support groups, government agencies and other helpful organizations.

Common Practices

United States obstetricians are more willing to request ultrasounds, determine the sex of the baby in utero, and provide pain-killing drugs during childbirth than physicians in other countries. At the birth it is common to take a blood sample from the baby and perform other tests. If you choose to have your baby boy circumcised, this will happen within a day or two of delivery.

Hospital stays after delivery are usually one to two days for a normal (vaginal) birth and five to seven days for a Caesarian Section (C-Section). No special care is provided or covered by insurance, once the mother and child leave the hospital. However you can arrange for help yourself. One option is to hire a doula.

Doulas

Doulas are becoming an increasingly popular resource, providing help throughout the entire birth process. **Birth doulas** offer pre-natal, labor, delivery and post-labor support. They usually charge a flat rate. **Postpartum doulas** offer services which include providing help with the new baby and other children, and doing the cooking and light housework. These doulas usually charge by the hour. Doulas are not medically trained, but rather provide encouragement, support and advice. Doulas are filling the need for many expectant families whose nearest relatives live too far away to offer help. The two types of doulas can be found at:

Birth doulas	Postpartum Doulas
Doulas of North America	National Association of Postpartum Care Services
801-756-7331	800-453-6852
www.dona.org.	www.napcs.org

La Leche League

Another resource is the La Leche League, an organization that provides education and support to women who wish to breastfeed. They have local meetings, play groups for children, and publications. In the Portland area, the La Leche League can be reached at 503-282-9377 or www.lalecheleague.org.

Feeling out of Control?

The U.S. health care system prides itself on having the latest equipment and medications. It also supports the philosophy that the woman has control of her health care choices throughout the birth process. However, having a baby in a foreign country, no matter how advanced the medical care, can be a frightening event. You may, in fact, feel that choices and events are quite out of your control. Our best advice is to find a support group through any of the resources listed above.

Children's Health and School

Vaccinations

Your child must be vaccinated to attend a public or private school. If your child is not vaccinated, s/he will not be allowed to attend. You will be asked by the school to complete a form listing the dates that your child received the various vaccines. The vaccinations required by the State of Oregon for your child to attend school are:

Diphtheria	Tetanus
Polio	Varicella (Chickenpox)
Measles	Mumps
Rubella	Hepatitis B
Haemophilus Influenzae	

It is likely that the types and timing of the vaccinations required in the United States are different than in your home country. Discuss the differences with your child's physician to determine which vaccinations your child needs. The physician is able to give the vaccinations (usually covered by insurance) or you may go to one of several free clinics. The school will provide you with a list of these clinics and the days they are open.

School Health Programs

Public schools offer free hearing and vision tests. In addition, they offer free fluoride supplements. Some water sources in the Portland area have been treated with fluoride to safeguard the health of your teeth. Your pediatrician will know which areas do not have fluoride in the water and may recommend a fluoride supplement for your child. Flouride supplements can also be purchased at drug stores. If your physician writes a prescription, a portion of the cost may be covered by insurance.

Health Insurance

[Note: Definitions of insurance terms can be found at the end of this chapter.]

Health insurance is vital to receiving quality health care. You have health insurance for the same reason you have other kinds of insurance: to protect yourself financially. You need to have a way to pay the medical bills in case of a serious accident or major illness. There are many insurance terms to learn and policy options to understand. It may seem unnecessarily complicated and overwhelming. It is. But do not despair. Americans struggle with understanding these choices, too. You cannot avoid the medical system if you are sick, injured, pregnant, or if family members need health exams or vaccinations. The best approach is to be prepared. Use all the resources available to you. Most health insurance companies have a customer service department to discuss claims and coverage. Ask questions until you feel comfortable with your health insurance.

How to Find Health Insurance

Your Home Country

First, do not overlook the option of being insured through your home country. This may be the best option for the following reasons:

> You are used to working with your home country insurance coverage in your own language.
> It may pay more of the medical bills and therefore be less expensive for you.
> You do not have to learn the United States medical insurance system.

You will need to determine for yourself if this option is possible.

Your Employer

The most common way to get health insurance in the United States is through an employer. This is known as group insurance and is generally the least expensive way to buy insurance. You may be offered several different plans to choose from. Note that businesses with 25 employees or more are required by law to offer health insurance. The employer will usually pay a portion or the entire monthly premium for this health insurance. The amount you pay will be deducted from each paycheck and your cost will depend on the type of insurance you select.

There are other places to find group insurance. Some examples are through your school if you are a student, or through a professional organization or club.

Private Insurance

If your employer is small enough to not offer insurance and you are not eligible for other group insurance, you can buy an individual policy from an insurance company. It will require effort on your part to look carefully at a variety of insurance companies and understand the plans they offer in order to make the best decision. Plans vary greatly in coverage, cost, and where you may be allowed to go for medical care, so it is worth your time studying the options.

Types of Health Insurance

Indemnity Plans

Indemnity (or fee-for-service) coverage is usually more expensive but is easier to un- derstand and use, and pays more of your bills. You pay a monthly premium and can choose to see any doctor or can change doctors at any time. You are also able to use any hospital you wish or see a specialist without first getting permission.

Managed Care Plans

The other type of insurance plan is the managed care plan, where you are required to select a primary care physician.

Open enrollment is the time, once a year, during which you can change your health insurance, or particulars such as your primary care physician.

Primary Care Physician

The primary care physician (PCP) manages the health care you receive. You must have authorization from your primary care physician for any medical tests, emergency room visits, consultations with specialists, second opinions from other physicians, etc. This authorization is called a referral. If your physician will not write a referral for a particular service, you can still receive the service without the referral, but your insur- ance will cover this service at a lower rate or not at all. If you wish to change primary care physicians, it is usually done once a year during open enrollment.

Your insurance company (directly or through your employer, school, or association) will provide you with the list of physicians from which to pick. Generally, this list in- cludes the following types of physicians:

> **Family Practitioner**: will see any member of your family for any
> health reason.
> **General Practitioner**: will see any member of your family for any
> health reason.
> **Internist**: will see any member of your family for any health reason.
> **Obstetrician/Gynecologist (OB/GYN)**: specializes in women's
> health care.

Mid-wife: specializes in women's health care.
Nurse practitioner: will see any member of your family for any
health reason.
Pediatrician: specializes in children's health care.

Review this list carefully before selecting an insurance plan. If you are interested in using a particular physician, be sure s/he is on the list and accepting new patients.

Types of Managed Care Plans

Health Maintenance Organizations (HMOs)

One type of managed care plan is the HMO (Health Maintenance Organization). An HMO can be a small group of local physicians, or a large, national organization including physicians throughout the United States, such as Aetna, Cigna, Blue Cross/ Blue Shield, or Kaiser Permanente. You choose your primary care physician from a list of physicians who belong to the HMO.

Preferred Provider Organizations (PPOs)

Another type of managed care plan is the PPO (Preferred Provider Organization). It offers a little more flexibility than an HMO in that you can select any physician to be your primary care physician, but if you choose from their preferred list of providers, you get a discount on your health care costs.

Paying for Health Care

Premiums

If you are receiving health insurance through an employer, your contribution to the cost of your policy will be deducted from your paycheck. If your insurance is not purchased through your employer, you will make monthly payments to the insurance company.

Co-Payments

When you visit your doctor you will be responsible for a co-payment (a per visit service charge), which will range between $5 to $20 depending on your insurance plan. You will either be asked to pay this amount at the time of your visit, or will be billed later, depending on your doctor's billing policy.

Deductible

Most plans also require that you contribute an annual amount to your health care. This amount is called a deductible. It is a specified amount of your medical bills that you must pay before the insurance company will begin paying.

Meeting the deductible means you have paid the entire deductible.

For example, a $250/$500 deductible means you are required to pay up to $250 for each individual in your family, but not to exceed $500 for the whole family.

The amount you pay in premiums and services not covered under your policy does not count toward the deductible. The deductible must be met each year.

Note that although the deductible is defined as the amount you must pay before insurance begins paying, some services, such as doctor's visits may be waived. In this case, your insurance will pay routine doctor's office visits even though you have not yet met the deductible.

Co-Insurance

After you have paid the deductible and the insurance company begins paying, you still may be required to pay a specified percentage of the bill, perhaps 20%. This is called co-insurance.

Cap on Out-of-Pocket Costs

Finally, your policy should specify a maximum amount that you are required to pay (usually $1000 - $5000). This is called a cap on out-of-pocket costs. Out-of-pocket costs may include co-payments, co-insurance and/or the deductible, depending on the insurance policy. When you have reached the cap, you no longer have to pay the pre-defined out-of-pocket-costs.

Example 1:
- Your cap is $1,000.
- Your insurance defines out-of-pocket costs as the deductible and co-insurance.

When you have paid $1000 in deductibles and co-insurance combined, the only payments you will continue making on any subsequent medical services will be the co-pay.

Example 2:
- Your cap is $1000.
- Your insurance defines out-of-pocket costs as co-payments and co-insurance.

When you have paid $1000 in co-payments and co-insurance combined, the only payments you will continue making on any subsequent medical services will be the deductible. Note, though in this second example, that when you reach this point, you have probably already met the deductible.

You will notice that different insurance plans often give you various choices for co-payments, deductible and co-insurance. The higher the deductible and co-payments and the larger percentage of co-insurance (all costs that are your responsibility), the lower the premium.

> ☞ **Often insurance representatives will use the words co-payments and co-insurance interchangeably. This adds to the confusion. Be sure that anyone discussing the terms of your policy speaks slowly, explaining terms clearly and precisely. Due to the complicated subject and its unique vocabulary, this is good advice for native English speakers and non-native English speakers alike.**

Forms You Can Expect to Receive

Bills

Each time you use a health care service, you will receive a bill from the provider of that service. For example, if you visit your doctor who then orders some blood tests, you will receive a bill from the doctor for the office visit and a bill from the laboratory for the blood tests. The first bills you receive will usually state that your insurance has been billed and you should not send any payment at this time.

Statements

You may receive a statement from each provider at the end of the month, repeating these charges.

Explanation of Benefits (EOBs)

After the insurance company has received the bill from the provider and acted on these charges, you will receive an Explanation of Benefits (EOB) which outlines what the insurance company has paid and not paid. An example is given on the following page.

The provider will then send you a second bill indicating what you are responsible to pay now that insurance has paid their portion. If you have any questions regarding services provided, you can call your provider. If you have any questions regarding the payments (and non-payments) made by the insurance company, you should call the insurance company customer service department.

Health Care Costs Which Are Your Responsibility

You are responsible for paying for the portion of insurance premiums not paid by your employer and the portion of medical bills not paid by your insurance company.

The following page shows two pie charts, which illustrate these costs. Pie chart 1 represents the various insurance premiums which you pay whether you use your insur-

1. Your Annual Insurance Premiums
(paid whether or not you receive medical care)

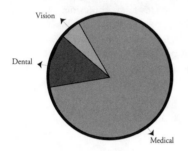

Complete Health Care Coverage

2. Your Medical Bills as a Result of Receiving Medical Care

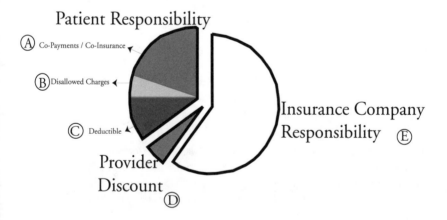

Insurance Company Name
Explanation of Benefits

Insured: *Person paying for insurance.*

Insured ID#: *Usually Social Security Number.*

Group: *Usually company name (employer).*

Group ID #: *Number used to identify the company (employer).*

PATIENT: *Person covered in this statement.*

CLAIM: *A number used for tracking the charges billed to insurance.*

PROVIDER: *Physician, or other health care professional, or facility (such as a hospital) that provided service to the patient.*

PAYEE: *Usually the same as provider; unless the provider is part of a larger company.*

Dates of Service : In the format of month-day-year.

Type of Service: A description of the medical, dental, or vision service provided.

Procedural Code: A number used by providers to identify the specific services provided to a patient.

Total Charges: The fees charged for the service.

(B) **Disallowed Charges:** The charges that an insurance company refuses to pay. This occurs when services are excessive (as determined by your insurer), or are not covered by your policy.

(C) **Deductible:** The amount a patient must pay for health care each year, before receiving insurance benefits.

(D) **Provider Discount:** A discount negotiated by the provider and the insurance company.

Remaining Covered Charges: The charges for services which are covered by your insurance company.

(A) **Co-Pay / Co-Insurance:** Co-payments are the amount a patient must pay each time s/he receives a service (for example, $10 per office visit). Co-insurance is the percentage of billed charges which the patient pays. These amounts are determined by your insurance policy.

(E) **Insurance Benefit:** The total amount the insurance company paid for this billed service.

Patient Responsibility: The amount the patient must pay.

Comments: Usually written in a code format. This section will give you the reasons behind the insurance company disallowing any coverage.

(patient's name) has met $ 00.00 of the $ 250.00 maximum for the 2001 benefit year.

ance or not. Pie chart 2 represents the full amount of a medical bill. The pieces of the pie represent the various payments made to pay the bill. You make some payments, the insurance company pays their share and a portion of each bill is simply written off by the provider.

Opposite the pie chart is a sample Explanation of Benefits letter which you will receive from your insurance company each time you incur health care expenses. (Note: to help you further understand your financial responsibility, we have cross-referenced the items you will find on an EOB with the pieces of the medical bill pie chart.) The EOB you receive will not look exactly like this and the terminology may be slightly different, but the information will be roughly the same. When you receive your first EOB, the information may seem overwhelming, but after studying it a few minutes, you should be able to figure out what your insurance company paid and did not pay, and why. The amount the insurance company has stated you should pay (called patient responsibility) should correspond to the amount appearing on your next bill as the amount due. You should pay this amount when you receive the bill. If you have any questions, call your provider or insurance company.

Covered Services

Medical Care

Medical Care includes general medical care, not including vision and dental care. This can include doctor's visits, emergency room visits, surgery, hospital stays, specialists, ancillary medical services, and pharmaceuticals. It is important for you to understand exactly what types of services are covered under your policy.

Vision Care

Insurance coverage for eye care is often a separate piece of health insurance. Ask friends, neighbors, colleagues, or your physician to recommend an eye doctor. Your insurance may require a referral from your primary care physician. Note that the medical doctor who specializes in eyes is called an ophthalmologist and is located in a medical office. An optometrist is someone who does not have a medical degree, but can examine your eyes, test your vision and fit you with corrective lenses. A good optometrist can recommend you see an ophthalmologist if they see any abnormalities, early signs of disease, or other vision problems. Ask your insurance company what types of services are covered and who can provide these services in order to be covered.

Dentist's Referral Service

*

Dentists

Dental Coverage

The care of your teeth is also a separate piece of health insurance. Ask friends, neighbors, or colleagues to recommend a dentist. You can also look in the Yellow Pages where you will find them listed alphabetically and by location. Look at the dental coverage closely. The most basic plans only cover routine cleanings once a year called preventive care. More costly plans will cover additional services such as fillings, crowns, root canals, etc.

Other Health Care Services

Health
*
Nutrition
*
**Fitness Con-
sultants**

The United States is better known for its technological advancements in medicine than for more natural, holistic methods. These services (sometimes called Alternative Health Care) are available if you know where to look and some may be covered by your insurance. Look in the yellow pages under the particular service you are looking for (such as acupuncture, homeopathy, massage, herbs). Natural food stores may also have consultants on their staff or can make recommendations. Before using these alternative forms of medicine, call your insurance to see if these services are covered. If your insurance does not pay, you may still use these services, but you will have to pay for them yourself.

Home health services can be provided in your home such as general nursing services and IV therapy. Assisted care (light housework, personal hygiene) is also available.

**H o m e
Health
S e r -
vices**

Hospice care, rehabilitation facilities, assisted living facilities, and nursing homes are available for longer-term care. Your physician or hospital can recommend a facility if one is needed.

Definitions

Cap: the maximum amount you will pay in out-of-pocket costs in one year.

Co-payments: usually refers to the amount the patient pays each time s/he receives a particular service, usually doctor visits.

Co-insurance: a portion (usually expressed as a percentage) of the medical bills that the patient is responsible for.

Deductible: the amount a patient must pay towards his/her health care each year before insurance will begin paying medical benefits.

Explanation of Benefits (E.O.B.): a report sent to the patient from the insurance company listing services provided by each provider and the related charges. It also shows the amount paid by the insurance company and the explanation of any non-payments.

Fee-for-Service: (see indemnity)

Group Insurance: insurance offered to a group of people such as employees of a company. The insurance company offers the insurance at a discount because of the large number of people being insured.

HMO (Health Maintenance Organization): a type of insurance coverage where the HMO provides health care to its members through a primary care physician. The primary care physician manages the type and amount of health care that a member receives.

Indemnity (also called fee-for-service): the type of insurance coverage which pays for medical costs regardless of who is providing the services. Primary care physicians are not used under a fee-for-service plan.

Individual insurance policy: the type of policy one would purchase directly from an insurance company, rather than being insured through a group such as an employer. This is often referred to as private insurance.

Managed care: refers to the use of a primary care physician to manage the type and amount of health care that a patient receives.

Open enrollment: the period of time provided annually for members of a group insurance program to modify their choices. This can include choosing a different primary care physician or modifying the amount or type of coverage, etc.

Out of area: a term describing services that are received by the insured (or his/her dependents) from health care providers other than those specified by the insurance company (for example, an emergency room visit while traveling in another city or country).

Out-of-pocket: the portion of payments for health services required to be paid by the patient, including co-payments, co-insurance, and deductibles.

Patient responsibility: health care costs paid by the patient.

PPO (Preferred Provider Organization): a type of health care coverage, which is a combination of an HMO and indemnity plan. You choose a primary care physician as with an HMO, but you can choose any doctor you wish. If you choose one from their preferred list of physicians, more of your health care costs will be covered.

Preexisting condition: any medical condition that has been diagnosed or treated before insurance coverage begins.

Premium: the cost to purchase an insurance policy. The premium may be paid once a year or set up as monthly (or other scheduled) payments.

Primary Care Physician (PCP): a physician who manages and monitors the type and amount of health care of a member of an HMO or PPO. This physician has the authority to recommend (or deny) further tests, procedures, or the patient's consultations with other physicians.

Private Insurance: a type of policy one would purchase directly from an insurance company, rather than being insured through a group such as an employer.

Referral: the formal written authorization given by your PCP to the insurance company allowing you to receive health care from someone other than your PCP.

Education

Chapter 9

Education

The school choices for both children and adults in the Portland area are varied and numerous. This chapter will discuss school options from pre-school (including public, private, and home schooling) through higher education. At the end of the chapter there is a glossary that defines terms and acronyms used in this chapter.

Education for Children

Aside from the issue of learning in English, one of the more difficult aspects of moving a family to a new country is that the education system may not parallel the system of your home country. You will have to determine whether course work in the United States is transferable to your home country. You may have to consider having your child repeat part of a school year. You will have to decide if the experience of attending public school in the United States is important, or whether to pay for a private school education. It is not easy, but there are solutions. This section will provide insight into the U.S. public school system, and steps to take to ensure that your child's education needs are met.

Attitudes about Public Education

Americans feel strongly that parental involvement is a key element for the success of a child at school. The common perception is that the higher the percentage of parents volunteering in a particular school, the higher the quality of education provided by that school. The reasons for this are two fold. First, because the parents are giving their time to the school, they obviously value their child's education experience. The second reason is that with recent tax cut measures, programs, teachers and staff in schools have been reduced. To maintain a certain level of education, schools rely on volunteers and community assistance to fill the void.

Americans tend to feel it is important to express an opinion in any decision-making process. This applies to education also. Schools may have a site-council with parent representatives. This council proposes, endorses or argues against programs and policies affecting the school. The power and authority of such groups varies between schools, but parents feel the need to have a voice in order to have their best interests represented.

Volunteering will Help You Understand the System

Whether you come from a country which believes in an autonomous school system or one which encourages parent involvement, you will find that volunteering in the classroom, attending field trips, and otherwise assisting the teacher(s) can give you a better sense of the type of education your child is receiving. You can then more easily determine if the school is meeting your standards or able to fit your child's learning style.

In addition, by volunteering for Parent-Teacher Association (PTA) committees and events you will get to know your children's friends, classmates, teachers, administrators and other parents. This can give you a feeling of community within the school and the understanding of resources available when you have questions or problems. Your child's school can be a rich source of friends and much needed support when raising a family, particularly in a foreign country.

The PTA is an organization that promotes parent involvement in the schools.

Permission Slips

One of the features of the American schools is asking the permission from a parent for a child to take part in activities. You should expect that you will be asked to sign forms which cover a wide range of subjects. Some activities for which your permission is needed are:

- waivers for sports participation (with health insurance information in case your child is injured while participating),
- permission slips for walks around the neighborhood and field trips,
- permission to take fluoride at school,
- permission to administer your child's medications at school, if s/he requires any,
- notification that you do not want your child photographed, and
- permission to print your address, and phone number in yhe school directory.

Permission slips and waivers ensure that the parents are aware of the activities and actions at the school. They protect the school administration from potential legal actions.

School and the Law

Federal law requires children to attend school by age seven. For continuity, all children begin the school year together in September. Children who are six years old by the first day of September enter the first grade so they will meet the requirement of being in school when they turn seven. Exceptions may be made, which can be taken up with the principal. Students must stay in school until they reach the age of 16 years.

If you arrive in Portland after the start of the school year, the school principal and teachers will work with you to determine the appropriate grade level for your child.

The School Year

The school year runs from the first week in September to the second week in June. A two-week Winter break extends from mid-December to the beginning of January. A one-week Spring break is taken in March. Students have half and full days off throughout the year for teacher training, parent/teacher conferences, and various holidays. In total, the school year is about 180 days, which compares with 240 in Japan and 210 in European countries. Throughout the year, there will be programs such as parent-teacher conferences, student performances and back-to-school nights at which your attendance, as a parent, is expected.

The School Day

Each public school has its own schedule for the school day. In general, elementary schools are open between 8:00 a.m. and 9:00 a.m. and dismiss classes between 2:15 p.m. and 3:15 p.m. Middle schools open as early as 8:15 a.m. and dismiss classes between 3:15 and 3:45 p.m. Some high schools start classes as early as 7:30 a.m. and dismiss classes as late as 3:45 p.m.

All students stay at school to eat lunch. (The exception is high schools with an open campus policy that allows students to leave the school grounds when not in class.) Students in all grades may bring their lunch or can purchase a lunch at the school cafeteria. Most public schools also offer breakfast. At some schools, this meal is free to all students. At other schools, there is a cost. Students of lower income families can qualify for free or subsidized meals.

Education System Overview

Preschools

Preschools, for children ages three, four, and five, are intended to offer a more structured learning environment than child care. Some elementary schools are part of a federal program that offers early childhood education. These schools offer programs (known as pre-kindergarten) for the year prior to kindergarten and full-day kindergarten at no charge.

Elementary School

Elementary School (also called primary school) is Kindergarten (K) through 5th grade. The ususal ages in each grade are:

Grade	Age
Kindergarten	5-6
1st Grade	6-7
2nd	7-8
3rd	8-9
4th	9-10
5th	10-11

Children do not have to attend kindergarten. However, public schools are required, at a minimum, to offer a half-day (two and a half-hour) kindergarten program in every elementary school. Some schools offer full-day kindergarten and will charge tuition of approximately $200/month.

Middle School

Middle School encompasses 6th, 7th, and 8th grades.

Grade	Age
6th	11-12
7th	12-13
8th	13-14

High School

High school (secondary school) includes grades 9 through 12.

Grade	Also Called	Age
9th	Freshman Year	14-15
10th	Sophomore Year	15-16
11th	Junior Year	16-17
12th	Senior Year	17-18

In the U.S. education system, some career choices are made during secondary school. Students can choose to attend vocational /technical high schools that will train them directly for a set of job skills. Students can also choose to complete college preparatory courses. College preparatory students do not specialize in any particular area. All high school students work towards earning a high school diploma.

Career specialization and training often occurs after high school in vocational schools, community colleges, and universities. Students are assisted in making career choices during high school through career counseling, school fairs and college entrance exams. Students become especially involved in this process during their final (senior) year when applying to universities or making decisions regarding a career path.

Higher Education

Higher education includes education after high school at a college or university.

Public or Private School

You have the choice of sending your child to the public schools in your neighborhood, a public school within or outside the school district, a private school, or home-schooling.

The vast majority of Portland area residents send their children to neighborhood schools. Many people choose their home based on the quality and reputation of the neighborhood school. Some parents choose to send their children to a public school in another neighborhood that offers a unique program to fit their child's interest or gifts, or special needs (known as Magnet schools).

Other parents choose to enroll their children in a private school.

A growing number of parents do not send their children to school, but instead personally instruct them at home. This is called 'home schooling' or 'unschooling'.

Public Schools

Public schools in the United States are schools funded by local, state, and federal tax dollars. Costs paid by the student may include school supplies, field trips, magazine subscriptions, and special programs, including sports and activities.

A school district is a group of several schools located in a particular geographic area. The district office administers policies and provides resources for its schools. Each school district hires teachers, decides curriculum and program offerings, and makes policies regarding discipline and other matters. Many of these issues are further clarified at the individual school level.

Local Portland Area School Districts:

Beaverton	503-591-8000	www.beaverton.k12.or.us
Lake Oswego	503-636-7691	www.loswego.k12.or.us
North Clackamas	503-653-3600	www.nclack.k12.or.us

Magnet Schools are public schools that offer special programs which draw students from all over the city to study in a specific field of concentration. There are Magnet schools for language, business, performing arts, etc.

Portland Public	503-916-2000	www.pps.k12.or.us
Riverdale School	503-636-8611	www.riverdale.k12.or.us
Tigard-Tualatin	503-620-1620	www.ttsd.k12.or.us
West Linn-Wilsonville	503-673-7000	ww.wlwv.k12.or.us
Vancouver WA	360-313-3000	www.vannet.k12.wa.us
Sherwood	503-625-8100	www.sherwood.k12.or.us

Private Schools

Private schools are funded by tuition paid by the parents. Private schools may be organized around a language (the French School, for example), a religion (Jesuit High School, for example) or a philosophy of education (Montessori School, for example). Class sizes may be smaller and usually, you will find better resources available to students.

The age of students that each private school serves varies among schools. Some may offer instruction from preschool through 12th grade. Others may focus on only a few grades.

Private schools often have programs where families can apply for financial assistance to help pay the cost of tuition. Some private pre-schools are co-operative schools that require parents to regularly volunteer in the classroom, and to assist in fund-raising to keep tuition low.

Charter Schools

Charter schools are publicly funded private schools. They are public schools that operate with independence from many of the regulations that apply to traditional public schools. The purpose of charter schools is to find more creative ways for educating students who may struggle within the traditional public school framework.

The founding idea of charter schools is that they are independent and are directly accountable (to parents, school districts, and taxpayers). They must be able to prove their worth through academic results and efficient financial management.

In the Portland area there are several charter schools. Charter schools can be targeted to elementary, middle, or high school students and are organized around a guiding education philosophy. Students who attend charter schools must meet the same testing standards as children in traditional public schools. If you are interested in finding more information about charter schools, speak with your district administration office listed above.

Finding a School

There are several sources for finding schools.

Schools

The book, <u>School Choices in Greater Portland</u> by Molly Huffman and Julie Powell, lists all public and private schools in the Portland area. It lists programs offered, standardized test scores, and other criteria to help you evaluate each school. It is available at local bookstores.

<u>Portland Parent</u> is a free magazine available throughout the city (at the library, schools, stores and recreation facilities). It has advertisements for private schools that give you an idea of what some schools offer. In addition, an annual magazine issue compares a large number of private schools. The information is presented in tables which makes it easy to see at a glance the features of a wide variety of schools from preschool through high school. The Portland Parent website is www.parenthoodweb.com. You can call 800-794-1018 to have a sample copy mailed to your home, or to find a distribution location near you.

Public schools are listed, by school district, at the end of the blue government pages of the phone book. You can always call a particular school to schedule an appointment to have a tour of the school, meet the principal and other school staff, and ask all of your questions.

Use the yellow pages to find private schools by location.

Most schools have web sites. The public schools can be found at the district websites listed above. These websites are very helpful, allowing you to determine your school by your home address, and listing special programs, test scores, education philosophy, and other general information. Individual neighborhood schools may have their own websites, available through the district website address. You can also search the web under education to find private school web sites.

Registering for School

A waiting list is created when space is not available for additional students in a class. When a space becomes available, the first name on the waiting list is given that place.

A realtor or the school district office can tell you which neighborhood school your child would attend according to your home address. Notify that school that you wish to enroll your child. The school will need a completed application, copy of the child's birth certificate, a record of vaccinations, and proof of your address (to verify that you live within the school's neighborhood boundary).

If you wish to send your child to a non-neighborhood public school, either within or outside the school district, you will need to get approval from the principal of that school.

To enroll in a private school, your child will need to meet the admissions requirements. Some private schools, particularly elementary schools, have waiting lists because there are more students than they have room to teach. Many private schools can help you apply for financial assistance.

Evaluating Schools

In order to find a school that is right for your child you will need to evaluate the quality of the school and determine if the type of school or its programs will fit your child's needs.

Do you and your child wish to have an American experience? If so, the public schools and many of the private schools would be a good choice. If your child is of high school age, you should ensure that courses studied here will be transferrable to your home country's education system. You may want to explore the International Baccalaureate as a option.

If your family is only here for a short time, you may want to consider one of the international schools that would allow your child to study in their native language, and follow a more familiar curriculum.

If your child is hoping to study in English but needs help with the language, you should focus on finding a school with a strong ESL program.

Does your child have 'special needs' for education? The U.S. laws require public school systems to provide educational opportunities for children with certain physical and mental disabilities.

Ask neighbors about the strengths and weaknesses of the neighborhood schools. Ask to speak with the president of the school PTA. The admission staff at a private school can give you names of parents who you can call to learn more about the school.

Evaluating Academic Strengths

In evaluating a particular school, you may want to answer these questions:

What is the average class size? (A large class with one teacher should alert you that students might not get the individual attention they need.)

How is reading and writing taught, particularly in the younger grades?

Are children grouped by ability level? If so, how is this determination made?

Is homework assigned? Is it evaluated by the teachers? Someone else? Do the students get regular feedback on their schoolwork?

Do students receive report cards? If so, how often and how are students evaluated?

When and how often are parent-teacher conferences held?

Can parents influence the choice of teacher for their child?

What are the average standardized test scores for the school?

Does the school use different teaching methods, based on a particular student's learning styles?

Does the school have any special accreditation?

If looking at high schools you might want to ask:

What percentage of students goes on to college? What other career and education options are students offered?

Does the school offer the International Baccalaureate program?

What are the average SAT scores? (The highest score possible is 1600. The average in Oregon is 1050. Nationally, the average is 1016.)

Which colleges do graduates attend?

Tour the School

In order to evaluate a school properly, you can call to make an appointment to tour the facility and meet with the principal. You will learn more about the school and the attitudes of the students and teachers if you tour when school is in session.

Does the school adequately house all the students?

Is there a large room to accommodate school-wide assemblies, performances, and physical education classes?

How does the library look to you? Is it inviting and organized to encourage reading and studying? Does it have magazines for students and teachers? Does it have adequate resources for the size of the school?

Does the school have a computer lab? Is the software and hardware current? Do students have easy access to a computer? If homework is expected to be done on computer, are computers available for this? Do students have access to the Internet? Is it supervised?

Special Programs

TAG is the acronym for Talented and Gifted. This program is for children with above average abilities.

Due to tax cuts, many public school districts have had to cut programs. If your child is interested in art or music, the sciences or some other area, look carefully at the programs offered at the various schools. Programs may vary between public schools in the same district. Magnet schools offer special programs to serve students with special interests and talents.

Specific questions to ask include:

Does the school have a TAG program or other similar offering to stimulate especially bright or talented children?

Are special classes such as music, art, and physical education taught by specialists or the regular classroom teacher?

Do the schools offer after-school activities? Is before-school and after-school child care available?

Administration, Teachers and Parent Involvement

Do the administration and teachers seem caring and concerned about the students' education?

Do they demonstrate a positive attitude towards the school, the district, and the school community?

Is there a policy or handbook regarding discipline and the handling of behavior problems?

Does the principal hire the teachers or does a central administration office assign them?

Is there a large percentage of parent involvement in the school?

Can parents be involved in the decision-making processes affecting the school, such as hiring the principal, program planning, etc.?

Is there an active PTA? You may want to call the local president or representative of the PTA to learn more about the parent's role in the school.

Standardized Testing and Public Schools

Oregon law requires all students in public schools to be tested when they are in the 3rd, 5th, 8th, and 10th grades. This series of standardized tests are called the Oregon Statewide Assessment (OSA) tests. Private schools have the option, but not the requirement, of participating. Currently, students are tested in reading, writing, math, and science. In coming years, the arts, second languages, and literature will also be evaluated.

Test scores allow teachers, parents and students to measure whether students understand the material taught in classes and are making progress toward successfully completing school. OSA scores are also used by the school districts to compare schools within school districts, statewide, and between demographically similar schools, using socioeconomic indicators. Administrators use this information to make policy decisions, evaluate programs and teaching methods.

If a student does not meet the performance standards established at a particular grade level, the student is strongly encouraged to seek additional help. Tutors, after school instruction using different materials or teaching techniques, and summer school are different options the student, teachers and parents can use to help a student meet the statewide standards. Tenth graders have several opportunities to re-test, if needed.

These tests are part of a broader assessment. Public school students who successfully achieve the 10th grade level test performance standards and meet other criteria will receive a CIM (Certificate of Initial Mastery). This acknowledges that the student has achieved a high level of proficiency in a subject. This is in preparation for the CAM (Certificate of Advanced Mastery) given to 12th graders who successfully complete a similar series of tests. The CAM also represents that the student has met a higher level of achievement than what is required to graduate.

The State of Washington has recently started a similar testing program. Scores are not available yet for evaluating schools.

SAT and ACT tests are given in the spring and fall of the high school students' Junior and Senior years. These national college admission examinations are an important element in the criteria for application and acceptance to most U.S. colleges and universities.

Additional Programs and Services

ESL

Both public and private schools offer English as a Second Language (ESL) programs. If your child is unable to read and write in English at his/her grade level, an ESL program makes sense. Not every public school offers such a program, so be sure to inquire. Refer to Chapter 3, 'Language' for resources on ESL programs offered to children.

International Baccalaureate

The U.S. high school diploma is not recognized at colleges and universities outside of the United States. High school-aged students who are planning to attend a university outside the United States may want to obtain the International Baccalaureate (IB) diploma, recognized world-wide.

A handful of high schools in the Portland area offer this program. It is a two-year program for students in their junior and senior years. However, because the course work is so rigorous, students are accepted into the program their freshman year in order to complete other state requirements early. This allows them to devote their time and effort to the program when the IB specific classes and testing begins in the 11th grade.

The IB program is particularly popular with competitive American students intending to attend U.S. universities. Admissions committees recognize this diploma as an outstanding academic achievement, giving these students a valuable credential at the more prestigious universities.

Students must apply to the IB program. Students are usually accepted, but there may be limits due to an over-subscription to the program. Inquire of your school district as to which schools offer the IB program.

Transportation

Bus service is available for public school students who live within the area served by the school. You can inquire at the school about eligibility, bus routes, location of bus stops, and pick-up and drop-off times. This service is free at the moment. If you choose to enroll your child in a school outside your boundary, you will be responsible for their transportation. Some private schools may offer transportation.

Extracurricular Activities

Public and private schools often offer programs beyond the academic. Sports teams, musical ensembles and lessons, and special interest clubs all are options for children after the normal school day ends. These programs usually require the student to pay to participate.

If your child rides the school bus, you should be prepared to arrange alternate transportation home for him or her, as these programs often end after the last school bus has departed.

Special Needs

In 1997, the U.S. Congress passed a law known as the Individuals with Disabilities Education Act (IDEA). This law re-established the principle of free appropriate public education for children with disabilities. Each school district must provide, to the best of its ability, an appropriate educational environment for each child with 'special needs'.

'Special Needs' children are those with physical or psychological disabilities.

If your child requires this type of support, and you wish to have him or her attend the public schools, you will need to contact your local school district to determine what opportunities are available to you.

There are, of course, private programs for children with special needs.

The community of families with children who have special needs is extensive in the United States. There are many support organizations in Portland, as well as national and international networks to assist you. Your library is a good first step in learning about the resources which could be the most useful to you and your child.

Home-Schooling

Home-schooling, also recently referred to as un-schooling, is a growing alternative to traditional schooling. There are a range of resources, including curriculum, support groups, books on how to home-school and organizations to help you with understanding the laws.

The Oregon Home Education Network is an organization that provides information regarding home-schooling in Oregon. It is a good place to start to learn the regulations and resources available for home schooling your child. The address is:

The Oregon Home Education Network   503-321-5166

   P.O. Box 218

   Beaverton, OR 97075-0218

You will need to notify your area's Education Service District (ESD) of your desire to home school. They will send you an application for you to complete. Local ESD offices are:

Clackamas	503-675-4028	www.clackesd.k12.or.us
Multnomah	503-257-1771	www.mesd.k12.or.us
NW Regional*	503-614-1427	www.nwresd.k12.or.us

(*for Washington, Tillamook, Clatsop and Columbia Counties)

If you are considering home-schooling, but would like your child to attend some classes offered at your neighborhood public school, you can arrange to do so. For example, some parents want their child to participate in the public school music, art, or physical education programs. Others arrange to have their children attend science classes because they do not have the appropriate equipment at home.

Your child will be required to take the OSA tests during grades 3, 5, 8, and 10. You may choose to have your child tested each year, to be sure your child is making the appropriate progress. There are fees for these tests.

The following is a list of resources you may find helpful in getting your home-school started. Many of the resources are Christian based, however most of their information is applicable to anyone wishing to home-school regardless of religion.

Most curriculums are not directed toward a particular faith. Resources using the term 'un-schooling' are associated with those persons interested in getting away from an institutional style of learning, rather than towards teaching a particular religious belief.

Books

Home Schooling in Oregon, The Handbook, Anne Lahrson, Out of the Box Publishing

Retail Stores

Stores carrying home-school curriculums:

School Supplies-Retail

Christian Supply, Main Store   503-256-4520

10209 SE Division, Portland

This store has the largest selection of materials for home-schoolers.

Exodus Provisions   503-655-1951

19146 Molalla Ave., Oregon City

This store carries new and used curriculums.

Education for Adults

Refer to Chapter 3, 'Language' for information on ESL for adults.

Higher education in the United States is available to anyone who has the academic credentials for admission, but it is paid for by the student, or student's family. In some cases (as with state schools) there is a lower tuition for residents of the state. But in general, the cost of higher education makes it a serious financial decision for any student.

Higher Education System

The higher education system in the United States is based on a model where, after a four-year program at a college or a university, the degree awarded is a Bachelor's Degree. After earning a Bachelor's Degree, a Master's Degree in a specialized subject area usually requires an additional two years. A Doctorate of Philosophy, also known as Ph.D., requires original research in a specialty field, which usually takes three years more. There are some programs which combine the work to earn both a Bachelor and Master Degrees into one five-year program, as well as programs which combine Master and Doctorate coursework.

Options

You may be interested in furthering your own education while you are in the United States.

You have several options, but first you should understand your reasons and goals for returning to school.

> Do you want to complete a degree (Bachelor's, Master's or Doctorate)?
>
> Do you wish a different degree from what you now hold?
>
> Are you simply interested in taking a class for enjoyment (for example, a drawing class or learning a new language)?

This chapter will explain the options available and the process of enrolling in classes.

Schools of Higher Education

The two types of schools beyond high school are colleges and universities. A college is a school that usually focuses on undergraduate education, although some colleges do award higher degrees. Some colleges offer a two-year associate of arts or sciences degree or a certificate in a given trade or field. These schools are called vocational, technical, and community colleges. Other colleges offer four-year Bachelor's Degree programs.

A university has both undergraduates and graduate students, awarding Bachelor's Degrees, Master's Degrees and Ph.D's. As an institution it will have several colleges within its structure. You may transfer from a two-year college program to a four-year college or university.

Colleges and Universities often offer special programs under the name of Continuing Education. These programs, for adult students, provide both non-credit and credit courses in a range of academic areas for professional development, life-long learning, and certification.

Most schools have an international students admissions advisor or department. This person(s) assists foreign students with registration procedures, program and course selection, and tuition. The following list includes state funded and private schools. The state funded schools are marked by a *.

Two-Year Colleges in the Portland Area

* Clackamas Community College	503-657-8400	www.clackamas.cc.or.us
* Clark Community College	360-992-2000	www.clark.edu
* Mt. Hood Community College	503-491-6422	www.mhcc.cc.or.us
* Portland Community College	503-244-6111	www.pcc.edu

Four Year Colleges and Universities in the Portland Area

Art Institute	503-228-6528	www.aipd.aii.edu
Concordia University	503-288-9371	www.cu-portland.edu
George Fox University	503-538-8383	www.georgefox.edu
Lewis and Clark College	503-768-7000	www.lclark.edu
Linfield College	503-434-2213	www.linfield.edu
Marylhurst College	800-634-9982	www.marylhurst.edu
Oregon Health Sciences University	503-494-8311	www.ohsu.edu
Pacific University	503-357-6151	www.pacificu.edu
*Portland State University	503-725-3000	www.pdx.edu
Reed College	503-771-1112	www.reed.edu
University of Portland	503-943-7911	www.up.edu
*Washington State University	360-546-9559	www.vancouver.wsu.edu
*University of Oregon	503-725-3055	www.pdx.uoregon.edu

At the start of each semester, each school publishes a catalog of courses to be offered. Portland Community College (PCC) sends a catalog to every home in the Portland area. To receive a catalog for a particular college or university, order one on the school's website or call the school directly.

Continuing Education

School of Extended Studies

The School of Extended Studies at Portland State University offers flexible and innovative programs. These programs are designed to meet the needs of adult students. This school includes programs for professional advancement, workforce development, degree completion, distance learning (using the internet), and personal enrichment.

Portland State University	503-725-3000	www.extended.pdx.edu

Applying for Admission

Two-year Colleges

If you are interested in attending a two-year college to earn a diploma, degree, or certificate, or to transfer credits to a four-year school, you will need to follow the admissions requirements. At a minimum this includes completing an admissions form and testing for placement in (or testing out of) reading, writing, and math. If English is not your first language, you will need to take a TOEFL test (Test Of English as a Foreign Language).

If you simply want to audit a course, it is relatively easy. You simply call the registration office, enroll in the course you desire, and pay the tuition.

Four-year Colleges and Universities

The admission standards are more rigorous and as a result, more complicated for a four-year school. You will need to be accepted into the university, into the specific college and then into the particular program that has your interest. If you wish to audit courses or are otherwise not planning on working towards a degree, you will need to determine the particular admission requirements for that class by speaking with the professor. If you are working towards a degree, you will need to take similar placement tests mentioned above under two-year colleges.

Transferring Credits

It is possible to transfer credits from one U.S. college to another. Many students choose to attend a community college with the intention of completing their education at a four-year college. It is important to determine that credits earned at the community college will indeed be transferable to the desired four-year school. Many community colleges have programs specifically designed to transfer credits to a specific university.

Students trying to transfer course work from outside the United States are at a disadvantage. These students may be asked to repeat classes. This will depend on the subject matter, the similarity of programs between schools, and/or the school's accreditation rating. When you discuss transferring credit to any U.S. university, you will need to be persistent. The individual(s) at the college or university who can give the approval for transfer of credits may be hard to identify.

Another difficulty you may experience is getting accepted into a program because the grading system in your home country may not easily translate to the standard used here. In the United States, your grade point average (GPA) is taken into consideration along with test scores and other criteria. The GPA has a scale of 1 to 4. A '4' indicates excellence, a '2' is the minimum needed to graduate. If your academic record is based on work with a different grading system, you may need to do additional course work, or convince the university that your previous education is appropriate and equally valid.

One college that may be able to help overcome these stumbling blocks is Lesley College, www.Lesley.edu in Cambridge, Massachusetts. They have established a degree program that allows you to take courses (which contribute towards your degree from Lesley) at partner universities all over the world. This is helpful for people who move often and do not want to interrupt their studies.

GED

If you do not have the equivalent of a U.S. High School diploma, but would like to continue your education in the United States, it is possible to earn a 'High School Equivalency Certificate' (also known as a GED).

The GED (General Education Development) is a program which prepares you to take examinations in five areas:

- reading,
- mathematics,
- science,
- social studies, and
- writing skills.

These examinations are scored on a scale of 20 to 80 points. You must receive a 40 on each of the five tests, and have an average score of 45 (from all of them) in order to earn a High School Equivalency Certificate. Some higher education programs require an even higher score. The preparation classes for the GED examinations are usually free at the local Community College. At Portland Community College (refer to the list above for contact information) the GED classes are found within the Adult Basic Education (ABE) program. To qualify for these courses you must be 18 years old. Special examinations are available for people with special needs.

TOEFL and TSE

The TOEFL (Test of English as a Foreign Language) examination or the TSE (Test of Spoken English) may be required of you to attend a university in the United States. Ask the International Student Admissions Office for more information specific to the university which you would like to attend.

You can arrange to take the TOEFL at the Sylvan Technology Center. The TOEFL examination costs approximately $120, and is given several times a year. You can choose a paper-based or computer-based test format.

Sylvan Technology Center	Milwaukie	503-659-9575
	Portland	503-254-2009

The closest TSE examination centers are in Washington State. The cost of the examination is approximately $125.

Further information about both the TOEFL and the TSE is available at www.TOEFL.org. This site has practice examinations, listings of exam locations throughout the world, and upcoming test dates.

Paying for Higher Education

Tuition is less expensive at a community college than at a four-year school. Many students choose to go to a community college for the first two years, because it is less expensive, and then transfer to a four-year school during the third year.

If you are simply interested in taking a class or two, and if similar classes are offered at both the community college and the university, you may want to consider the lower cost of tuition at the community college.

Tuition varies with residency status, at state funded schools. Qualifying residents pay a much lower tuition than non-qualifying residents. Each school's residency requirements vary, but International students tend to be charged the non-qualifying residents' fee. It may be worthwhile for you to check these rules carefully. Be sure to check with your employer or spouses' employer. The company may have an agreement with a school. Your type of visa, paying Oregon State Taxes, and the fact you have lived in this area for more than one year, may qualify you for the resident tuition.

Private colleges and universities do not make a distinction between residents and non-residents.

Financial aid and/or scholarships may be available to you. The financial aid office and the international student affairs department can help you in this area. A little time spent completing forms may be time well spent.

Glossary of Terms

ACT: standardized test used for college admissions. Not as commonly used by colleges as the SAT.

BA or AB: Bachelor of Arts Degree.

Benchmarks: standards which students are tested against to see if they are learning material presented in school, or if they may need some additional help.

CAM (certificate of advanced mastery): not completely implemented, certificate asserts that a student has met a high level of proficiency in various subjects as measured through a series of tests and other criteria in the 12th grade.

Charter Schools: Schools which have been given special permission by the state to use radically different teaching methods in order to reach students who are not doing well in a conventional school setting.

CIM (certificate of initial mastery): this certificate asserts that a student has met a high level of proficiency in various subjects as measured through a series of tests and other criteria in the 10th grade.

Foundation: a non-profit organization established for the purpose of fund raising for a school or district.

Language Immersion: a program in which all academic subjects are taught in a language other than English. These programs are designed to teach a second language to English speaking students.

Learning Styles: the various ways people learn, such as auditory, visual, sensory, and kinesthetic.

MA, MEd, MS, MBA: Master of Arts, Master of Education, Master of Science, Master of Business Administration.

Magnet Schools: certain public schools that offer special programs which draw students from all over the city. Examples include: language immersion programs, early foreign language programs, school-within-a-school, special learning programs for refugees, early childhood education, accelerated programs, sign language, multi-age classes, the International Baccalaureate program, performing arts, business and technical schools.

Oregon Statewide Assessment: The series of tests that public school students are required to take at 3rd, 5th, 8th, 10th, and 12th grades in order to receive CIMs and CAMs.

Parent Teacher Conferences: meetings between the parents and teachers in order to discuss the student's school progress, usually held twice a year.

Ph.D: Doctorate of Philosophy.

PTA (Parent Teacher Association): an organization that promotes parent involvement in the schools and helps foster communication between parents and schools. Examples of their activities include: displaying student artwork, organizing after school classes and activities, parades, potluck dinners, story times, ski swaps, bike swaps, field days, fun runs, and fund raising events. A PTA newsletter tells of upcoming events, meetings and general information of importance to parents.

SAT (Scholastic Assessment Test): standardized test used for college admissions.

Site-Council: an organization of school administrators, teachers, and parents that makes decisions regarding policies and programs.

TAG (talented and gifted): a program designed to stimulate the minds of particularly bright or talented students.

Safety

Chapter 10

Safety

When you have an Emergency   Call 911

This single number will connect you with all police, fire, and medical services. When you call 911, you will be asked whether you need police, fire or ambulance and to give the nature of the emergency. Speak slowly and clearly. Stay on the telephone until the emergency services arrive. If you call from a cellular phone, you will be asked for the street address or a landmark near you so that the emergency response team can find you.

Remember that 911 is only for emergencies. Refer to the last pages of this chapter for the non-emergency police telephone number for your community.

Poison Control   503-494-6161

If someone swallows a substance that you think might be poisonous, or such a substance gets on their skin or in their eyes, call the above number. It is staffed 24 hours a day, seven days a week.

Many people have Ipecac in their first aid kits. This drug will induce vomiting. However, before you give Ipecac to anyone, call the regional poison control center because there are some substances, like gasoline, with which it should not be used.

Usually the word 'safety' is used in the context of people, and the word 'security' is used with objects.

American Attitude Toward Safety

Americans are safety conscious. The laws about safety issues may seem like common sense to you, but they are in place to protect and benefit all citizens. For example:

- If you ride a motorcycle in Oregon you must wear a helmet, but helmets are not required in all states.
- In road construction areas you are required to drive at slower speeds, and can be steeply fined if you do not.
- Seat belts are required for the driver and all passengers in any seat in the car and any position of the seat, while the vehicle is in motion.
- Children less than four years of age (and weighing forty pounds or less) are required to sit in an approved child safety seat. For more information on child safety seats refer to Chapter 11, 'Local Transportation'.
- Homes and cars have security systems.
- You may have to wear an identification badge when at work.
- The playground equipment on which children play must pass a safety inspection.

All of these are everyday examples of the concern for safety in American society.

Sport Safety

Bicycles

When riding a bicycle in Oregon you will most likely share the roadway with automobiles. Even in places where there is a bike path, it may be part of the street and differentiated only by a white line. For that reason it is important that your bicycle be equipped with reflectors (and lights if you plan to ride at night). You also should be certain to wear reflective or bright colored clothing. Anyone on a bicycle under age 16 (even children sitting in a bike seat on a parent's bike) must wear a helmet . Most adult bicycle riders also wear helmets.

In-line Skates and Skate Boards

It is wise when you (or your children) in-line skate to wear helmets and padding to protect your wrists, elbows, and knees. Pavement is brutal on exposed skin and cars with thoughtless drivers can appear seemingly out of nowhere, regardless of how careful or confident you are on skates.

Skiing

Many recreational alpine skiers are wearing helmets to protect their heads from a fall on ice or hard-pack snow, or collision with a fixed object such as a tree, a chair-lift tower, or a rock.

Personal Safety

You may have some concerns about your personal safety while in the United States. Television, movies, and reports of crime in the United States might make you think this is a dangerous place. In truth, the reporting of crime is exaggerated. Portland is probably no more dangerous than your hometown.

If you are smart about yourself, your family and your belongings, the chances that you will be a victim of a crime are very low. If it does happen it will probably be a 'crime of opportunity.' This means that by taking actions (listed below) you can significantly reduce the chances of being a victim.

Below are recommendations, given by state and local authorities, for action you can take in specific situations. These apply to any place that you live; they are not unique to the United States.

On the Street

To 'hitchhike' is to travel for free by getting rides from passing vehicles.

Be aware of your surroundings and where you are.

Remember that your safety is more important than your property.

Walk facing traffic - not only for your physical safety but also to prevent a car from pulling up behind you.

Try to walk with someone else. There is safety in numbers. Robbers prefer lone targets.

Street crime rates are three times higher at night. If you often walk alone in the dark, it is a good idea to get a personal attack alarm or a can of mace, and keep it where it is easily accessible. A personal attack alarm is a device that: makes a very loud sound, can give off an odor, and can spray a thief with an indelible stain. You can find mace and alarms at electronics stores and hardware stores.

Do not take short cuts through dark alleys, parks, or deserted areas.

Never hitchhike or pick up hitchhikers.

Carry your pocketbook or wallet close to you with the clasp or zipper toward you. Carry your keys in your pocket rather than your pocketbook so that you do not loose them if your pocketbook is stolen.

If you become the victim of a street crime, do not resist! People who resist are 3.7 times more likely to be hurt.

Wallets and Purses

Carry your wallet in an inside pocket. If someone bumps into you in a crowd, immediately check for your wallet or purse.

Avoid carrying a large amount of cash.

Memorize your PIN (access code for your bank card). Do not carry a copy of your pin code in your wallet or purse.

A thief only needs a second to take your coat off a rack, your checkbook off the counter, or your briefcase/bag/pocketbook set down on a chair. Be aware at all times.

Only carry your passport when you need to.

Keep mobile phones out of sight and avoid leaving them in your car.

Children's Safety

There are some basic rules to teach your children that can help them act safely. The chances that they will become victims are very low. Teach your children:

How to determine an emergency situation and how and when to call 911.

Their full name, address and telephone number, including area code.

Their father and mother's full names and work telephone numbers.

How to use a telephone to call home.

To be alert and to tell an adult they trust if something makes them feel uncomfortable.

Not to take dares from their peers or to follow their peers into situations that make them feel uneasy. They should trust their instincts in any situation that makes them feel uneasy.

Who to ask for help if you are not around or they get lost.

How to use locks in both your home and car.

To always keep the doors locked when they are at home or in the car.

That anyone they do not know is a stranger.

To stay away from cars occupied by strangers and **never** accept a ride or give directions. They should rapidly walk away from the car in the opposite direction the car is pointed. An adult should not be asking a child for directions.

Never open the door to strangers or tell anyone on the phone or at the door that they are alone.

It is okay to say no to an adult if the adult is making them uncomfortable.

Never to let anyone touch them where their underwear or swimming suit should cover.

It is okay to run and scream for help if they are being made to do something that makes them feel uncomfortable. Child abductors in prison today say that when their potential victims yelled for help, they left them alone.

Never to accept gifts of any kind from a stranger and to tell a parent about it immediately.

How to describe a person's appearance and/or their car.

To stay near parents while in a store or other public place. If they are separated from you they should stay in one place and/or find the nearest check out counter or clerk to ask for assistance.

What to do if they get lost in a crowd.

Never to go into a public restroom alone.

As a Parent

There are many things you can do to make certain that your children are in a safe environment. Some of these are to:

Be aware of changes in your child's behavior.

Encourage your children to communicate with you about anything that makes them feel uncomfortable.

Work out and rehearse an escape plan in case of a fire or other house emergency.

Check out your child care and school's policies on absent children. Are parents called when a child is absent?

Never leave your children unattended.

Make sure your children are taking the safest route to school, friends' houses, and stores. Help them to determine where to go on these routes if they need help.

Teach your children that they should have a buddy with them when they go somewhere without an adult.

Know where your children are at all times.

Know their friends' addresses and phone numbers.

Always leave a phone number where you can be reached.

Listen when your children tell you they do not want to be with someone and find out why.

Check out all child care and after school programs thoroughly. Look at certifications, staff qualifications, rules on parental permission for field trips, reputation, and policies on parental participation and random visits.

Check all references of any child care provider.

Have your child check in with you or a neighbor when they get home. Agree on rules for having friends over, and for going to a friend's house when no adult is home.

Do not mark your children's name on their clothing in a prominent place. Everyone responds when someone calls him or her by name. If you need to mark clothing with your child's name, mark the inside.

Get to know your neighbors.

Have a code word, selected in advance, that lets your children know this is a safe person to go with or talk to, if an emergency occurs and someone, other than you, needs to pick-up your children. You should stress the importance of the word remaining a secret.

Home Security

Burglary is a crime of opportunity. Burglars do not choose victims, they choose opportunities. Statistics show that burglary is a crime of convenience. 25% of burglaries occur through unlocked doors and windows. The best protection against home burglary is to keep your doors and windows locked.

If you were locked out of your house, would you be able to get in? Chances are good that if you have a way to get in, so does a burglar.

Most burglars will spend no longer than 1-4 minutes trying to break into a home. If you can delay the burglar with good locks, good lighting, and aware neighbors, you decrease their opportunities at your home.

Home Security Survey

Are all entrances lighted?

Are all accessible entrances to your home (skylights, crawl spaces, or vents) protected?

Are all the entrances locked, including garage and inside doors?

Is your porch and/or yard lit at night?

Are your house numbers clearly visible and attached?

Are your doors and windows free of shrubs so they can be clearly seen from the street or a neighbor's house?

Are exterior doors secured with a deadbolt lock?

Does your overhead garage door lock?

Are exterior doors thick enough to withstand excessive force?

Are lock strike plates anchored to the doorframe with 3" screws?

Do doors that swing out have non-removable hinge pins?

Are sliding glass doors and windows secured against forcing the lock or lifting them out of their frames?

Is there a peephole viewer on windowless doors?

Are double-hung windows secured with a pin or extra lock to discourage jimmying?

Are the locks new?

Are ladders and garden tools locked away so they can not be used to gain access to unsecured second story windows?

Doors, Locks, and Windows

The most common way of forcing entry is by kicking or prying a door open. The following makes it more difficult for a burglar to get in, thereby discouraging them from entering your home.

Locks: The best locks are deadbolts with a 1-inch throw bolt made of metal parts and a steel bolt.

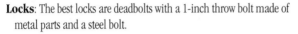

Dead bolt

Strike Plate: The strike plate must be attached to the doorframe with screws that measure 3" to ensure they fasten securely into the double two-by-four behind the doorframe. Never rely on a chain lock as a security device.

Door Re-inforcers: A door re-inforcer is a simple metal channel that wraps around the door at the lock area. This strengthens the door and helps to prevent the wood around the doorknob and deadbolt from being broken.

Strike Plate

Double Doors or French Doors: Install 1" flush bolts or bolt locks at the top and bottom of the doors.

Sliding Glass Doors: Sliding glass doors need special attention. To prevent both door panels from being lifted up and out of their tracks, secure the stationary panel with a screw from the inside through the door and frame. Insert a couple of screws into the top rack above the sliding door just far enough so the door barely clears them. It is also helpful to brace the sliding door with a metal rod, cut broomstick, or dowel to prevent the door from opening.

It is also a good idea to keep your house keys with you at all times. Never allow people you do not know to come in contact with your house keys. This includes parking garages, places of auto repair, a coat check, or loaning your keys to casual acquaintances. Instead of hiding keys around the outside of your house, give an extra key to a neighbor you trust.

Lighting and Landscaping

Lighting may be one of the best deterrents to nighttime crime. Burglars prefer darkness when they are burglarizing a home. Leave outside lights on during the night and try not to come home to a dark house. However, do not leave the lights on during the day, as this may indicate you are not home. Electric timers can be of help in switching lights on and off at certain times of the day.

Floodlights are useful in lighting up yards, driveways, and garages. When installing, make certain the area the floodlight illuminates is not disturbing to your neighbors.

The lighting should aid you in detecting unwanted persons as well as allowing your neighbors to easily see someone prowling around your home.

Keep your yard clean and trim shrubs and hedges so they do not hide doors or windows.

Marking Your Property

Mark your valuables with an engraving tool (which can be purchased at a hardware store or borrowed from a local library). Marking your property with your driver's license number serves as a deterrent to burglars and it helps police identify and return stolen property. Marked items are often not taken because they are difficult to pawn, fence, or sell. It is a good idea to make a list of your belongings to use as a reference in case your home is burglarized. You can also photograph or video your possessions in case you ever have to prove ownership.

☞ **Pawn & Fence: refers to the practice of taking property to a business which will consider the item as collateral and give a cash loan. When you repay the cash you get back the item. A thief will take your items to such a business to get cash.**

Alarms

A home alarm system can be a good investment, especially if you have many valuables in your home, live in an isolated area, or in a neighborhood with a history of break-ins.

Check with several companies before you buy so you can decide what level of security fits your needs. Do business with an established company and check all references before signing a contract. Determine if your main concern is for your safety while you are inside your house, or property protection when you are away. Some things to consider when inquiring about a system are:

- a battery back up in case of power failure,

- a fire sensing capability,

- an information display to monitor the system in case of problems, and

- an audible bell versus silent monitoring by a security company.

If you do purchase an alarm, you will need to purchase an alarm permit from your town. This is an annually renewed permit that is available through your alarm company.

Ask your neighbors to be alert to possible break-ins if the alarm is activated. Give your alarm code to a trusted neighbor so they can turn it off once your home is found to be secure.

Learn how to use the system properly and avoid setting off false alarms. Neighbors will stop paying attention and the local police will fine you after the second false alarm.

Deterrence

Some less expensive options include a sound-detecting socket that plugs into a light fixture and makes the light flash when it detects noise. There are motion sensing outdoor lights that turn on when someone approaches. You can have lights with pho-tocells that turn on when it is dark. There are audio-tapes of barking dogs that can be triggered by motion or sound. You can display Security Company warning stickers in the windows of your home, even if you do not have an alarm. All of these can help make your home a place that is not worth a thief's efforts.

Dogs are Not a Deterrent

While it might seem that a dog would be a good defense against burglars, dogs are unreliable as your only security device. Dogs can be easily bribed with food. When you travel, either take your animal with you or board it in a kennel. Dogs will warn you when you are home, but are ineffective when you are not.

Travel/Vacations

When you are away from home for a weekend or longer, the best security procedures are those that make your home look lived in. A neighbor or friend watching the house, periodically opening and closing curtains, and turning lights on and off is preferred, but there are other things you can do to make your house look occupied while you are away.

Use timers on lights in the living room and bedroom.

Use a timer on your stereo or television.

Leave curtains open a little so neighbors or police can see if someone is inside, but not open enough for a potential burglar to determine if anyone is home or not.

Ask a neighbor to park one of their cars in the driveway.

Stop your mail and newspaper deliveries or ask a neighbor to pick them up for you.

Do not leave a message on your answering machine indicating you are not home.

Hide valuables. Do not leave them in obvious places.

Have someone mow your lawn, rake leaves, or shovel snow when you are away.

Other Tips

Do not put empty boxes that contained expensive equipment such as computers or electronics out for garbage collection without collapsing them flat. You do not need to advertise what you have added to your home.

Do not put your name on your mailbox.

Thieves may telephone your house to see if you are there. Turn down the ringer volume on your telephone to ensure that it can not be heard from the street.

Burglars can do more than steal; they can also assault if they are surprised (by someone returning home or by entering an occupied home). If something looks suspicious when you arrive home, do not go in. Call the police from your neighbor's house or a cell phone. If you are home and you think you hear someone entering, leave the house and call the police. If you cannot leave the house, lock yourself in a room and call the police. If an intruder enters your room while you are asleep, pretend to continue sleeping.

Guns are not necessary for security. Because of the heated debate in the United States about gun control and media attention about violent crime, you may be under the impression that all Americans own guns. The fact is that less than half of Americans own guns, and you are more likely to be injured in a car accident than with a gun. Portland is a safe city. If you want more information you can contact your local police office for statistics on crime and advice on security in your neighborhood.

Be A Good Neighbor

There are two programs which can help you get to know your neighbors, and create a safer place to live. The Neighborhood Watch Program and the Block Home Program are offered by local police departments. They will help you establish it in your neighborhood if one does not already exist.

Neighborhoods with the **Neighborhood Watch Program** have fewer burglaries. Police officers do not know your neighborhood as well as you do, nor are they there as often as you. You can recognize when something out of the ordinary is happening. Neighborhoods with the Neighborhood Watch Program have bright orange signs posted on the light poles. Benefits of participating are:

Improved livability as you get to know your neighbors and look out for each other.

Improved home security.

Partnership with the local police, access to their resources, and a monthly newsletter.

The **Block Home Program** is designed to provide children with a safe place to go if they ever feel lost, frightened, or threatened in any way. Participating homes are given stickers that are displayed in the front window to let local children know that it is a safe haven for them. These programs are usually sponsored through an elementary school.

In any case, if you spot something suspicious in your area, call the police immediately. Do not try to stop a criminal yourself. Instead, get a good description of the person and his or her vehicle and call 911.

Home Fire Safety

Houses in the Portland area are usually built with wood. This makes fire safety very important. The following lists ways to prevent a fire in your home.

Fireplaces or Barbecue Grills

Learn to use your fireplace or grill safely. If you have a wood burning fireplace, have the chimney cleaned annually. Do not ever use gasoline to light a fire. Use only qualified starters (charcoal lighter fluids, starter logs, etc.) which are specific to the type of fuel you are burning. Do not burn charcoal indoors (it is poisonous). Always have a multipurpose fire extinguisher near by.

Electrical Appliances

Check lamps and ceiling fixtures to make sure wiring is intact. If an appliance smokes or smells, turn it off immediately. Examine electrical cords before use and replace any that are frayed or cracked. Do not overload (plug too many devices into) electrical outlets. Ensure that appliances (a clothes iron, for example) are shut off when not in use.

Candles

Be sure that candles are sitting in a nonflammable holder that will contain the wax as it melts and prevent the candle from burning into the surface on which it is placed. Position candles away from materials which could ignite from heat or flame (such as lamp shades and curtains). Keep matches in places where children cannot reach them.

Smoke Detectors

Smoke detectors can give you precious minutes to escape a burning house safely. Install them on every level of your home, especially outside sleeping areas. Test and vacuum dust from detectors monthly (dust can impair their effectiveness). Replace detector batteries twice a year (a suggestion is do it when you adjust your clocks in the spring and fall).

Visible House Number

The fire department cannot respond quickly if they cannot find your home. Make sure that your house number is visible from the street. It should be well lighted so it can be easily seen at night. Some local fire departments have volunteer programs that make home address signs. Contact your local fire department for more information.

Fire Escape Plan

Develop a plan for escaping a fire in your home. Try to establish two ways out of every room. Make certain that your children know what to do in case of a fire. Fire routes should not include elevators. Select a meeting spot outside of the house where everyone will gather in case of a fire. Practice your plan every month if possible.

Fire Extinguishers

Place fire extinguishers at every level of your home, especially the kitchen, basement, or garage areas where there is the greatest danger of a chemical or electrical fire. Practice how to use them. Check them monthly to make sure they are in working condition. You can purchase fire extinguishers at home improvement stores, hardware stores and department stores like Fred Meyer.

In Case of Fire

Get out of the house as quickly and safely as possible. If you must get through smoke to escape, keep low. The cleanest air will be 12 to 14 inches above the floor. Crawl on your hands and knees to get to the nearest safe exit. If possible, cover your mouth and nose with a damp cloth or handkerchief. Call 911 from a cell phone or a neighbor's house. Do not go back into the house once you are outside. Group your family members in the place you have designated as the meeting spot.

Disaster Planning

Disasters are unpredictable. It is always a good idea to be prepared for the unexpected.

Portland winters are notorious for ice storms. If ice laden trees fall on electrical lines, you could be without power for several days. There have been instances in the last ten years of flooding, severe thunderstorms, and windstorms. FEMA (Federal Emergency Management Agency) recommends that you establish an emergency plan for a 72-hour period of time when you have no electricity, heat, or running water. You can find out more from the FEMA website www.fema.gov, or go to your local library.

Home and Family Preparedness

Know how to shut off the gas, water, and electricity in your house or apartment.

Your home should have at least one easily accessible fire extinguisher. It should be able to extinguish all types of fires (food, chemical, and electrical).

Maintain an emergency supply of food and water. This should include a supply of canned or dried foods that do not require cooking. You should store several gallons of water for each person.

Have a battery-operated radio (with extra batteries) to listen to disaster updates.

Have a supply of candles and matches.

Have a battery-powered flashlight (with extra batteries).

Keep a list of emergency numbers by the telephone. If the electricity is off, cordless telephones will not work. Keep a simple corded phone accessible for emergency use. A cellular phone may also work.

Have easy access to blankets and warm clothing. If the electricity is off, your home's heating system may also be off.

Have an agreed upon place for family members to reunite if you become separated. Also agree upon an out-of-area friend or family member whom your family members can call to report their whereabouts and conditions if unable to reunite in the designated place.

Develop a plan for how you will care for your pet.

Earthquake Preparedness

The Northwest is a geologically active area. The area has volcanoes (many dormant) and, at times, is subject to earthquakes. Although there have not been severe earthquakes in recent Portland history, it is prudent to be prepared.

Whether you are in your home, school, or office, it is important to know how to protect yourself during an earthquake. DUCK, COVER, AND HOLD are the key words for earthquake preparedness.

DUCK- drop to the floor.

COVER- take cover under a sturdy desk, table, or other piece of furniture. If that is not possible, stand close to an interior wall and protect your neck and head with your arms. Avoid windows, hanging objects, and tall furniture (which could fall). If you are outside, move to an open or clear area away from buildings, trees, electrical poles and wires, etc.

HOLD- if you are under a piece of furniture, hold onto it and move with it. If you are next to an interior wall, stay where you are until the ground and building stop shaking.

Some additional suggestions:

If you are in a high rise building, move to an interior wall, protect your head and neck with your arms, and do not be surprised if the sprinkler system and alarms turn on.

If you are driving a car, pull over to the side of the road; avoid overpasses, power lines, and other hazards. Stay in your vehicle.

If you are in a crowded store or public place, move away from display shelves and things that could topple onto you.

If you are on the sidewalk near a building, duck into a doorway to avoid falling bricks and glass.

Automobile Security

There is a variety of security devices to deter a car thief. Alarm systems, car stereos with removable control panels, and clamps that lock your steering wheel are all commonly used devices. Here are some additional things that you can do to deter crimes:

Never leave your keys in the ignition.

Lock your car, even if it is parked in front of your home.

Have a copy of your Vehicle Identification Number and license plate number in your wallet along with your driver's license.

Keep your home and car keys separate. When you take your car for service, do not give your house keys with your car key.

Never leave packages visible in the car.

Maintain your car so that you do not have to leave it in a strange place. Ensure that there is enough gasoline to get to wherever you want to go and back. If your car needs to be parked for an extended period of time, remove the battery.

If you often drive alone, get a cellular phone for security.

Do not open your car door or roll down your window to speak to a stranger.

Metro Area Emergency Services

Any Police, Fire, or Accident Emergency   911

Poison Control   503-494-6161

Portland Crime Prevention Offices

Non-Emergency Telephone Report Unit   503-823-3333

Use to report vandalism, theft, and burglaries that have already happened, or to add information to a report already filed.

Police Information Line   503-823-4636

For information on police services, referrals, and rumor control during emergency situations.

District Coalition or Neighborhood Office   503-823-4519

Police Bureau website   www.portlandpolicebureau.com

www.ci.portland.or.us

Beaverton Crime Prevention Offices

Non-Emergency Telephone Report Unit   503-526-2665

Use to report vandalism, theft, and burglaries that have already happened, or to add information to a report already filed.

Police Information Line   503-526-2260

For information on police services, referrals, and rumor control during emergency situations.

Neighborhood Resource Office   503-526-2243

Police Bureau website   www.ci.beaverton.or.us/police

Gresham Crime Prevention Offices

Non-Emergency Telephone Report Unit   503-823-3333

Use to report vandalism, theft, and burglaries that have already happened, or to add information to a report already filed.

Police Information Line   503-618-2313

For information on police services, referrals, and rumor control during emergency situations.

Community Safety Specialist   503-618-2332

Police Bureau website   www.ci.gresham.or.us/police

Lake Oswego Crime Prevention Offices

Non-Emergency Telephone Report Unit   503-635-0238

Use to report vandalism, theft, and burglaries that have already happened, or to add information to a report already filed.

Police Information Line   503-635-0250

For information on police services, referrals, and rumor control during emergency situations.

Neighborhood Resource Office   503-635-0250

Police Bureau website   www.ci.oswego.or.us/police

Tigard Crime Prevention Offices

Non-Emergency Telephone Report Unit   503-629-0111

Use to report vandalism, theft, and burglaries that have already happened, or to add information to a report already filed.

Police Information Line   503-639-6168

For information on police services, referrals, and rumor control during emergency situations.

Neighborhood Resource Office   503-639-6168

Block Home Program   503-620-1620

Police Bureau website   www.ci.tigard.or.us/police

Washington County Crime Prevention Offices

Non-Emergency Telephone Report Unit   503-629-0111

Use to report vandalism, theft, and burglaries that have already happened, or to add information to a report already filed.

Sheriff's Information Line   503-846-2700

For information on police services, referrals, and rumor control during emergency situations.

Neighborhood Resource Office   503-846-2700

Block Home Coordinator   503-846-2579

Police Bureau website   www.co.washington.or.us/sheriff

Clackamas County Crime Prevention Offices

Non-Emergency Telephone Report Unit   503-655-8911

Use to report vandalism, theft, and burglaries that have already happened, or to add information to a report already filed.

Sheriff's Information Line   503-655-8218

For information on police services, referrals, and rumor control during emergency situations.

Neighborhood Resource Office   503-655-8218

Police Bureau website   www.co.clackamas.or.us/sheriff

Multnomah County Crime Prevention Offices

Non-Emergency Telephone Report Unit   503-255-3600

Use to report vandalism, theft, and burglaries that have already happened, or to add information to a report already filed.

Sheriff's Information Line   503-255-3600

For information on police services, referrals, and rumor control during emergency situations.

Police Bureau website   www.co.multnomah.or.us/sheriff

Local Transportation

Chapter 11

Local Transportation

This chapter is about traveling around the Portland metropolitan area. For information about travelling to other parts of the United States and beyond, see Chapter 12, 'Long Distance Travel.'

There are three common modes of local travel: automobile, bicycle, and public transit (bus or train). Americans love their cars and, because of suburban housing developments and centralized shopping malls, you may use your car more than you did in your home country. As the city's population grows, traffic and pollution are becoming increasingly problematic. Many residents are finding that biking or taking the bus to work is actually faster than driving, and offers surprising benefits. A few moments to read a book on the bus, or the clarity that results from a bit of exercise on your way to work can make driving seem like a waste of time. Regardless of how you choose to travel around Portland, it will be different than in your home country. This chapter will help you learn how the local transportation options differ from what you are used to, and how you can best take advantage of them.

Maps

Get a city road map and spend some time familiarizing yourself with the major routes around the city. Knowing the names of the main roads, and where they go, will help in finding the addresses of new friends, shopping locations, and restaurants. You can purchase maps in bookstores, supermarkets, drug stores, card shops, and gas stations. You can also get them from the AAA (say 'triple A'), the American Automobile Association of Oregon. There is more information about this organization later in the chapter.

The Portland Chamber of Commerce distributes a large map that covers the entire metropolitan region. It includes most streets and an index. You can get this map by calling 503-228-9411, or by visiting the website at www.pdxchamber.org.

The Rand McNally Company is another map publisher. The maps they sell are smaller in overall size. The company offers several styles. The 'King of the Road' series is specific for each section of the city. The 'Easy Finder' series is laminated for durability. In addition to finding these in local stores, you can purchase these on their website at www.randmcnally.com. This site also offers a selection of guides for exploring Oregon and the Northwest.

Other maps available are the Pittmon series, published by Oregon Blueprint, and the Goush laminated maps.

There are several websites that will give you free detailed directions to where you are going, in or outside of Portland. You can print these as a map, or as a written set of instructions. Two such sites are www.digitalcity.net and www.mapquest.com.

There are also maps that are specifically for bicycle routes. For a listing of bicycle maps and guides, turn to the 'Bicycles' section at the end of this chapter.

Automobile Transportation

Roads

The U.S. road system has the following categories of roads:

Interstate Highways are identified by red, white, and blue, shield-shaped signs with the route designated by a number. Odd numbered roads travel north-south. Interstate 5 (I-5), I-205, and I-405 pass through Portland. Even numbered roads travel east-west (for example, I-84). Interstates have limited access which means that you can only get on and off at certain places called entrances or exits. In less populated areas, entrances/exits may be 20 miles or more apart. Interstate highways usually have speed limits of 55 mph and higher. Each state can set its own speed limits (maximum speed) for these roads, so when you are traveling across state borders, pay attention to the posted limits. Also be alert that the speed limit will be reduced when the interstate passes through a densely populated area.

U.S. Routes are identified by black and white, shield-shaped signs showing a route number. In Portland, these routes are US26, US30, and US99. These roads are generally divided two lane highways. Access on these roads is not limited to exits and they may have stoplights and cross traffic. Maximum speeds on these roads will be posted.

State Routes are identified by uniquely shaped, black and white signs showing the route number. The Oregon State sign is an oval shield; the Washington State sign is a silhouette of President George Washington. State Routes will have stoplights, and many access roads.

City and residential streets have no standard sign color for showing street names, though they are usually rectangular. The maximum speed on city streets range from 20 to 50 mph.

Toll Roads do not exist in Oregon and Washington at this time. But you may find such roads (often known as 'turnpikes') when you drive in other states.

Speed

Any speed limits you see posted will be the maximum speed in miles per hour. In some areas there will be speeds posted specifically for trucks. The following chart gives miles per hour equivalents of kilometers per hour.

MPH	KPH
25	40
50	80
55	90
65	105
70	113
75	120
84	140

Speeds in the United States are taken seriously. Traveling at 120 kph or more, although it may be common in your home country, will quickly draw the attention of the police. Speeding tickets (as well as accidents and other traffic violations) will be recorded against your driver's license. When you renew your automobile insurance each year your driving record will be checked. If you have received any moving violations, your insurance premium may increase. This 'black mark' on your driving record is removed after three years.

Road Signs

International road signs are not used in the United States. The United States uses its own system of signs which have meaning based on their shape and color.

The standard shapes (regardless of color) and their meanings are:

 An octagon always means stop.

 A pennant means No Passing Zone.

 A diamond shaped sign means hazard.

 A triangle with the point down means yield.

 A trapezoid is used for recreational guides.

A vertical rectangle is used for regulatory signs.

  A horizontal rectangle is used for route guide signs.

  A pentagon means school.

  A circle is for railroad crossing and civil defense evacuation routes.

The different colors used in highway signs have distinct meanings:

Orange is for construction and road maintenance signs.

Yellow is for warning and school zone signs.

Brown is for recreation or cultural interest signs.

Blue is for motorist services signs.

Green is for mile posts and route guide signs.

Red is for Stop and Yield signs.

Black on red or white is for regulatory signs.

☞ **To familiarize yourself with all road signs see the U.S. Department of Transportation website at: <u>www.ohs.fhwa.dot.gov/mutcd/</u>, or you can look in the driving manual for the State of Oregon.**

Portland Area Road Names

The highways in the area are often referred to by a nickname. If you listen to traffic reports on the radio you will hear the announcer talking about the Sunset, the Banfield, the Glenn Jackson Bridge, the Freemont Bridge, and others. Here is a translation:

Inbound: the direction towards the center of Portland.

Outbound: the direction away from the center of Portland.

The Banfield: I-84.

The Sunset: U.S. Route 26 from Portland going west.

The Glenn Jackson Bridge: the bridge on I-205 crossing the Columbia River (near the airport).

The Freemont Bridge: the north end of Portland at the I-405/I-5 junction.

The Marquam Bridge: the south end of Portland at the I-405/I-5 junction.

The Interstate Bridge: on I-5. crossing the Columbia River, near Jantzen Beach.

Portland Bridges

There are eight bridges in downtown Portland. Two of them are interstate routes and the rest of them allow local access from one side of the river to the other. Each has a unique architecture and history. If you are interested in learning about these there are walking tours of the bridges given by several tour guide services. The Portland bridges are (from north to south):

Fremont (has flags displayed on top)

Broadway

Steel (MAX crosses the river on this bridge)

Burnside

Morrison

Hawthorne

Marquam

Ross Island

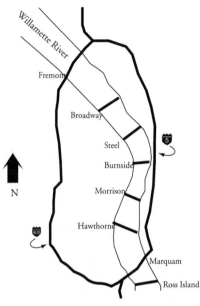

N

In addition, the St. John's Bridge is north of the city near Sauvie's Island and the Sellwood Bridge is south of the city near Lake Oswego.

Bridges in Downtown Portland

Driving a Car

To drive legally in the United States you must have both a valid driver's license and a legally registered vehicle. In Oregon, the Oregon Department of Transportation's Driver and Motor Vehicle Services (DMV) manages these processes. In Washington, it is the Washington State Department of Licensing. In both states, the processes are comparable. This chapter will explain the process for the state of Oregon. At the end of this section you will find the relevant information for the state of Washington.

Driver and Motor Vehicle Services (DMV)

This state department is responsible for registering automobiles and motorcycles and for issuing and renewing driver's licenses.

☞ **The word license refers to more than one thing. A driver's license is a small card with your name, address, and picture. An automobile license plate is the metal plate with letters and numbers that is attached to the front and rear of your automobile.**

The DMV has two types of offices: there are ten full service offices and five express offices. The main DMV telephone number for questions is 503-299-9999.

Full Service Offices conduct all business regarding registering and titling your car, and getting your driver's license. These can be found at the following addresses:

Beaverton	14250 SW Allen Blvd.
Hillsboro	1300 SW Oak
Gresham	2222 E Powell Blvd.
Lake Oswego	3 Monroe Parkway
Mc Minnville	1661 SW Hwy 99W
Portland	8710 SE Powell Blvd.
	8260 N Interstate Ave.
	1836 NE 82nd Ave.
	1502 SW 6th
St Helens	500 N Columbia Highway

DMV Express Offices do not offer driving tests, knowledge (learners permit) tests, nor will they inspect your vehicle's ID number (a part of the vehicle registration process). However, you can get your automobile registered, your driver's license renewed, and pick up all DMV forms.

Beaverton	3405 SW Cedar Hills Blvd.
Clackamas	8428 SE Sunnyside Rd.
Portland	990 Lloyd Center
	9904 SE Washington
Hillsboro	NW185 and Cornell Rd.

Getting an Oregon Driver's License

If you intend to be in Oregon for less than a year, you may drive with a valid home country license and an international license. If you plan to own a car or motorcycle, or live here beyond one year, you must get an Oregon license within one year of arriving.

Automobile Driving Schools

Driving Instruction

There are many driver education schools in the Portland area. The cost for this training is split into two parts. One part will assist with getting the learners permit (the knowledge test). It will cost approximately $40 for a two-hour tutorial (in a classroom). The practical driving skills are taught in a car. The school will pick you up at your home. Lessons are 90 minutes long. You can arrange for sets of lessons (4, 6 or 8) or you can pay by the lesson (about $100 per lesson). There is a discount if you purchase a set of lessons. Six lessons cost approximately $400. Driving schools can also provide a car for you when you take your practical test.

Motorcycle Driving Classes

There are Motorcycle Driving Classes given by Team Oregon, which is sponsored by the Oregon Department of Transportation. Locally, the classes are taught in cooperation with Portland Community College. In these you spend a weekend learning to drive a motorcycle safely. After passing both a written and a practical exam, you are given a certificate to take to the DMV to get the motorcycle endorsement on your license. You must be at least 15 years old to enroll.

Team Oregon   www.orst.edu/dept/team-oregon.   541-737-2459
                                                                       800-545-9944

It is also possible to enroll through Portland Community College.

PCC   www.pcc.edu.   503-244-6111

Oregon Driving Manual

To learn about the driving rules for Oregon, get a copy of the Oregon Driving Manual. Since international road signs are not used in the United States, pay close attention to the section on street signs (One Way, Do Not Enter, No Parking between certain hours, etc.). You will need to know specific details about U.S. signage, as well as all of the other information in the manual, to pass the examination. Copies of the Oregon Driving Manual are available at DMV offices or from the DMV website at www.odot.state.or.us/dmv. Currently the Oregon Driving Manual is available in English and Spanish languages.

Examinations

To get a driver's license you must pass three examinations: a knowledge test (learner's permit), a practical driving skills test, and an eye exam.

Learner's Permit

This test is a knowledge test that measures your familiarity with Oregon's driving rules. It is given on computer terminals at DMV full service offices. You do not need an appointment to take this test, it is given on a 'first-come, first-served' basis. At times there are long lines; you should go into the DMV prepared to be there for several hours. After passing this test you are issued a learner's permit. This permit allows you to drive a car as long as a fully licensed driver accompanies you. You must have a learner's permit before you are allowed to take either of the other driving tests.

Driving Skills Test

The second test is the driving skills test. You must make an appointment for this test and it is given by an inspector at a DMV Full Service Office.

For the driving skills test, you must have a road-worthy vehicle. The inspector will check the car to be certain that the following are in good working order: brake lights, fenders, rearview mirror, turn signal lights, seatbelts, muffler, foot-brake, horn, tires, functioning inside passenger door handle, headlights, and tail lights. If your car does not have these in good working order, the inspector may refuse to give the test.

The driving skills test is a way for the inspector to evaluate your driving skills. You will be asked to drive in traffic, make turns, park, turn the car around, etc.

Eye Exam

The last test is an eye exam. This test is designed to test your ability to see the road in various weather and traffic conditions. It is usually given after you successfully complete your driving skills test, and before your license is issued. There is no appointment for this test. If you need to wear glasses to drive, it will be noted on your license.

Other Oregon DMV Functions

Automobile Registration and Title

If you purchase a car through a dealership, after you provide them with proof of your auto insurance they will do the paperwork for getting your car registered and getting your name on the title. If you purchase a new car, this will involve getting a set of license plates. Initially you will have a paper permit that must be displayed in the rear window of the car until the license plates are delivered. If you purchase a used car, registering it simply involves getting the name changed on the registration and title papers. If you purchase from a private seller, or bring your car with you from out of state, the DMV will require you to complete an 'Application for Title and Registration' (available at all DMV offices). At the time of sale, the seller must 'sign over' to you the title of the car, in addition to any bill of sale that you get. Submit the old title with the DMV application and they will transfer ownership of the car to you. When you receive your new title in the mail, keep it in a safe place. It is the legal document that proves your ownership of the car.

Department of Environmental Quality (DEQ)

If your car is more than three years old and if you live within the Portland Metropolitan Area, your car will be required to pass an emission test every two years. The date of the next required test is on a sticker on the car's license plate. Simply transferring the registration of a car to your name does not require a DEQ inspection unless the car is from outside of the Portland area. Antique vehicles (manufactured before 1975) are exempt from DEQ emissions testing. The DMV has a map of the DEQ testing jursidiction and a list of the DEQ testing centers.

Washington State Department of Licensing

You must get a Washington State driver's license and register your car within 30 days of establishing residency in Washington. Read the section on Oregon Driving for a general description of what to expect when you get a driver's license and register a car. Consult the Washington State Department of Licensing for specific information.

Offices

Main Office	www.wa.gov/dol	360-902-3900
Main Vancouver office		1301 NE 136th Ave
Express office		5411 Mill Plain Blvd

Driving Manual

The driver's manual is available in Vietnamese, Chinese, Russian, Japanese, Spanish, and Korean, in addition to English.

Emissions Check Stations

Emissions checks are required on all vehicles produced after 1976. Vehicles must be tested every two years. Odd production year cars in odd years, even years in even years. All cars older than three years must be tested. All cars must be tested when sold, regardless of year of production.

Emissions stations are open Tuesday through Saturday from 9 a.m. to 5 p.m.

West Vancouver	14110 NW 3rd Ct.	360-574-3731
East Vancouver	1121 NE 136th Ave.	360-254-2173

Driving Tips

Seat Belts and Child Safety

Seat belts are required for all drivers and passengers in either the front or back seats of the car while the automobile is in motion.

Children less than four years of age (and weighing forty pounds or less) are required to sit in an approved child safety seat. Find information about different kinds of child safety seats, their installation, and safe usage from the Child Safety Resource Center at 503-656-7207.

Approved safety seats can be purchased at local department stores like Fred Meyer, Target, and WalMart. There are different safety seats for infants (weighing less than 20 pounds) and toddlers. If you are a member of AAA, you can borrow a child safety seat (for a maximum of 30 days) with a deposit of $60 (great for when you are traveling and need a rental car!).

General Advice

The roads in Portland are often wet, so use caution. In the winter it can be difficult to tell when the water on the road has turned to ice. If you are in doubt about the road conditions, slow down.

The best advice is to drive defensively. Be aware of the cars around you. Watch to see what is coming several cars ahead. Leave a distance of several car lengths between you and the car in front of you. Finally, be comfortable with the vehicle you are driving. If you are still adjusting to driving a left hand drive car, go to a vacant parking lot to practice before you attempt to drive in rush hour traffic.

Stop Lights

In the United States, stoplights are placed in the center or far side of an intersection. A solid white line across your lane on the roadway indicates the place where you stop your car. In places where there is a crosswalk for pedestrians, this white line may be set back from the intersection.

'Rush Hour' refers to the busiest traffic periods in the work week, usually from 6 a.m. to 9 a.m. and from 4 p.m. to 7 p.m.

Road Dividers

As is common in many countries, double yellow lines mark the divider for traffic on most roads. On a highway, the traffic dividers are often concrete. A painted white line, groupings of raised bumps, or small reflective markers may separate lanes. The type of lane marker used is dependent on the area's winter weather. Areas that use snowplows rely on reflective paint that is not damaged by a plow blade. If the area is more prone to heavy fog, reflective markers and bumps are more often used.

Traffic Calming Devices

In residential areas with heavy traffic use, you may find speed control features such as bumps and 'round-abouts' (also known as rotaries) to slow traffic. If these features are present, they will be identified with signs and white paint on the road to alert you before you reach them.

Traffic Reports

Traffic reports are available to tell you the condition of the roads, in and out of the Portland Metropolitan Region. These are available on-line at television station websites and from the Oregon Deptartment of Transportation. Radio stations and television news reports often give local traffic reports as part of their news.

The Oregonian newspaper publishes planned road closures and detours due to construction and other information regarding ongoing or long-term traffic delays.

The following websites provide traffic reports:

KATU	www.katu.com
KGW	www.kgw.com
KOIN	www.koin.com
Oregon Department of Transportation	www.odot.gov
Washington State Department of Transportation	www.wsdot.wa.gov
Commuter's check - video cameras all over the state	www.trip-check.com

Headlights On

In the Pacific Northwest it is common to drive with your headlights on. Driving rules mandate that you use your headlights whenever you use your windshield wipers. In addition, many people use their lights to ensure that they are seen by oncoming traffic. This is particularly important when traveling on roads that do not have a solid center divider, especially in less populated areas.

Right on Red

You will see many drivers who make a right hand turn when the traffic light in their lane is red. This is legal provided that there are no cars coming from the left, and providing that there is no sign prohibiting it. Not all states in the United States allow turning right at a red light.

Exit only Lanes

In the Portland area, highway exits can be in the right or left lane. Exits will be posted on green overhead signs on the highway. There are some cases where the travel lane turns into an Exit Only (posted in yellow) lane. The words 'Exit Only' mean that cars in that lane must exit. The 'Exit Only' lanes do NOT indicate that it is impossible to get back onto the highway once you have exited.

Parking Lots and Meters

If you are parking in the city of Portland, at the airport, or in another heavily populated area, you will find parking garages and parking meters which require you to pay for the time you are there. Parking meters take coins (usually quarters (25¢), dimes (10¢), or nickels (5¢)). Metered spaces have a limited length of time (prominently noted on the meter) that you cannot exceed regardless of how much money you have put in (15, 30, 60, and 90 minutes, or up to three hours). They will also have a sign giving the hours during which they apply. There are many commercial areas such as shopping centers and malls that have free parking.

At parking garages that charge for their spaces, pick up a ticket as you drive in and pay the cashier as you drive out. The airport parking areas will accept a credit card for payment, but most other parking areas only take cash. Some paid parking areas in downtown Portland will provide two hours of free parking if you make a purchase at a nearby store. To take advantage of this you must carry your parking ticket with you and ask the store clerk to validate your parking. Some retailers require that you spend over $50 in order to earn a stamp, others do not.

Buying Gasoline

There are three grades of unleaded gasoline available in Oregon and Washington (based on octane rating). These are known as Regular (87), Plus (89), and Premium or Super (91). Regular is the least expensive. There is only one grade of Diesel.

It is illegal to pump your own gas in the state of Oregon. When you drive into a gas station the attendant will ask whether you want to pay with cash or a credit card and which grade of gasoline you want. Paying with cash will be less expensive at some stations; at others the fuel is the same price regardless of which form of payment you use. At some gas stations, you can simply hand your credit card to the attendant and s/he will complete the transaction at the pump. Other stations may require you to go to a central kiosk to pay.

You may pump your own gas in Washington State. When you drive into the gas station there will be signs on the pumps indicating 'full service' or 'mini-serve'. Full service means that they will pump the gas for you, wash your windshield, check your oil, etc. The price of gasoline in these lanes is higher because of the service provided. Mini-serve is where you serve yourself.

Winter Driving Advice

Change in Fuel Mixture

In the winter (November 1 to May 1), by Oregon law, alcohol (10%) is added to the gasoline for pollution control. The gas station pumps display a sticker with this information when this is in effect. If you own an older car, the engine may need adjustment to run smoothly on this type of fuel. Some gas stations sell the same fuel, with alcohol, all year long. Check the pump when you purchase gas, or ask the attendant.

Black Ice

In the winter, Portland is notorious for its icy streets. This phenomenon is called 'black ice' because the road looks wet, but is actually frozen. In some areas there are small signs along the road, which turn blue when the temperature is at the freezing point indicating that ice may be present.

There are two main tactics for driving in icy conditions. One is to increase the distance between you and the car ahead. The other is to reduce your traveling speed. This tactical advice also applies to rain in the summer and early fall. In the first major rainstorm after a period of clear weather, oil and rubber residues from cars traveling over the road surface mix with the water and make the roads as slick as if they were covered in ice.

Practice your ability to control your car on the ice in a vacant parking lot. This is a good way to get the feel of how to handle a car in slippery conditions. Primarily you need to learn to use the brake sparingly. Do not drive fast and do not crowd the car ahead of you. Secondarily you need to learn what to do if the car does slide. Turning the steering wheel in the direction of the slide will help you gain control of the car.

Driving Instruction

There are several Portland companies that offer driving classes to help drivers learn to drive defensively. They have ways of simulating icy road conditions, even in the summer!

Traction Devices

Tires

If you are going to ski at Mt. Hood, travel to the east of the state or to California by car in the winter, you are required by law to have traction devices for your car's tires. Traction devices can be chains or traction tires. Traction tires can be studded tires or special snow/ice tires (labeled with a symbol of approval or issued with a certificate) that will ensure that your car will be able to handle the snow or ice. Studded tires are only allowed on Oregon roads between 1 November and 1 April. If you have questions as to the most appropriate tire for your car, talk with a salesperson at a tire store. When you travel in snow zones, you will see signs posted that inform you of the need to install your chains. There are places along the road to 'chain- up' if driving conditions require. If you have been advised that traction devices are required and you do not use them, you may be fined.

Windshield Replacement

There are many towns in Oregon that use gravel on the roads in the winter to provide increased traction. Unfortunately these gravel pieces can be thrown up against your windshield, occasionally damaging the glass. Reduce this type of damage by increasing the distance between you and the car in front of you.

Glass-Automobile

*

Windshield Repair

If you have a damaged windshield, you will need to get it repaired. Check with your auto insurance to see if you have glass replacement coverage as part of your policy. If you do, the insurance company can refer you to a repair company. Depending on your policy, you may have to pay part of this cost.

There are companies that can come to your home or place of business to either repair the chip or replace the glass. Occasionally you may receive a telephone call solicitation from a company offering to repair your cracked or chipped windshield. You may also find a coupon for such repair in the advertising flyers that are delivered to your home.

What to do in an Accident

With a Car or a Pedestrian

1) Stop your car (if possible, pull off the road to a safe place). Do not leave the accident scene.

2) Call 911 (the emergency number - explain what happened, where you are, and what type of help you need).

3) Give aid to any injured persons. Do not try to move an injured person unless s/he is in a life-threatening location.

4) Turn on the hazard lights of the car(s). Set up flares in the road to warn on-coming cars of the accident

5) Exchange information with the other driver, the injured passengers or pedestrians, and any witnesses of the accident. Provide your driver's license number; your name, address, and birthdate; make, model year, and license plate number of the car; and the car's insurance company name and policy number. Make sure you get this information from the other driver. Do not admit responsibility.

6) Write down the name and badge number of the police officer and ask how to get a copy of the police report for your insurance company.

7) Do not accept money offered by the other driver to settle the claim. It will compromise your insurance claim.

8) If you have a camera, take pictures of the damage, the positions of the cars before they are towed away, skid marks, etc.

9) Report the accident to the DMV using an accident report form if there is more than $1000 damage, and/or if someone is injured (regardless of how minor). This report must be filed within 72 hours of the accident.

10) Keep a copy of your accident report form.

11) Report the accident to your insurance company.

12) If you have a leased car provided by your employer, notify the company's Hu man Resources Department.

☞ **Accident report forms are available from the police department, the sheriff's office, or a local DMV office.**

With a Parked Vehicle

Pull off the main traffic route. Attempt to find the driver. If it is not possible to find the owner, leave a note with your name, address, telephone number, driver's license number, your auto license plate number, insurance information, and a description of what happened. Report the accident to your insurance company.

With an Animal

Stop and move the animal to a safe place. If you cannot find the owner, report the accident to the nearest police department.

Buying a Car

If you plan to own a car in Oregon, you must have an Oregon driver's license. The process of determining what you can afford and what style you need will be the same in the United States as in your home country. Your needs and financial resources will dictate whether you buy a new or a used car, and if you lease or purchase. Some aspects of buying a car in the United States may surprise you: the fact that most Americans borrow money to buy their car rather than paying for it in cash, that there are so many choices of car dealerships and car models, or the prevalence of automatic transmissions.

New or Used?

There are many places to find cars for sale. Locally you can use car dealerships, the newspaper's classified sections (Saturday's papers have a special section on automobiles), and the internet. Car dealerships have both used and new cars. Some dealers only sell used cars with a one-year warranty and some dealers offer cars on an 'as is' basis with no guarantees. Use the Internet to learn about the costs and options which are available on most new cars. Look at the manufacturer's websites to get more information (www.ford.com, www.honda.com, www.jeep.com, etc.). Regardless of how you find your car, be certain you understand what you are signing before you sign your name. If you need assistance in understanding a contract or need help in getting it translated for you in your native language, be sure to get it before signing your name (refer to Chapter 3, 'Language' for translation resources).

Lemon Law

Oregon has a law familiarly referred to as the Lemon Law (Oregon Statute 646.315-375). If you purchase a new car which develops a problem that cannot be fixed within four attempts, the dealership must replace the car, or provide you with a full refund. You must provide documentation of the attempt of service, and the problem cannot be a result of your neglect. The lemon law is appropriate for the first 12,000 miles of driving or one year, which ever comes first. There is no lemon law for used cars. If you decide to purchase a used car without a warranty, arrange to take it to an independent garage, for a fee of usually one hour of labor, to have it checked for major problems.

Cash, Financing, or Leasing

The option of leasing is only available with new cars. Leasing means that you agree to use a car for a certain period of time, drive it a certain number of miles, and pay for certain maintenance costs during that time. At the end of the agreed upon time period, you give the car back to the dealership. When you lease a car, you are borrowing money to finance the lease. This is different from buying a car with financing. In this latter case, you pay the money on the loan, and own the car outright.

*Financing-
borrowing
money to pay
for something.*

A used car must be bought, either with cash or through financing. If you find the car you want at a dealership, they will probably be able to offer you a financing plan for the purchase. You can also borrow money from your bank.

Insurance

Once you have made your decision you will have to get automobile insurance before registering and driving the car. There are many insurance companies which can sell you insurance.

**Automobile-
Insurance**

Some types of insurance coverage are required, other types are optional. The cost of the insurance will be directly related to the amount of deductible you decide to have.

Coverage Required by Law

Bodily Injury Liability: pays for injury to anyone if you are responsible for an accident.
Property Damage Liability: pays for property claims if you are responsible .

Additional Coverage Required if you have a Car Loan

Collision Coverage: covers damage to your car when it is caused by impact with another object.
Comprehensive Physical Damage Coverage: covers damage to your car when it is caused by theft, fire, vandalism, flooding, hail, and other perils, but not damage caused by collision or overturning.

Optional Coverage Choices

Medical Payment Coverage: pays for personal injuries regardless of who was responsible for the accident.
Uninsured/Underinsured Motorist Protection: pays for injuries to you or your family if in an accident and the responsible party has limited insurance coverage.

If you do not have liability insurance at the time of an accident, your driving privileges will be suspended for one year.

Rental Reimbursement: this covers the cost of a rental car if your car needs repair from an accident.

Towing and Labor Coverage: covers the costs of towing service in an emergency.

A separate policy option, called Umbrella Liability Coverage can be purchased. It provides $1 million or more beyond your normal liability, and will additionally apply to your automobile, homeowner, rentor, or boat liability coverage.

Shop around to a few different agents to ensure you are getting what you need and want. Once you find the insurance plan that best fits your needs, you must give the Insurance Company the vehicle identification number (VIN), color, make, model, year, etc. The insurance company will then give you a policy number, which is your proof of insurance. In a few days you will be sent a form to keep in your glove compartment proving that you have insurance. You must carry this form in the car.

Automobile Parts and Repairs

If you purchased your car new, take it to the service department of your dealership. If you bought your car used, there are many options for service. There are private garages that specialize in cars made by certain manufacturers, or others that specialize in a certain type of problem (brake repair shops, oil change/lubrication shops, muffler shops, transmission repair shops, etc.). You will need to spend some time finding the repair facility with which you are most comfortable. Refer to Chapter 6, 'Making Your House a Home' for more information on automobile service and repair.

If you want to repair your car yourself you will find many car parts stores. Stores will include the word 'Import' if they provide parts for cars made outside of the United States. The wrenches and sockets needed for repair of an import car are 'metric' in measurement. The wrenches and sockets needed to repair an American-made automobile are 'standard' (American term) in measurement. For obvious reasons, other tools will fit both American and imported cars.

AAA (the American Automobile Association)

The American Automobile Association is a membership organization that can provide a variety of services for you and your car. Membership is offered at several levels (ranging from $55-$100 per year) and second drivers can be added for a fee (approximately $30/yr.). Benefits of membership include:

- emergency roadside assistance, anywhere in the United States , if your car breaks down,

- maps and guides for travel anywhere in the world,
- local and national savings at museums, excursions, car rentals, etc.,
- full service travel agency,
- insurance for auto, life, homeowners, and renters,
- free American Express Traveler checks, and
- competitively priced Visa and MasterCard, with special member benefits.

The local AAA offices can be found at:

600 Market Street Portland, 97201	503 222-6734
8555 SW Apple Way Portland 97225	503-243-6444
6 Centrepoint Drive #100, Lake Oswego. 97035	503-973-6555
10365 SE Sunnyside Rd, Clackamas 97015	503-241-6800

Car Sharing

If you do not need a car every day, Car Sharing may be a good option for you. Car Sharing is an organization that offers its members the opportunity to use a car occasionally. You pay only for the hours and miles driven. The insurance, gasoline, and repairs are included in the rate per hour. This company currently offers service to 'close-in' Portland neighborhoods, but is expanding to the 'further-out' suburban areas also. The membership process entails an application and a non-refundable $25 fee. To become a member you must be over 21, have a good driving record (no more than two moving violations or insurance claims in the last three years), and a solid credit record. Once accepted you make a refundable $250 security deposit which is repaid when you discontinue membership.

Car Sharing Portland Inc.   503-872-9882   www.carsharing-pdx.com

Car Rentals

Rental rates for automobiles are based on the size of car (compact, economy, midsize, luxury, etc.), and the length of time you will use the car. Some car rental companies will charge an additional fee for the number of miles driven.

Automobile Rental

You will be given the option of adding insurance coverage to your rental contract. This will add several dollars per day to the rental rate. Before you rent a car, check with your credit card company or your personal automobile insurance to see if you are insured for driving a rental vehicle with their policies. If you do not need to take out insurance on the rental car, you will be asked to initial that such coverage is declined. If you have no insurance, have declined the coverage, and you have an accident with the rental car, you will be held liable for the cost of repairs.

You will also be asked to choose, at the time of rental, between returning the car with a full tank of gasoline, or purchasing a tank of gasoline so that you can return the car with a low fuel level. If you return the car with low fuel level, and you have not purchased the tank in advance, you will be charged a premium price for a full tank of gas.

Finally, before you drive out of the parking lot, walk around the car and inspect it for damage. Note any damage on the contract you have, and ask the lot attendant to confirm it. This will protect you from false assertions that existing damage was done to the car while in your possession.

Renting a car can be particularly useful when you have guests, and need a larger vehicle for a short time. It can also be helpful if your automobile is being repaired and you need transportation. You can access any travel website to do comparison shopping of rates.

Taxi Services

Thirty taxi service companies service the Portland area. Some of these are independent companies and some are part of a national company. To use a taxi, call the service in advance to arrange to be picked up. If you call expecting a cab immediately, you may have to wait for service if they are busy.

Taxi

If you are traveling to the MAX light-rail station nearest you, you may be able to take advantage of the shuttle bus services Tri-Met provides. Look at the MAX station for more information, or call Tri-Met at the number listed in the following section on Public Transportation.

If you use a taxi for regular travel within the local area, you will be charged a rate per minute and based on the distance of the trip.

If you are traveling from the airport to your home, use this rough guide to know what you can expect to pay. Remember to add 10% to the cost as a tip for the driver.

> Airport to downtown Portland: $20 - $30
>
> Airport to Vancouver: $15 - $25
>
> Airport to Gresham: $20 - $30
>
> Airport to Hillsboro: $40 - $50
>
> Airport to Beaverton: $30 - $40
>
> Airport to Tigard: $30 - $40

Public Transportation

Portland has an extensive public transportation system comprised of bus and train service. Tri-Met provides bus service in the Portland area. MAX is the light rail train system currently serving the Portland area from Gresham in the east to Hillboro on the west side. C-Tran provides bus service to the Vancouver area. The Tri-Met organization also offers ride-sharing programs for people who want to car pool to their work or school.

MAX is an acronym standing for Metropolitan Area Access.

Tri-Met

Tri-Met is the name of the department of regional government that manages the public transportation system in the Portland area including bus service and MAX. The name Tri-Met refers to the three Portland Metropolitan Counties (Multnomah, Washington, and Clackamas). Tri-Met offers many ways for you to get information about the routes that will work best for you. Visit an office, telephone the help line, or visit their website. You can also pick up local transportation maps at public libraries and neighborhood centers.

Contacting Tri-Met

Tri-Met's offices are at Pioneer Courthouse Square (701 SW 6th Ave.) and 4012 SE 17th.
Information is available online at www.Tri-Met.org, or telephone Tri-Met:

Customer Services and Personal Assistance Trip Planning
       Weekdays 7:30 a.m.-5:30 p.m.
       503-238-RIDE (503-238-7433)

General information
       503-238-RIDE (503-238-7433)
       TTY 503-962-5811
       Fax 503-962-3092

Senior & Honored Citizen Information
       503-962-2455
       TTY 503-962-5811
       Fax 503-962-3092

Bikes on Tri-Met
   24-hours, recorded information
   503-962-7644

Public Carpool Matching Service
   24-hours
   Dial 503-CAR-POOL (503-227-7665)

Lost and Found
   Weekdays 9:00 a.m. - 5:00 p.m.
   503-962-7655

Vandalism Hotline
   503-962-7666

Basics of the Bus System

In the TriMet Bus system there are service area symbols and bus line numbers to help you manuever around Portland.

The Tri-Met service system is divided into seven service areas, each of which has a color and a symbol.

 Red Fish - North, Northwest, and Northeast Portland

 Purple Raindrops - Northeast Portland

 Blue Snowflake - East to Gresham and Troutdale

 Brown Beaver - Southeast Portland

 Green leaf - South to Oregon City, Lake Oswego, and Tualatin

 Yellow Rose - Southwest to Tigard, King City, and Sherwood

 Orange Deer - West to Beaverton, Hillsboro, and Forest Grove

Courtesy of TriMet

You should know in which service area your home is located. This is important if you plan to travel on the bus to and from downtown Portland. Many bus lines travel through several service areas; the bus line number cannot be the only guide in finding the correct bus home. Some buses will have the same line number but be going in opposite directions. The transit mall on SW 5th and 6th is marked with the service area symbols to help you determine the correct bus stop. If you have questions ask the driver.

Buses have a number clearly displayed on the front. On bus stop signs the lines which stop are labeled.

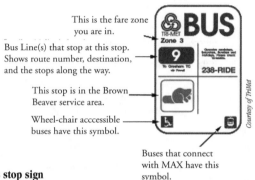

This is the fare zone you are in.

Bus Line(s) that stop at this stop. Shows route number, destination, and the stops along the way.

This stop is in the Brown Beaver service area.

Wheel-chair acccessible buses have this symbol.

Buses that connect with MAX have this symbol.

Example of a bus stop sign

Cost

Tri-Met system fares are based on the number of zones through which you travel as you go from here to there. If you begin in Zone 3 and travel to Zone 1 you will need to purchase an 'all zone' fare. Likewise, if you travel from Zone 3 to 2 you need to purchase a '2-zone' fare. A '1-zone' fare is for travel within a single zone. The same rates apply for bus service or for MAX. All transfers between bus and MAX are free, as long as you do not go beyond the zone for which you have paid. If you decide that you need to travel further than you originally anticipated, you can add an additional zone to your transit ticket for 30 cents. Fares are assessed by age. Children under six years old are free with an adult rider. Youths 18 and under and senior citizens have discounted rates. Tickets are discounted if you buy ten or more at a time. Call the Tri-Met office to determine the exact route and the fare needed to travel anywhere in the system.

Tri-Met fares as of September 2000:

Cash	10 Tickets	Monthly pass
All Zone: $1.50	$14.00	$ 54.00
2-Zone: $1.20	$11.00	$ 43.00
1-Zone: $1.20	$10.00	not available

Passes

You can purchase a day-pass for $4. This pass is valid all day on Tri-Met and C-TRAN. It is also possible to purchase monthly passes. In the summer months, a special pass ('The Summer Blast Pass') is available for youth under age 18. This pass is valid from June through August on both Tri-Met and C-TRAN. Some Portland area companies provide annual transportation passes as a benefit for their employees. You may arrange for a ticket or pass to be delivered by mail each month to your home. Call the Tri-Met number above for more information.

Getting on and off the Bus

As you board the bus, show your pass to the driver or put the exact fare or a ticket in the fare-box. If you are transferring from one bus to another or to MAX, ask the driver for a 'transfer'. This paper will allow you to board the next bus or MAX without additional charge. Transfers are valid one-way only. You may not re-board the same bus route on a transfer.

If you are unfamiliar with your destination, ask the driver, when you board the bus, to tell you when to get off. If you recognize your destination, press the driver notification button or pull the notification cable as you get close to the place you want to get off. This notifies the driver to stop at the next bus stop. The Tri-Met bus drivers are very helpful and will assist in whatever way they can.

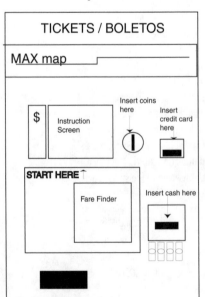

Paying for MAX

You must purchase your MAX ticket before you get on the train. At each station there is a ticket vending machine that looks like this:

Unlike other vending machines that require money to be inserted before you make a selection, MAX ticket machines require you to choose your tickets before inserting your money. After you have selected your tickets, pay for the fare with a credit card or cash. No debit cards are accepted at the machines. If you buy a single ticket, it will be stamped with the current date and time.

If you purchase multiple tickets, you will need to validate (stamp with the date and time)the ticket you are about to use.

The ticket tells you which end to stamp. Once you stamp your ticket, it is valid for ninety minutes.

While there are times when you will ride MAX and no one will ask to see your ticket, be advised that if you do not have a ticket, or your ticket is not validated, you may be fined.

Validation Machine

Traveling in Downtown Portland

Fareless Square

The downtown area of Portland that is bounded by I-405, the Willamette River, and NW Irving is called Fareless Square. Travel on MAX trains or Tri-Met buses within this area is free at any time. When you leave the Fareless Square area you must have a valid ticket or pass. The Fareless Square includes the main transit center in downtown Portland.

Vintage Trolley

The Vintage Trolley uses the MAX tracks to go from the Lloyd Center to downtown Portland. It is a free trolley service. The entire trip takes 40 minutes. It is wheelchair accessible but for only one chair at a time.

Call 503-228-6687 for more information.

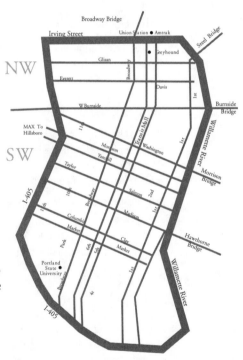

Fareless Square

Central City Streetcar

This service (planned to begin service in 2001) will travel north-south along the west side of the Willamette River. The two miles of track will go from Good Samaritan Hospital on NW 23rd to Portland State University at SW Mill. Streetcars are scheduled for every 10 minutes. Stops are placed every two or three blocks. Tri-Met passes, fares, and transfers are honored. There will be no charge for riders within the Fareless Square. This route is wheelchair accessible.

Other Tri-Met Services

Tri-Met also offers services for bikes, carpools, and vanpools (for larger groups of people traveling to the same destination on a regular basis). Call the numbers at the beginning of this section for more information. Use the Park and Ride system. Parking is available at outlying public transit stations where you board your bus or MAX. Parking is usually free, but space is limited. You can ride your bike to the station and lock it in a bike locker or you can transport it on the train or bus.

Taking your Bicycle on the Bus or on MAX

You need a bike permit and a valid ticket to travel with your bike on Tri-Met. Tri-Met bike permits are available at local bike shops and at the Pioneer Square Tri-Met office. In order to get the permit you must pay $5 and watch a short film that instructs you on the use of the bus bike racks. Call the Tri-Met bike number (at the beginning of this section) for further information.

When you travel on the bus, you are responsible for securing your bike on the bike racks on the front of the bus. When you get to your destination, tell the driver that you will be removing your bike. Do not leave your bike on the bus! It is very common for people to forget that they brought their bike with them.

There are special areas on MAX where you can sit with your bike. Get on the train after everyone else.

> ☞ **If the bike rack on the bus or the special seating section on the train is already filled, you must wait until the next bus or train.**

C-TRAN

C-TRAN is the public transportation system for Clark County in Washington State. It offers 37 bus routes with over 2000 stops, carpool, and vanpooling services. Bike racks are available on all C-TRAN buses and there are bike lockers on many routes. C-TRAN offers special transportation services for people who cannot use the regular route service (elderly, physically disabled, etc). Classes are available to teach people how to utilize public transportation.

C-TRAN includes commuter routes into Portland, as well as Vancouver, Battle Ground, Camas, and La Center.

Tri-Met tickets, transfers, and passes may be used on C-TRAN. C-TRAN tickets, transfers, and passes are honored on Tri-Met as well.

For information about C-TRAN call 360-695-0123 or 503-283-8054, or visit their website www.c-tran.com. Their main offices are on 7th Street in downtown Vancouver and there is a branch office at the Vancouver Mall.

Cost

There are two C-TRAN system fares. One is for 'C-zone' travel. The other is for 'all-zone' travel (regardless of the number of zones you travel). The C-zone fare is approximately one dollar and the all-zone fare is about $1.50. The C-zone fare covers Clark County. The all-zone fare allows you to travel to and from the Portland area.

Reduced fares are available for senior citizens (62 years and older), disabled citizens, and Medicare cardholders. Children under six years old are free with an adult rider.

Call the C-TRAN office to determine the exact route and the fare needed to travel anywhere in the system.

Passes

You can purchase a day pass for $3. This pass is valid all day on C-TRAN and Tri-Met. It is also possible to purchase monthly passes. These can be purchased at the C-TRAN offices. In the summer months a special pass ('The Summer Blast Pass') is available for youth under age 18. This pass is valid from June through August on both Tri-Met and C-TRAN.

Low-income citizens and youths (18 years old and younger) qualify for a pass discount. There is no cash fare discount.

S.M.A.R.T.

South Metro Area Rapid Transit is a bus service that brings people from the further-out areas to the Tri-Met system at the Park and Ride lots at Barbur and Tualatin. It is also a commuter service for the cities of Wilsonville, Oregon City, and Salem. Information is available at www.ridesmart.com or call 503-682-7790 or 503-570-1585.

Bicycles

Most Americans use their bicycles for recreation rather than for reliable transportation. If you are interested in recreational riding with a group of people, there are organizations which sponsor rides every weekend. This information is published in the A&E (Arts and Entertainment) section of the Friday Oregonian. It can also be found posted on bulletin boards at local bike shops.

There are a growing number of people commuting to work by bicycle. With roadways increasingly clogged with cars, bicycling is often faster than driving, and many people like the chance to squeeze some exercise into their busy schedules.

Riding a bicycle in Portland means that, in most instances, you are sharing the road with cars. For this reason helmets are recommended for adults and required for children ages 16 and under. Some routes have designated bicycle lanes (meaning that there is a strip of paint delineating the bike lane from the car lanes), but most routes do not. If you plan to use your bicycle for commuting to and from work, ask other cyclists at your work about the routes that they take. Explore to find the roads that work best for you.

Yellow Bicycles

Downtown Portland has a system of free bicycles. These bicycles are painted bright yellow, and are available for anyone to use. You can save yourself time getting from one end of the city to another, however by the time you complete your business, the bike may have been borrowed by someone else. The yellow bike program is sponsored by the Community Cycling Center. Additional bikes are added each year.

Ride Smart Rules of the Road

There are several rules of the road that will make biking safer for you and for the drivers around you:

1) Be predictable. Obey the traffic lights and signs as if you were a car. Do not ride against the traffic. Use hand signals to indicate your intentions. Do not pass on the right of a car unless there is a bike lane, or the car is making a left turn.

2) Do not weave among stopped cars.

3) When you are traveling the same speed as traffic, ride in the center of the lane. If you are traveling slower than the normal traffic, stay to the right. If you are turning left, you have two choices: ride in the left lane and turn with the cars, or cross the road as a pedestrian would.

4) You may not ride on the sidewalks in downtown Portland. In other areas, if you need to ride on the sidewalk, you must yield to pedestrians. When you want to pass give a verbal warning ("coming up on your left") or ring a bicycle bell.

5) Be alert. Expect the unexpected and ride defensively. Make eye contact with drivers. Learn to look over your shoulder to check the road behind you. You can also use mirrors.

Riding on State and Federal Highways

While it is legal to travel by bicycle on Federal and State highways, you should always check with a local bike shop to ensure that the route you plan to take is not closed to bike travelers.

In Portland it is forbidden to ride a bicycle on the following routes:

- I-5 from Delta Park to the 217 Interchange,
- I-84 from the I-5 interchange to the Sandy River (exit 18),
- I-205 from the Columbia River to the Highway 43 overpass in West Linn,
- I-405 is entirely off limits,
- Highway 30 from Northwest 23rd to I-405, and
- US 26 W from downtown Portland to the west end of the Vista Bridge Tunnel.

Bicycle Maps and Guidebooks

Oregon Bicycling Guide (from ODOT)	503-986-3300
Oregon Bicycling Manual (from ODOT)	503-986-4190
Portland Bicycle Program	503-823-2925
Multnomah County Bicycling Guide	503-248-5050
Getting There by Bike, Washington County	503-693-4943
Clackamas County Bike Map	503-650 3706
Cycle Clark County Washington	360-737-6118

Available in Bookstores and Bicycle Shops

Rubber to the Road- 30 rides around Portland

Bike There Map

Local Transportation

Long Distance Travel

Chapter 12

Long Distance Travel

Because of Oregon's location on the western coast of the United States, Portland has a great number of options for transportation.

If you are interested in exploring more of the state itself, the Northwest region, or any of the other states by car, you can get all the information you need from the Automobile Club of America (AAA). Refer to Chapter 11, 'Local Transportation', for more information on AAA. It is also possible to rent a motor home for your journey.

**Motor Home
Rent & Lease**

This chapter gives you the basics about traveling by train, airplane or bus.

Traveling by Air

Portland has an airport that is serviced by ten domestic airlines and seven international airlines. Because of the 'hub and spoke' system (make a picture, in your mind, of a wheel) used in the United States, when you travel from Portland to the East Coast or to Europe and beyond, you will be routed through a 'hub' city. The most common ones are Denver, Minneapolis, Dallas/Ft. Worth, and Chicago. In the 'hub and spoke' system, the airlines use a central major airport, halfway across the country, to make connections with most of their flights. Each airline has a different airport as its hub city (United Airlines uses Chicago, NW Airlines uses Minneapolis, for example). Seattle, San Francisco, Vancouver B.C. and Los Angeles offer non-stop flights to Asia, Europe and the East Coast of the United States.

Getting Tickets

There are many ways to arrange air travel. You can work with a 'travel agent' in your neighborhood. You can call the airlines directly (or go to their websites) to arrange for your itinerary. You can work with on-line reservation centers on the Internet.

E-tickets

When you purchase a ticket, whether through a travel agent or on the Internet or by telephone, you will be given the choice of a paper ticket or an e-ticket. With an e-ticket you receive only an itinerary, but an electronic record of the reservation is in the airline computer system. When you check-in for a flight with an e-ticket you must show positive identification (a passport or driving license with a photograph on it).

There is a fee for printing a paper ticket. The disadvantage of a paper ticket is that it can be misplaced or lost, and it is your responsibility. The advantage of a paper ticket comes IF your flight is canceled. With a paper ticket you can more easily transfer to another airline. They will honor your ticket. If you have an e-ticket, transferring to

another airline is more difficult to do. Different airline computer systems do not currently share reservation information. You will need to get written proof from a ticket agent of the original flight.

Travel Agents

Airlines have reduced the fees that Travel Agents earn when they sell airline tickets, so you may find that Travel Agents are more interested in helping you set up an entire trip than arranging only airfare. These types of trips are known as 'packages'. Many people appreciate this kind of assistance because all travel arrangements can taken care of in advance. Airfare, hotel (you are usually offered several choices at different levels of service), transportation to and from the hotel (known as transfers), and activities and meals can all be planned and arranged in advance. In a 'package' you typically are traveling independently of others. A Travel Agent can arrange package travel on a cruise ship, or by train also.

Travel Agents also set up tours. A 'tour' is a 'package' trip where you travel with a group of people.

Do it Yourself Reservations

This can be done in two ways. You may prefer to travel on one airline (to accumulate frequent flyer miles). You can arrange reservations by calling that airline directly or by visiting its Internet website. Call the airline to use your accumulated 'frequent flyer' miles, or to upgrade your ticket with miles. In some cases you may need to go to an airline sales office in order to complete your transaction. The telephone representative can direct you to the office closest to you.

The airlines that service Portland are:

Domestic Service

Alaska Airlines	800-426-0333
American West	800-235-9292
Delta Connection	800-221-1212
Frontier Airlines	800-432-1359
Hawaiian Air	800-367-5320
Horizon Air	800-547-9308
Sky west Airlines	800-241-6522
Southwest Airlines	800-435-9792
United Express	800-241-6522

International Service

Air BC	800-766-3000
American Airlines	800-433-7300
Continental Airlines	800-525-0280
Delta Airlines,	800-221-1212
Northwest Airlines	800-225-2525
TWA	800-221-2000
United Airlines	800-241-6522

Because of the alliances formed between airlines to provide worldwide transportation, you may find that the airline you use in your home country is affiliated with an American carrier, and you can credit miles flown in the United States on your home country air mileage program.

Finding Airline Websites

Find the website address of any U.S. based carrier at www.faa.gov.

International carriers that service Portland can be found at these websites:

Air BC	www.airBC.com
American	www.aa.com
Continental	www.continental.com
Delta	www.delta-air.com
NW/KLM	www.nwa.com
TWA	www.twa.com
United	www.ual.com

Getting the Least Expensive Ticket

The airline websites will usually give you the least expensive ticket available at the time, but if you are not certain which airlines fly to your desired destination, you can choose to go to a 'travel' website and explore your options there.

When you use these websites, you will be asked to become a member. This usually entails nothing more than signing up with your name, address, and establishing a password that will let you access their services. The reason for this is to allow them to track your purchasing, so that they can sell more appropriate web site advertising. You will need to have a credit card to purchase a ticket.

Airline ticket pricing is not consistent. You will find that prices vary according to time of year, destination, day of the week, popularity of the route, etc. Prices can change dramatically within a few minutes. If you choose to purchase your tickets through a

travel website, make sure that you understand the restrictions that can be placed on the fare that you are given. In most cases there is an additional fee to change the ticket in any way.

There are full service travel agents on-line. Some of them are:

Travelocity	ww.travelocity.com
Expedia	www.expedia.com
Preview Travel	www.preview.com
Trip.com	www.trip.com
Places to stay	www.placestostay.com
Priceline	www.priceline.com
Adventureseek	www.adventureseek.com

Travel Information Websites

In addition there are some specific websites which might help you learn about places in the United States and around the world.

The National Parks Service has a website www.nps.gov. This site will tell about each national park. Usually to make reservations to stay either in a hotel or in a campground you are required to contact the park vendor by telephone. Contacts for each park are given.

City search www.citysearch.com will provide you with details about most cities within the United States. These ideas will include cultural opportunities, special things happening when you plan to be there, finding a hotel or restaurant.

www.towd.com is a central directory of Tourism Offices, worldwide. You can get the 'official' version of what the city has to offer through the links of these pages.

The Lonely Planet www.lonelyplanet.com is a great place to get insight into any country on which they have a guidebook published. It also can keep you up to date on possible problems you may run into (for example if you are planning on trekking in Nepal, certain passes may be closed at certain times of year). The website will have updates on such things.

Miscellaneous Information Websites

If you have concerns about health matters in your destination, contact the Center for Disease Control at www.cdc.gov/travel.

If you have concern about political unrest or safety information on any country, the U.S. State Department travel page is www.travel.state.gov.

If you have a physical disability and want to travel, the Access-able Travel Source at www.access-able.com can assist you with plans.

If you want to stay in touch via the Internet while on the road, there is a listing of cybercafes around the world in the Internet Cafes Guide at www.cybercafe.com.

Portland International Airport (PDX)

Getting to the Airport

There are several ways to get to the airport: automobile, taxi or shuttle, and public transportation.

Parking Options

If you drive yourself, you will need to park.

Parking is available on airport property in three lots.

The **short-term** lot is the parking structure by the main terminal building. This is for parking for less than one day, with a cost of $1.50 per half-hour (maximum of $16/day). In the short term parking structure, the sky-bridge to the terminal is on level four.

There is a **long-term** parking lot near the parking structure with a cost of $12/day.

The **economy** parking lot is on the road leading to the airport just after you get off of I-205. The cost is $8/day (as of summer 2000). In this lot there is a code for keeping track of where you park. When you leave your car here, be sure to note the row you park in, as well as the color (red or blue), and number of the bus stop where you get onto the shuttle bus to the terminal. It will make your return to the car much less confusing.

The long term and economy lots provide free shuttle buses to transport riders to and from the terminal. In all of the parking lots, if you lose your parking ticket you will be charged a maximum fee, so put your ticket in a safe and easily remembered place.

There are off-site private parking lots known as 'Park and Fly' lots on NE 82nd Avenue. These lots provide security, and a shuttle service to the airport. Some travel agents will provide discount coupons to park in these lots.

Do not park in the airport area hotel parking lots. If a car is there without being registered at the hotel main desk, it will be impounded and towed.

Taxi Services, Airport Transportation

You can get to the airport by shuttle, limousine or taxi.

Airport Transportation

*

Taxi

A taxi or limousine will pick you up at your home and deliver you to the airport. You must arrange this ahead of time. A taxi is usually about $25 from downtown Portland to the airport. If you live in Beaverton or any other location on the West Side, it will be more expensive. A limousine will always be more expensive.

You can also get an airport shuttle from your area to the airport. Some of the shuttles have regular routes and you meet them at a local hotel at a specific time. Some will come to your door and get you. In either case you need to call ahead and arrange for transport.

One national company offers a service for business travelers which helps to manage the details of frequent travel. Once you have applied for a VIP card, **USA Ground Transportation** can be used to arrange for travel to and from the Portland airport or any other airport in the United States. The cost of each ride is slightly higher than the cost of a taxi but each use is charged to your credit card. No cash is needed, except for the tip for the driver. This service also awards airline frequent flyer miles. You can reach them at 1-877-872-7433 or on their website at www.usaride.com.

Public Transportation - Bus and Light Rail

You can go by public transportation. At this writing (summer 2000) buses are the only public transportation to the airport; however, as of summer 2001, there will be a direct MAX route.

Public Bus service from downtown Portland to the Airport is on Route 12 also called the 'Sandy Blvd. route'. It will take approximately 40 minutes from the downtown transit center on SW 6th to get to the airport (this will vary with time of day and day of the week). You can call TriMet, or go to their website, to get a detailed schedule of where and when to get the Sandy Blvd. Bus in order to get to the airport in time for your flight.

Departures and Arrivals

Several options exist for checking on airport arrival and departure schedules. You can check the following websites to determine if the flight you are taking, or expecting to meet, is on time.

Portland Airport	www.portofportlandor.com
KGW	www.kgw.com
KINK	www.kinkfm102.com

Most airlines have a dedicated telephone number that can be called to check on the arrival or departure time of a flight. In many cases, the entire transaction is auto-mated. You enter (using the keypad on your telephone) the flight number (when prompted) and it will tell you the projected time of arrival (departure) of that flight. If there are several cities on the flight route you will be asked to specify the city about which you are interested.

PDX airport	877-739-4636

Domestic Service

Alaska Airlines	800-252-7522
American West	800-235-9292
Delta Connection	800-325-1999
Frontier Airlines	800-432-1359
Hawaiian Air	503-282-3790
Horizon Air	800-547-9308
Sky west Airlines	800-241-6522
Southwest Airlines	800-435-9792
United Express	800-241-6522

International Service

Air BC	800-488-1800
American	800-233-5436
Continental Airlines	800-525-0280
Delta	800-325-1999
NW/KLM	800-441-1818
TWA	800-893-5436
United	800-241-6522

Reaching Someone While They are Traveling

'Will Mr. Jones please pick up a white paging telephone for a message'

If you have an emergency and you need to reach someone, call the airport at which they are expected and leave a message for him or her. In Portland call 1-877-739-4636.

Train Travel

Because of the immense travel distances in the United States, long distance train travel is less popular than in some other countries. It is possible and is a wonderful adventure, if you have the time. To travel across the country from Portland to New York City will take a minimum of three days. To travel to Seattle will take four to five hours. To travel to San Francisco will take a full day.

Train Service

AMTRAK is the passenger train carrier in the United States. The train routes generally travel east-west or north-south, and share the railroads with freight trains.

Train travel takes longer and is less expensive for the same class of service than air travel. There are several classes of tickets available depending on the length of travel. If the trip is shorter, you can choose between coach and first class. But if you are going to travel overnight there are deluxe sleeping accommodations, moderate sleeping accommodations, and coach seating (and these are priced accordingly). A dining car and lounge are also a part of the journey.

Tickets

You can make reservation for AMTRAK by contacting a travel agent. You can visit the Amtrak website at www.amtrak.com. You can also purchase tickets at the train station.

Train Station

The trains leave the Union Station in downtown Portland. Union Station is located on the west side of the Willamette River at 800 SW 6th, at Irving Street. This is near the TriMet Bus Transit Center, and the Greyhound Bus Terminal.

Parking

There is short-term pay parking available at Union Station but long-term parking is not possible. If you are going on a longer journey it is better to arrive and depart by taxi or public transportation.

Bus Travel

The least expensive way to travel long distance throughout the United States is on the bus. On a long distance bus trip you can expect to stop briefly for meals. Some routes offer movies. All intercity buses have bathrooms.

Greyhound

The major bus service for traveling around the country is Greyhound. You can learn about Greyhound routes, fares and services by telephone (503-243-2310 or 800-231-2222), by visiting their website www.greyhound.com, or by going to the bus station. The bus station is located next to the train station in Portland on 550 NW 6th (at Irving).

When planning a bus trip, remember that it takes three days to travel to New York from Portland. It takes 20 hours to get to San Francisco. On many routes there are 'Express' buses that travel with fewer stops. 'Local' buses stop at more towns along the way, therefore an Express bus trip will get you there faster.

Ameripass

A discount pass, called Ameripass, is available for anyone (with additional discounts available for seniors (over age 62), children (under age 12) and college students).

This pass allows you to travel on any Greyhound Bus route within the United States, with as many stops and layovers as you would like, in a specific period of time, for a single price. Passes are available for 7, 10, 15, 30, 45 and 60 day periods. International travelers can get an additional discount if they purchase the Ameripass via the website at least 21 days before starting travel. But anyone can purchase the pass in person at a Greyhound station.

Other Intercity Bus Services

There are other bus services which run smaller bus route systems. One that services the West Coast is called Green Tortoise. This bus system has a commuter bus that travels up and down the West Coast once a week (it is 20 hours from San Francisco to Portland). It also offers trips to other parts of the western United States.

Started in the 1960's, this bus service holds true to its' 'hippie' roots. Buses have sleeping cots (bring your own sleeping bag). It has leisurely food stops, where everyone shares a meal. It's promotional materials promise any trip to be an adventure (wherever you go). It is however the least expensive way to travel by bus on the west coast. Look at their website www.greentortoise.com or call 1-800-867-8647.

Legal Matters

Chapter 13

Legal Matters

This chapter gives a brief overview of the legal requirements of living in the United States as a foreign national (not a United States citizen). It also gives an overview of regulations regarding working, and foreign national responsibilities regarding state and federal taxes. This chapter is simply an overview. If you are a foreign national, you should get more complete information from the offices listed below.

Visas, Immigration, and Residency

Immigration and Naturalization Service (INS)

Portland District Office
511 NW Broadway
Portland, OR 97209

There is no local telephone number for the INS. The National INS Customer Service number is 1-800-375-5283.
www.ins.usdoj.gov

Social Security Administration   800-772-1213   (7 a.m.-7 p.m.)

Portland	158 SW Yamhill
	2625 SE 98th
	1235 NE 47th
Beaverton	1190 SW 2nd
Milwaukie	1741 SE Mcloughlin Blvd.

These offices are open 9 a.m. to 4 p.m., Monday-Friday.

Federal Tax Information

The walk-in assistance office for the Department of the Treasury, Internal Revenue Service is located at 1200 SW 3rd, Portland. It is open from 8 a.m. to 4 p.m., Monday-Friday.

Taxpayer information	800-829-1040 or 503 -221-3960
Tax forms	800-829-3676
Federal tax website:	www.irs.treas.gov

State of Oregon Tax Information

The Oregon Department of Revenue is located at 955 Center Street NE, Salem 97310

Taxpayer information	503-378-4988
(from January to April)	800-356-4222
Oregon Department of Revenue	www.dor.state.or.us

How to Enter, Stay, and Leave the United States

Visas

What is a Visa?

A United States visa is needed if you plan to live in the United States. Normally you apply for a visa at an American Consulate office in your home country. The visa issued classifies the visit as business, tourist, exchange visitor, etc. It is valid for a specific length of time and allows multiple visits.

Visas are categorized into two classes - Immigrant Visa and Non-immigrant Visa.

Certain foreign nationals staying in the United States for less than 90 days do not require a visa (see Visa Waiver Program description below). A Non-immigrant Visa will allow you to stay in the United States for more than 90 days for purposes of education, business, tourism, etc. If you plan to live and work in the United States permanently, you will need an Immigrant Visa. A relative that is a United States citizen or your United States employer will need to petition the INS on your behalf for an Immigrant Visa.

Types of Non-Immigrant Visas

Different kinds of visas are issued to people depending on their purpose for entering the United States:

Visa Type	Appropriate for
A	diplomatic and other government officials, including their families and employees
B	temporary visitors
C	aliens in transit
D	crewmen
E	international traders and investors
G	representatives to international organizations, including their families and employees
I	representatives of foreign media , including their families
J	exchange visitors, including their families
R	religious workers

Visa Waiver Program

A Visa Waiver Program exists between the United States and certain countries. Nationals who are planning to stay in the United States for less than 90 days may enter the country without a visa (visa category B). The countries that have this cooperative agreement with the United States are:

Andorra	Argentina	Austria
Australia	Belgium	Brunei
Denmark	Finland	France
Germany	Iceland	Ireland
Italy	Japan	Liechtenstein
Luxembourg	Monaco	The Netherlands
New Zealand	Norway	Portugal
San Marino	Singapore	Slovenia
Spain	Sweden	Switzerland
The U.K.	Uruguay	

There are a few restrictions that apply to this specific type of entry to the United States. You must:

- plan to be in the United States for less than 90 days,
- have a valid passport,
- have a return ticket, and
- present a complete INS-Form I-94 when you arrive.

You may not extend or change this non-immigrant status.

If you are denied admittance you have no right of review.

Arrival and Departure Record

A visa only allows you to travel to the United States. It does not guarantee that you will be allowed to enter. The Immigration and Naturalization Service (INS) can deny entry. When you arrive in the United States you must complete an INS form I-94. This is the first step in the creation of an Arrival and Departure Record. The inspector at immigration will endorse the I-94 with the date, place of arrival, category of your visa, the length of time you may stay, and any special conditions that may apply. The inspector will keep the arrival part of the form, and give you the departure part of the form, which you must keep with you. When you leave the United States you surrender the departure part of the form to the airline representative or customs officer.

If you decide you want to stay longer than the authorized limit on your INS Form I-94, you must apply for an extension with the INS. The decision to grant an extension rests solely with the INS.

Green Cards

If you want to live and work in the United States permanently as a foreign national rather than a naturalized citizen, you must have what is known as a Green Card or more formally, an Alien Registration Receipt Card.

To be issued a Green Card (which is actually pink in color) you must do the following:

- receive approval for an immigrant petition filed by a family member or employer on your behalf,
- receive an Immigrant Visa Number from the United States State Department, and
- apply to the INS to modify your status to permanent residential status. If you are outside the United States, this is done through a U.S. Embassy.

Immigrant Visa Number

U.S. law limits the number of Immigrant Visa Numbers that are available annually per country. This means that even if you are approved for Immigrant Visa status, you may not get an Immigrant Visa Number immediately. In fact, it can take several years if you come from a country where there is a high demand for U.S. Immigrant Visas. You do not apply for an Immigrant Visa Number; the U.S. State Department will issue it to you. This means that you must wait until it is issued. You must have an Immigrant Visa Number before you apply for Permanent Resident Status.

Family Eligibility

Immediate relatives (parents, unmarried children under age 21, and spouse) of a U.S. citizens do not have to wait for an Immigrant Visa Number.

All other immigration cases based on family are prioritized in a preference system.

First preference: unmarried adult children (over age 21) of U.S. citizens.

Second preference: spouses of legal permanent residents, and the unmarried children of legal permanent residents and their children.

Third preference: married children of U.S. citizens and their children.

Fourth preference: siblings of U.S. citizens, and their spouses and children under age 21.

Business Eligibility

Immigrant Status based on employment is granted according to the following preference system.

First preference: workers with extraordinary abilities (outstanding professors, researchers, and certain multinational executives and managers).

Second preference: members of professions holding advanced degrees and persons of exceptional ability.

Third preference: skilled workers, professionals, and other qualified workers.

Fourth preference: certain special immigrants including those in religious vocations.

Fifth preference: employment creation immigrants.

Permanent Resident Status

To be a legal resident of the United States you must apply for Permanent Resident Status. Forms are at the local INS offices. Once you submit them you will be asked to go to an INS office for a personal interview.

If you are planning to travel outside the United States during the process of application, you must notify the INS before you leave. This process is called 'getting advance parole'. If you do not apply for advance parole and you leave the country, your application for Legal Permanent Resident Status will be abandoned and you will not be allowed to re-enter on your return. If you are denied residency, the process to remove you from the country will begin immediately. You may appeal the decision to an immigration judge. If you appeal, the INS has to prove that the facts you presented were untruthful, and that the application was properly denied. If the judge decides to deny your application you may also appeal this ruling within 33 days.

There are many community based non-profit organizations that can help you through the process of gaining legal resident status. Contact the local INS office for resources.

Registering Children Born in the U.S.

If your child is born in the United States s/he is automatically a U.S. citizen.

The hospital where you deliver your baby will complete and file all the necessary forms to register the birth with your town or city, and apply for a social security number for the child.

It will be your responsibility to register the child with your home country. To get an original birth certificate, you will need to go to the Clerk's office in city or town hall.

Passports

You have the choice of getting a U.S> Passport for the child or getting one from your home country. Be sure to do this before you plan to travel outside of the country. To get a U.S. passport for your child you will need to apply in person with:

- a completed application (except for your signature - do not sign until in the office with the agent),
- proof of citizenship of the child (apostilled (see below) original birth certificate),
- valid identification for yourself,
- two identical 2x2 inch passport photos (can be color or black and white), and
- the fee (ranging from $45- $60).

The www.travel.state.gov website has the application process explained in detail, as well as application forms which you can download, and addresses of local Portland offices where you can apply in person. Any questions you may have can be answered by the:

Seattle Passport Agency
   Henry Jackson Federal Building
   915 Second Ave.
   Suite 992
   Seattle, WA 98174-1091
Hours: 8 a.m. to 3 p.m., Monday-Friday, excluding Federal holidays
Automated Appointment Phone Number: 206-808-5700

Passport Photos

You can get passport photos taken in many photo-developing shops. The passport photo size used in your home country may be different from the required passport photo size in the United States. Be sure to check with your consulate or embassy to ensure that you are providing the correct size, and the correct head orientation.

☞ **It is difficult to take a photo of a baby. A suggestion is to lay the baby on his or her back on a white blanket and stand over the child with the camera. Use indirect lighting rather than a flash in the child's face. Remember that the passport photo must have a head image that is 1 to 1 3/8 inches from chin to top of hair, and both ears must be visible.**

Registration and non-U.S. Passports

You may be required to obtain a passport before registering your children in your home country. You can visit your home country's consulate or contact the embassy (the closest embassy may be in San Francisco or Washington D.C.). Registration of the child in your home country may involve a lot of paperwork. In some cases, in addition to the child's original birth certificate (with apostille) you may need to provide proof that you are the parent of the child, your marriage license; and if you have been married and divorced you may have to provide copies of those licenses and forms also.

Embassies and Consulates

If you do not know where to find your nearest home country embassy or consulate, you can ask the embassy in Washington D.C. To find the address and telephone of any embassy in Washington D.C. access www.embassy.org/embassies.

Apostille

An apostille is a form from the Secretary of State verifying that a notary public is in good standing with the state. The Secretary of State can only verify notaries located in their state.

When you get an original birth certificate be sure to ask if it is notarized. To get the birth certificate apostilled, you must send it to the Secretary of State. They will affix a seal proving that the person who notarized the form is in good standing. To confirm the appropriate fee to send and the correct office to send it to, call the Notary Office in Salem at 503-986-2593.

Working in the United States

If you are not a U.S. citizen or a legal permanent resident and you want to work in the United States, you need to apply for an Employment Authorization Document (EAD). If you are a legal Permanent Resident, your Alien Registration Card verifies that you may work in the United States.

There are some situations where you may not be allowed to work in the United States, perhaps because you are the partner/spouse of a temporary immigrant. You may be wondering what to do with your time each day. Portland has a large number of non-profit organizations in which you can invest yourself. Ranging from snuggling sick babies in the hospital to helping build homes, from helping at the zoo to cleaning up the coastline. Volunteering is a part of the "American" culture. For more information on being a volunteer refer to Chapter 7, 'Making Portland your Home'.

Employment Authorization Document

You need to apply for an Employment Authorization Document (EAD). If you are

- an asylum seeker,
- a refugee,
- a student seeking a particular type of employment,
- an applicant for Permanent Resident status,
- a person in (or applying for) temporary protected status,
- a non-American fiancé of an American citizen, or
- the dependent of a foreign government official.

Social Security Number

The Social Security program in the United States provides economic support to retired and disabled workers, based on contributions made over one's working life-time. It is based on contributions (at a rate of 6.2%) taken from each worker's wages (the current maximum amount per year is $4724.40). A nine-digit number assigned to you (your social security number) tracks your contributions and benefits. In addition, this unique number is used for verification of identification and credit references. If you work for a U.S. company and/or are paid in the United States; you will probably need to have a Social Security Number (SSN).

Getting a social security number is easy and free. If you are over age 18, you must apply in person to the local Social Security office. You will need this number if you are working for a U.S. company and getting paid in U.S. dollars.

To apply you must have an address at which you can receive the card in 14 days. If you are not a U.S. citizen you must provide a document from a Federal, State or local agency explaining why you need a Social Security Number and that you meet all of the requirements for benefits or services. If you do not qualify for a Social Security Number you may get an Individual Taxpayer Identification Number (ITIN).

To Get a Social Security Number

If you have never been assigned a number before you must go to a Social Security office and apply in person. You must provide original documents, not photocopies, certified by the custodian of record. Notarized copies are not acceptable. You will need to provide:

- proof of age, usually an original birth certificate. If you were born outside of the United States, your passport is acceptable. If you have difficulty providing either of these documents, call the Social Security office to arrange for an alternate.
- a document with the correct name that you want on the card. Your driver's license, employer ID, passport, marriage or divorce record, or an adoption record are all acceptable.
- if you have alien status, a current form issued by the INS. Forms I-551, I-94, I-688B, or I-766 are acceptable. A receipt showing that you have applied for (but not yet been granted) such documents is not acceptable. If you are not authorized to work in the United States, you can be issued a Social Security Number if you are in the United States lawfully and need a social security number for a valid non-work reason. The organization requesting that you have a social security number must provide a document stating why. Your social security card will be marked with a statement that you cannot work, and the INS will be notified.

If you have lost your card you will need to provide proof of identity (photo identification such as a driver's license or a passport).

If you are changing your name (for example, if you get married or divorced) you need to provide documents which contain both the old and the new name.

If you have any questions about the information that is needed, call ahead to ensure that you have all the documents you need before you get to the Social Security office.

Starting Your Own Business

If you start your own business, you will be responsible for all appropriate taxes and for understanding the legal rules that apply to any American business. These rules include registration, reporting, collecting, and payment of both employment taxes and income taxes. It is appropriate to consult with both an accountant and a lawyer who can assist in setting up the necessary systems.

Government Resources

The Business Information Center in Salem is a one-stop resource center for starting your own business. If you call, they can check if the business name you want to use is available and then will forward, by mail, the appropriate forms you need to completely register your new business. The Business Information Center consolidates forms and booklets from the following state divisions:

> Department of Revenue
>
> Employment Department
>
> Workers Compensation Division
>
> Department of Consumer and Business Services
>
> Corporation Division of the Secretary of State's Office
>
> Oregon Economic Development

The State of Oregon has a division for small businesses called the Small Business Development Center. This office publishes the Oregon Business Guide that can help you understand the steps towards starting your own business. The guide is available from the Business Information Center or on-line from the Secretary of State's office at www.sos.state.or.us/corporation/corphp.htm.

The Business Information Center

> Corporation Office
> > Secretary of State
> > Business Registry Division
> > Public Service Building, Suite 151
> > 255 Capital Street NE
> > Salem, OR
> > 503-986-2200

Other business related offices:

> Internal Revenue Service
> > 1220 SW Third
> > Portland, OR
> > 503-221-3960

> Oregon Department of Revenue
> > Oregon Tax Forms
> > PO Box 14800
> > Salem, OR 97309-0920

Oregon Employment Department
 Tax section
 875 Union St. NE
 Salem, OR 97310
 503-378-3524

Department of Consumer and Business Services
 Business Administration Division
 21 Labor and Industries Building
 Salem, OR 97310
 503-945-7881

Occupational Safety and Health Administration
 Department of Consumer and Business Services
 Labor and Industries Building, Rm. 430
 350 Winter Street
 Salem, OR 97310
 Salem: 503-378-3272
 Portland: 503-229-591

Steps to Starting a Business

There are some basic considerations and requirements for starting a business in Oregon. Steps you should take:

- protect your idea (copyright, patent, or trademark).
- select a business name.
- determine the best business structure: sole proprietor, corporation, or partnership, and the tax implications of each.
- check state licensing requirements.
- check local licensing requirements.
- check for appropriate zoning at the business location (talk to both the city and the county clerks).
- obtain income tax information.
- arrange for a personal property report.
- check on other taxes that may apply to your business.
- check with the federal department of environmental quality (if appropriate).
- obtain a federal tax number.

Legal Matters

- determine if you must comply with the Americans with Disabilities Act (ADA).
- determine if you must register with any state licensing boards.

Contact the above listed offices for further information. If you will have employees, there are additional rules and regulations with both the state and the federal government.

Taxes

For tax purposes an alien is a person who is not a U.S. citizen. Aliens are classified as resident and non-resident. Resident aliens are generally treated the same as U.S. citizens; they are taxed on their worldwide income. Non-resident aliens are taxed on income from sources within the United States.

Accountants

*

Tax Return Preparers

*

Tax Advisors

U.S. tax law is not simple and allows for a great deal of variability depending on your circumstances, such as type of visa, residency status, and other qualifying benefits you may have. You will probably be quite frustrated by the process and the number of forms that you are required to complete. Many Americans also find it frustrating. While it is possible to complete your taxes independently, it will take a great deal of time to understand the nuances of U.S. tax law. We recommend that you consult with a tax professional. Inquire as to the experience that the tax preparer has, with respect to your specific needs as a resident or non-resident alien. Your embassy may be able to supply you with a list of experienced tax professionals.

Resident Alien Status

You are a resident alien (for tax purposes) if you meet either the Green Card Test or the Substantial Preference Test.

Green Card Test

You are a resident alien if you are a lawful permanent resident at any time during the calendar year. You are considered a lawful permanent resident if you have been issued an Alien Registration Card (also known as a Green Card).

Substantial Preference Test

You will be treated as a U.S. citizen for tax purposes if you meet the following criteria:

You must be physically present in the United States for 31 days during the current year, and 183 days during the 3-year period that includes the current year in the following distribution:

The sum of

- all of the days in the United States in the current year,
- 1/3 of the days in the United States in the last year, and
- 1/6 of the days in the United States in the year before the last.

For tax purposes, the term United States includes all 50 states, the District of Columbia, and the territorial waters of the United States. It does not include U.S. possessions, territories, or U.S. airspace.

ITIN

If you are working in the United States and you do not have a social security number, you will be issued an Individual Taxpayer Identification Number (ITIN), as a resident or non-resident alien. The ITIN number is for tax purposes only and it does not entitle the holder to benefits, nor does it change your employment or immigration status under U.S. law.

Income Taxes

Federal

Regardless of your classification as resident or non-resident alien, the U.S. tax year covers the period from January 1 to December 31. The taxes that are due must be filed and paid by April 15. U.S. tax law allows extensions for filing correct tax returns, but the actual tax must be paid by April 15, or fees and interest are charged.

U.S. tax law is based on an increasing rate of taxation with increasing levels of income. There are deductions for dependents, business expenses, etc. There are some instances where your income may be exempt from U.S. tax laws.

If you are a resident alien, you will use the same 1040 forms that American citizens do. If you are a non-resident alien, you will use a special tax form called a 1040 NR. There

*A 'short form'
is a simplified
version of the
tax form.*

is a short form for both (designated by the letters EZ appended to the form number) for individuals with no dependents.

Tax forms and free assistance can be found at the local IRS offices and IRS satellite offices, and by calling the IRS hotline.

State

State income taxes are based on federal taxes. You must attach a copy of your federal tax form to the state form. State taxes are also due on April 15.

Other Taxes

Purchase Based Taxes

Sales taxes are collected at the time of purchase. Oregon does not have a sales tax, but the state of Washington does. If you make a substantial purchase (auto, appliances, bedding, etc.) in Washington, you are not subject to the sales tax if you show your Oregon driver's license. When you travel in the United States you should be aware that local tax laws will differ; your purchases may cost more than you expected. Many large cities charge additional room and city taxes for hotel room rentals, and there may be a specific sales tax on restaurant food and service.

Property Based Taxes

Local taxes are billed by the county or city on a specific schedule. Water usage and sewage processing costs will be billed to you quarterly. Property taxes will be billed annually, usually in the autumn. For further information refer to Chapter 5, 'Finding your Home'.

Shopping

Chapter 14

Shopping

This chapter covers the purchase of two general types of items, household goods and food. Refer to Chapter 6, 'Making Your House a Home' for help with specific furnishings purchases. Refer to Chapter 11, 'Local Transportation' for help with buying a car.

You have a lot of choices in the United States when you go shopping. Not only in the number of items to choose from but also in the number of ways that you can buy. You can shop in person and visit small specialty shops or you can go to discount warehouse stores. You can order things by catalog using the postal service (known as placing a 'mail order'), a toll free telephone call, or over the Internet. Some retailers (like Nordstrom, or Smith and Hawken) offer all of the above methods; some (like Amazon.com, Homegrocer.com or Kozmo.com) have only one. As a result of having so much choice, you may be overwhelmed.

This chapter will explain the 'consumer mentality' in the United States and how to use it to your advantage. Because of the growth of suburban residential areas in the Portland region and the concentration of retailers in shopping malls, you probably will have to travel to shop for food, clothing and other items when you choose to shop in person.

Paying a Fair Price

The most important thing to keep in mind when you go shopping is that you will find the exact same item available in a range of shops at a range of prices. There are stores that specialize in discounted items, and stores which offer exceptional customer service for an added premium.

There are some basic guidelines that you can follow to ensure that you are paying a fair price for something:

Discount means a reduction in price. Other words to look for are SALE, Reduced, Special.

    You pay more in a small town than you will in a large city. This applies to gasoline, milk, etc., anything where transportation costs are added onto the price.

    You will pay more for food at a convenience store than you will in a supermarket.

    You will be able to buy almost anything on sale if you are willing to wait.

    You can find good condition, and less expensive, used clothing (especially for fast growing children).

Shopping as a Game

Being a smart shopper (informed consumer) is an attitude encouraged by the retail community. Shopping in the United States is somewhat like a game. Americans feel as if they won when they pay less for something than someone else; and they feel as if they lost (or were taken advantage of) when they find the same item later at a lower price. Americans pride themselves on getting a good deal. And will tell you about it! However, it is rare that you can "haggle" with a salesperson over a price (except in purchasing a car).

Another part of learning to be a smart shopper is taking advantage of sales. There are traditional times of year when items are sold at a discount. For examples - sheets, towels, bedding are on sale in January and February. Cars are on sale in June and July, just before the new models are delivered. Some stores have sales in November, to encourage early Christmas purchases. The days after Christmas are a great time to get wrapping paper and Christmas cards for next year. If you want to buy furniture, purchase in the late fall.

The other facet to American consumerism is the reality that you can shop anytime. Most retail stores are open seven days a week. Some food stores, and pharmacies are open 24 hours a day. With the Internet and toll free order numbers you can order what you want at your convenience.

Shop by Catalog

If you shop by catalog, you have several choices in how you place your order. The traditional catalog shopper placed an order by completing the order form included in the paper catalog, and mailing it to the company. Now orders by telephone are most common and mail order companies have a toll free (800 or 888 area code) telephone numbers for order placement. It is increasingly popular to order over the Internet.

The advantages of shopping by catalog are:

- You can make decisions and choices at your own pace.
- No sales person is trying to force you to buy.
- You can compare prices for the same or similar items (if you use the Internet).
- You can easily return items that do not fit your expectation - size, color, or functionality. The cost to you is the cost of return shipping.

The disadvantages of shopping by catalog are:

- The delay in the time between making the decision to buy and when you have the item in your hands. There is no assurance that the item you order is available and can be shipped immediately. This is especially true for popular items such as toys in December.

- You must use a credit card. You risk, although remotely, having someone steal your card number over the Internet or the telephone or from the mail. .

- You can not try things on until you have already paid for them. It may take several orders to get the correct size.

Catalogs and Mailing Lists

You will receive catalogs of all sorts of products in your mail (such as clothing, gifts, wines, computer supplies, and gardening products). Library circulation rooms have current or past copies of catalogs, or ask friends to share.

Catalog companies regularly trade their mailing lists of potential customers. Once you place an order you will be on a mailing list for other companies carrying similar items. If you do not want to have your name and address shared, request that your name be marked in their database. In the United States having a reliable customer database is a large asset to any catalog sales company. If you receive catalogs you do not want, call the company that sent it and ask to be taken off of their mailing list.

Local Retail Shopping

Shopping Hours

Most stores are open in the evenings. Most stores are open seven days a week. There are exceptions to these general statements, of course. The opening hour can range from 8 a.m. to 10 a.m. You can always telephone a specific store and ask for its hours.

Most stores post an open/closed sign with their hours somewhere in the entry area of the store.

Some grocery stores are open 24 hours a day, seven days a week.

Internet in Portland

There is a website that you can use www.dailyshopper.com that will give you a search index for items on sale in local Portland area stores. If, for example, you want to purchase a barbeque grill, you enter the brand for which you are looking and it will tell you which stores have it, at what price, and how long it will be onsale. It does not guarantee that by the time you get there the store will still have stock. Most stores will issue a rain check if you try to buy an advertised sale item that is already sold out.

A rain check means that you can purchase the item at the sale price when the sale is over.

271

Clothing Size Charts

The U.S. sizes and equivalent international sizes:

Ladies Wear

Dresses and Skirts

USA	10	12	14	16	18
Britain	32	34	36	38	40
Europe	38	40	42	44	46
Japan	9	11	13	15	17

Shoes

USA	6	7	8	9	10
Britain	4.5	5.5	6.5	75	8.5
Europe	36	38	39	40	41
Japan	23	24	25	26	27

Men's Wear

Suits

USA	36	38	40	42	44	46
Britain	36	38	40	42	44	46
Europe	46	48	50	52	54	56
Japan	S	M		L		LL

Shirts

USA	14.5	15	15.5	16	16.5
Britain	14.5	15	15.5	16	16.5
Europe	37	38	39	41	42
Japan	37	38	39	41	42

Shoes

USA	6	6.5	7.5	8.5	9.5	10.5
Britain	5.5	6	7	8	9	10
Europe	39	40	41	42	43	44
Japan	24.5		26		27.5	28

Children's Wear

Most Clothing

USA	3	4	5	6	7	8
Europe	98	104	110	116	122	128

Note that the numbering system for children's clothing and shoe sizes are related to the age of a 'typical' size child.

Infant clothing sizes are assigned newborn, 6 months, 12 months, 18 months and 24 months sizes.

Stores and Where to Find Them

There is no logic to the distribution of stores at the various shopping areas. Nationally known stores are found along side unique specialty shops. in every large mall, as well as specialty shops that are unique.

A Mall is a grouping of stores that usually surround a covered central walkway. A mall will have a great variety of stores, from large department stores to small specialty shops, and restaurants. At a mall you can find clothes and shoes, books and music, toys and gifts. A mall does not have a supermarket. Often a movie theater is nearby. In the surrounding area of large malls, you will find many other retailers (electronics, computers, toys, books and furnishings).

The local large malls in the Portland area are:

The Lloyd Center Mall (NE Portland)
The Washington Square Mall (One and Two) (SW between Tigard and Beaverton)
The Clackamas Town Center (SE- off of I-205)
Pioneer Courthouse Place (One and Two) (SW- downtown Portland)
Jantzen Beach Center (off I-5, by the Columbia River)
Vancouver Mall (WA state, off of I-5)

Smaller malls with regional and smaller chains stores.

Beaverton Mall (Cedar Hill Blvd.)
Beaverton Town Center (US 26, and SW Canyon Rd.)
Mall 205 (I-205 and SE Washington)
Eastport Plaza (SE 82nd)

There are also **shopping centers** where the shops face a central parking area. Supermarkets are usually found in shopping centers. Many times you will find services

within a smaller mall or shopping center such as medical offices, family restaurants, the post office, and the library.

Factory Outlet stores and Discount Malls, have brand name retailers selling their items at a discount. This is a way for the retailers to get rid of last years inventory.

Suburban Portland has not been designed for shopping easily on foot or bicycle. There are some neighborhoods in 'close-in' Portland where it is possible. Many town centers have been turned into wall to wall shopping areas with concrete parking lots which are difficult to maneuver on foot (Beaverton is a good example).

General Types of Retail Stores

The following is a general list describing of the types of stores you will find in the Portland area. We associated each type with a few representative names of stores. This list is meant to explain the differences between stores, as well as to provide assistance when you have to look for items you need. It is not exhaustive, nor is it meant to recommend that you purchase from these retailers.

National Department Stores (Sears, JC Penny, Montgomery Ward)

They have almost everything (appliances, clothing gifts, toys, etc.) except food.

Specialty Department Stores (Nordstrom, Emporium, Meier and Frank)

These stores specialize in clothing for everyone, accessories, cosmetics, shoes and small gift items. Some carry kitchen and household furnishing items.

Discount Department Stores (WalMart, Target)

These stores carry toys, office supplies, clothing and shoes, gift items, kitchen and household furnishing items.

Specialty Electronics Stores (Frye's, Good Guys, Magnolia HiFi, CarToys, Standard Appliance, etc.)

These stores are national chains that carry everything electronic from car stereos, to cell phones, to televisions and kitchen appliances.

Specialty Chain Stores, (Office Depot, Toys R Us, PetSmart, Borders Books and Music, etc.)

The name says what it sells.

One Stop Shopping (Fred Meyer)

Here you can get food, household supplies, clothes, gardening supplies and plants, hardware, music and electronics, books, home decorating supplies, and toys.

Super Market Chains, Grocery Stores (Albertson's, Thriftway, Safeway)

You can get food, over the counter and prescription drugs, paper products, household-cleaning items, beer and wine, pet foods.

Membership Stores (like Costco, BiMart)

These types of stores have a membership requirement. You may be required to be part of a larger group, such as an employee of a certain company, but often you can be a member simply by paying the fee. At this type of store you can purchase items at lower prices than normal retailers, however you are usually required to purchase these items in larger quantities, for example, you can not get only one can of soup, you must buy three. This type of purchase is useful if you use an item frequently but it means that you must have room to store the additional packages. Because of store purchasing methods, you can not be sure that what you want will be there each time you go. These stores carry food items and a variety of other things (tires for you car, items of clothing, computer equipment, over the counter drugs etc). The trick to shopping in a store like this is that not everything will actually be at a better price. You have to be an informed buyer.

Convenience Stores (7-eleven, Star Mart)

Historically these stores provided groceries when regular food stores were closed. Now with most supermarkets open most hours, these stores carry a limited selection of groceries, and are better known for their snacks: coffee, soda, chips etc.

Discount Drugstores (Rite Aid, Hi School Pharmacy),

hese stores began as prescription drug outlets, but have grown into providing a myriad of items, based on the communities' needs. All carry cosmetics and health products. Some carry plants and hardware, some carry clothes and games.

Second Hand (used item) Stores (Goodwill, Salvation Army, Vintage Clothing Shops, Consignment Clothing Shops, etc.)

These places offer you good quality used items. It is a chance to spend less money, but you need to have the patience to spend the time to search out what you want. Good quality children's clothing can be purchased here at a significantly lower price.

Factory Outlet Stores

These brand name stores offer closeout inventory at a discount. They are, by law, forbidden to be located within 30 miles of a city where the same items could be found at full retail, so you will find these malls outside of the Portland area (Woodburn, Troutdale, Lincoln City) on well traveled roads.

Outdoor Gear

If you are looking to get outdoor sporting clothes, equipment, you have several places to turn. REI is a membership store that is open to the public. Oregon Mountain Community is an independent outdoor store. GI Joe's is a regional chain for sports and automobile parts. There are also specialty stores that focus on particular sports, such as bicycles, skis, and water-sports.

Special Portland Retail Options

Powell's Books

Powell's is located in downtown Portland and has several satellite stores which specialize in art, technology, travel or food. This independent bookstore buys and sells new and used books. For many travelers, it is a destination in Portland. Powell's (and most other book stores) have an in-house coffee shop in which you can take a book to browse before you purchase. They also sponsor book signings and lectures. You can pick up a monthly list of 'what is going on' from the front of the store.

Saturday Market

Located on the road which runs under the Burnside Bridge in downtown Portland in Old Town, is a market which is open April to December on weekends. It is called the Saturday Market, but do not be fooled by the name. It is open on Sunday also. It is outdoor in the summer, and somewhat covered in the winter. It is a place for artists and craftsmen from all over the northwest to come and display their wares. During December Saturday Market is also open during the week. If you are looking for a unique gift, or an entertaining day, it is a great place to visit. There are usually street musicians, and performers and vendors with unusual snacks in addition to the crafts-people.

The Children's Store

The Children's Store is a store which benefits Portland-area children's charities. Each fall the store opens in a different prominently located space. Proceeds from the store go to local charitable programs for children. You can purchase holiday cards, gifts, toys, etc. The Oregonian and radio announcements will inform you when the store opens, and where the store is located for the season.

Food Shopping

The typical American shops for food one or two times a week, due in part to the ample size of refrigerator and freezer space and package sizes. If you are accustomed to shopping daily for fresh meats and produce this may take some getting used to. You will need to go to a specialty butcher to find food like wild game or to a 'European baker' or natural food store to find breads that are really whole grain. You will find the international food section of the Supermarket carries foods for Asian and Central American tastes.

The supermarkets offer the convenience of only having to stop at one place to get all of your food needs. When you go grocery shopping you should expect that someone will pack your groceries in bags that the store provides. You may choose to use your own bags and boxes, which you bring with you. Many supermarkets will give you a 5-cent credit for each one used. Do not be surprised if someone offers to push your shopping cart to your car and transfer your groceries to it. This is a service many markets offer. This person does not expect to be tipped for this service.

In Portland there are no fees for using a shopping cart.

In Oregon you will be charged a per bottle charge as a deposit on bottles and cans for soda, beer, water, etc. In Washington State you will not be charged this fee. Every store that sells products in returnable containers must have a way for those to be returned and for you to get your money back. In some places there are machines which will accept the returnable bottles and cans. In other stores there is a person who will accept them. If you have bottles that are rejected as returnable you can recycle them. Refer to Chapter 6, 'Making your House a Home' for more on recycling.

Things are Different

One of the biggest differences you will see in an U.S. supermarket is the quantity of items in every category. Cleaning products, cold drinks, snacks, cold cereal, cat litter. It can be overwhelming. One strategy is to create a list of what you want to buy. Then, when you are becoming disoriented by the decision of which kind of cookies to choose, you can be reminded of what you actually need to purchase.

When you get to the check out stand (the conveyer belts where the total price for your groceries is calculated) you will be asked by the cashier "Paper or plastic". This is not a question about how you will pay for your groceries. It is a question about the type of bag in which your groceries will be packed. Most stores will give you a small credit if you bring your own shopping bags and boxes with you, but expect to get an odd look if you start to pack your own groceries in them.

You have the choice of using cash, check, credit card or debit card to pay for your groceries. When you use a debit card you may be asked if you want 'cash back'. This refers to putting a higher charge on your debit card than the value of the groceries and giving you the difference in cash.

You may be surprised at the range of low fat, no fat, or sugar-free products. This can be seen in dairy products especially (such as milk, cheeses, and yogurts).

Milk, Yogurt and Cheeses

All milk products sold in stores must be made from pasteurized milk. Milk is labeled according to the fat content. 'Whole' milk has a rating of 3.5% fat. 2% milk, 1% milk and 'skim' (less than 1%) are also available. You will also find 'milk' made from soy or rice. You must refrigerate dairy products.

There are varieties of coffee creamers from which to choose. Half-and-Half (similar to single cream) is located in the refrigerator dairy case. Non-dairy flavored creamers are located with coffee and tea. Condensed milk is located with the baking supplies. For cooking there is heavy cream, whipping cream and low fat whipped products with stabilizers in them to get them to hold their shape. There are some aseptic packages for non-diary coffee creamers, soy and rice milks, etc. but that type of packaging for standard milk is not common.

The most popular yogurts in the United States are low fat (the most common) and 'Swiss style' (fruit flavor and bits mixed through out). You will have a choice of many flavors. It is possible to find yogurt that is made of whole milk, has the fruit on the bottom, or is plain, but you have to search for them.

Many markets now have cheese counters at which they sell imported cheeses. In general, the Deli Counter at the market sells sandwich cheese that is sliced to your order. The most popular domestic cheese in the United States is Cheddar in varieties from extra sharp (aged) to mild (green or young). You can also find domestic Swiss, Muenster, and Brie. 'American Cheese' is a blended product. Oregon is renown for its Tillamook Cheese, which is manufactured in Tillamook Oregon (about an hour from Portland on the Coast). You can visit the factory and watch them manufacture the cheese in large batches.

Food Handling

There are some foods that are handled in a different way in the United States. An example is fresh eggs. Eggs are always refrigerated. The reason is that the eggshell, when it is washed, looses its ability to protect the egg from air born contamination. USDA graded eggs are washed. Therefore when you buy eggs you will find them in the refrigerated section of the store and you must keep them in your refrigerator at home.

Nutritional Labeling

Nutrition Facts	
Serving size 1 Cup (240 mL)	
Servings about 4	
Amount per Serving	
Calories 100	**Calories from Fat** 5
	% Daily Value *
Total Fat 0.5 g	1%
Saturated Fat 0g	0%
Cholest. Less than 5 mg	1%
Sodium 760 mg	32%
Total Carb. 22g	7%
Fiber 1g	7%
Sugars 13g	4%
Protein 2 g	
Vitamin A 15% • Vitamin C 10%	
Calcium 2% • Iron 2%	
*Percent Daily Values are based on a 2000 calorie diet.	

Serving size on which the nutritional information is based.

Number of servings in this container

These nutrition items are required to be listed on any prepared food

This is the "typical" calorie intake for an average size person.

Labels on prepackaged food of all kinds must have nutritional information on them. You can use this information to compare the nutrition content of foods. If you are following a special diet (low fat, low salt, low carbohydrate), these labels can be especially useful. In addition you can check the ingredients list on each product. Items in the ingredient list are given in descending order by volume. You can determine if there is a lot of sugar in the product, or if chemicals and preservatives are used that you want to avoid. You may be surprised at how little nutrition is to be found in many commonly eaten U.S. foods.

Weights and Measures

When you purchase food in the United States, you will be using pounds and ounces for weight, and ounces, cups, pints, quarts and gallons for liquids. Refer to Chapter 1, 'Basics' for U.S. Standard to Metric equivalents and conversion tables. You may find it difficult to find meat and fish portions prepackaged in smaller sizes. Ask the butcher at the meat and fish counter or the staff at the deli to package the amount you actually want.

Coupon Clipping

If you choose to use the supermarkets for your basic groceries you can save money by using coupons. There are two types of coupons: Manufacturers Coupons and store coupons.

Manufacturers' Coupons

Manufacturers coupons are issued by the company that makes or distributes the food item and can be used in any supermarket that accepts coupons. Manufacturers' coupons are found in the Sunday edition of the Oregonian, and at times, in the mail to your home. These are colorful multi-page pamphlets, with coupons on each page. Cut out the coupons for the items you would like to buy. When you shop, hand them to the

cashier. The cashier will subtract the value of the coupon from your total shopping bill. (Notice that each manufacturer coupon will list an expiration date; after this date the coupon is not valid).

In Store Coupons

In-store coupons are offered by a particular store or chain of stores (such as Safeway, Thriftway, Albertsons, or Fred Meyer). They can not be used at any other store. The supermarket chain offers special products at a discount to entice customers to shop at their store. These coupons may be delivered by mail (in a coupon book or a special advertising page). They are also delivered in the Oregonian. The Tuesday Oregonian contains coupons in the special section called "Food Day". Special in-store coupons and food bargains begin on Wednesday, the day after the store flyer comes to your home.

Some stores double the value of coupons, or offer special food discounts, on a specific day of the week, usually a Tuesday (referred to as 'Tightwad Tuesday'). The stores do this to entice buyers to shop on a slow business day.

Club Cards

In addition to coupons, you can save money by getting a specific store's 'club card'. Some stores ask you to register with them, and in return you are given a buying card which will offer you additional discounts on sale items. This means that each time you purchase anything using the card, the computer system tracks your preferences. At some point in the future you may receive promotions for other similar products. You have the choice when you register for the card to tell them that you do not want to receive any promotional materials or offers.

Internet Food Resources

You can even purchase your groceries on the Internet. www.HomeGrocer.com will deliver groceries to your house at a scheduled time. They offer fruits and vegetables, in addition to packaged and dry goods, meats, fish and dairy products. It can be very helpful if you have a difficult time getting to the food store. Delivery is free if the total bill for your grocery order is above $75. Because there are a limited number of deliveries each day, it may mean that your order can not be scheduled for delivery on the day you place it. HomeGrocer does deliver on Sunday. You should tip the driver $5 per delivery.

If you live within the Portland city limits and want to get a video and a pizza delivered to you, visit the www.kozmo.com web-site. This company offers snacks and entertainment delivered straight to your door (usually by bicycle) within an hour. When you

join Kozmo.com, you give them a credit card to which all purchases are charged. You should tip the delivery person a few dollars cash.

The following list of websites provides you the chance to get food and other items from home. Some of these sites are in the United States and others are in your home country.

African	www.accramarket.com
	www.afrifood.com
Asian	www.asianmall.com
	www.asianestore.com
	www.maruwa.com
	www.pacificrim-gourmet.com
Australian	www.autraliapresents.com.au
	www.cravings.com.au
British Foods	www.britishmailorder.com
	www.britishaisles.co.uk
	www.britishexpress.co.uk
	www.bbcamerican.com
	www.ukgoods.com
	www.britsabroad.co.uk
	www.estorek.com
	www.expatexpress.co.uk
	www.expatshopping.com
	www.expatriate.co.uk
Dutch	www.holland-america.com
	www.dutchmarket.com
French	www.france-ok.com
German	www.germancorner.com
New Zealand	www.kiwi-ingenuity.com
Russian	www.russianfoods.com

Local Sources for Favorite Foods

There are also local specialty stores sell things that you may miss from home, and that are not a part of the American diet. This type of food is referred to as "ethnic" food. The list which follows provides places to go to find foods your neighborhood supermarket might not carry.

Specialty Supermarkets

Asian Foods

Anzen Imports   503-233-5111
736 NE MLK, Portland

OTA Tofu   503-232-8947
812 SE Stark, Portland

Asia Supermarket and Herbalist   503-255 1718
8211 NE Brazee St., Portland

Uwajimaya   503-643-4512
10500 SW Beaverton Hillsdale Hwy., Beaverton

Hong Kong Marketplace   503-526-9360
12050 SW Allen Blvd., Beaverton

European Foods

Foti's Greek Deli   503-232-0274
1740 E Burnside St., Portland

Scandia   503-643-2424
10020 SW Beaverton Hillsdale Hwy, Beaverton

Dutch American Market and Import   503-646-1518
12125 SW Canyon Rd., Beaverton

S&N Russian Food   503-771-8873
6433 SE Foster Rd., Portland

Scottish Country Shop   503-238-2528
3568 SE Powell Blvd., Portland

Edelweiss Sausage and Delicatessen   503-238 4411
3119 SE 12th Ave., Portland

Victors European Meat Market   503-684-2580
13500 SW Pacific Hwy., Tigard

General Gourmet Foods

Pastaworks

3735 SE Hawthorne Blvd., Portland   503-232-1010

Nature's Fresh Northwest

17711 Jean Way, Lake Oswego	503-635-8950
4000 SW 117th, Beaverton	503-646-3824
3016 SE Division, Portland	503-233-7374
3535 NE 15th, Portland	503-288-3414
6344 SW Capitol Highway, Portland	503-244-3110
2825 E Burnside, Portland	503-232-6601
Marketplace 8024 E Mill Plain Blvd., Vancouver, WA	800-357-3470

Zupan's

3301 SE Belmont, Portland	503-239-3720
2340 W Burnside, Portland	503-497-1088
7221 SW Macadam, Portland	503-244-5666
8225 SW Apple Way, Beaverton	503-203-5962
19133 Willamette Dr., West Linn	503-635-6281

Haggen Food and Pharmacy

8515 SW Tualatin-Sherwood Road, Tualatin	503-612-8400
18000 NW Evergreen Parkway, Beaverton	503-690-5900

Elephant's Deli

13 NW 23rd Place, Portland   503-224-3955

City Market NW (4 shops in one place)

735 NW 21st Ave., Portland

Trader Joe's

4715 SE 39th, Portland	503-777-1601
Beaverton Town Square	503-626-3794
15391 SW Bangy Road, Lake Oswego	503-639-3238
New Seasons	503-292-6838

7300 SW Beaverton-Hillsdale Hwy., Portland

Indian/ Pakistani Foods

Fiji Emporium   503-240-2768
7814 N Interstate Ave, Portland

Taj Mahal   503-646-2838
4130 SW 117th Ave, Beaverton

India Emporium   503-646-0592
10195 SW Beaverton Hillsdale Hwy., Beaverton

Sriders India Imports   503-620 8665
11945 SW Pacific Hwy, Tigard

Mexican Foods

Becerra's International Groceries

3022 NE Glisan St., Portland   503-234-7785
18929 E Burnside St., Gresham   503-667-4444
Su Casa Imports and Bakery   503-648-5779
1050 SE Walnut St., Hillsboro

Mid Eastern Foods

Golden Loaf Bakery Deli and Grocery   503-231-9758
1334 SE Hawthorne Blvd., Portland

International Food Market   503-520-1850
12070 SW Allen Blvd., Beaverton

Rose International Emporium   503-646-7673
6153 SW Murray, Beaverton

Thai/Vietnamese Foods

Manila Imports and Exports   503-641-4545
12155 SW Canyon Rd., Beaverton

Thai & Etc   503-644-5599
12940 SW Canyon Rd., Beaverton

Specialty Spices

Oregon Spice   503-238-0664
1630 SE Rhine St., Portland

Whole Grain Foods

Bob's Red Mill   503-654-3215
5209 SE International Way, Milwaukie

Summer-time Farmer's Markets

From May to October, there are local neighborhood outdoor markets, called Farmer's Markets, where you can go to purchase fresh produce, crafts, plants, etc. These markets are usually on Saturday morning from 8 a.m. -1 p.m. Some sites are also open on Wednesday evening.

Each market has its own unique character. Some have musicians who entertain; some have food stands for snacking. In early Spring, you can find many flowering plants. In late summer you will find honey, and homemade food items. Some Farmers Markets only allow legitimate farmers to sell. Some allow anyone to set up a display table to sell their wares (for a fee). Beaverton has a very large Farmer's Market.

In the spring, The Oregonian newspaper will give a list of the outdoor markets in the area. The list with day, open hours, and locations of area Farmer's Markets (from summer 2000) is below.

Beaverton	mid May - late Oct.	Sat. 8 -1:30 p.m.	SW Washington between 3rd and 5th.
Canby	mid May - late Oct.	Sat. 9 - 1 p.m.	Railroad Parking lot
Cedar Mill	June - Sept.	Sat. 8:30 - 1:30 p.m.	NW Cornell at Saltzman
Forest Grove	mid May - late Oct.	Sat. 9 - 1 p.m.	19th and Ash
Gresham	mid May - late Oct.	Sat. 8 - 2 p.m.	Roberts Ave between 4th and 5th
Hillsboro	May - late Oct.	Sat. 8 -1:30 p.m.	Courthouse Sq., at 2nd and E. Main
		Tues. 5:30 - 8:30 p.m.	
Hollywood	mid May - late Oct.	Sat. 8 -1 p.m.	NE Hancock, between 44 and 45th
Lents	mid May - late Oct.	Sat. 9 -2 p.m.	SE 91st and Foster Rd
Milwaukie	mid May - early Oct.	Sat. 10 - 2:30 p.m.	Across from City Hall
Molalla	mid May - late Oct.	Sat. 9 - 2 p.m.	Next to fire station
Portland SE	early Apr. - late Nov.	Wed. 2 - 7 p.m.	3029 SE21st
Portland	mid May - late Oct.	Sat. 8 - 1 p.m.	Park Block at PSU
	June - late Sept.	Wed. 10 - 2 p.m.	SW Salmon and Park
Sandy	early May - Labor Day	Sun. 10 - 3 p.m.	US26 and OR 211
Tigard	late May - Oct.	Sat. 8 - 1 p.m.	SW Hall, near Washington SQ.
Vancouver	early April - Oct.	Sat. 9 - 3 p.m.	Ester Short Park, at 6th and 8th

The cost of an item at a farmer's market will not necessarily be less expensive than at a supermarket or farm-stand, however it will be very fresh.

You can purchase in larger quantities if you wish to make a favorite homemade specialty. Oregon, more than many other states, has a tradition of preserving food for winter eating. This summer and fall activity of home preserving may include preparing jam and jelly, canned fruits, dried meats, and frozen vegetables. If you are interested in learning home preserving, the public library is a great resource to find how to do it safely.

Holidays

Chapter 15

Holidays

The word 'holiday' in the United States means special days for remembrance and celebration. When you take time off from work and school for rest and relaxation it is called a vacation.

The holiday celebrations in the United States will be appreciably different than in your home country. Some holidays will have the same dates but be celebrated with American interpretations and traditions. Some holidays will be entirely new to you. This chapter describes the special days in the United States. Each entry gives the date, name of the holiday, and a little insight into what you should expect to see and experience at each of these. The chapter contains two lists. The first list is the national holidays celebrated in the American calendar. The second list contains the other days that have special meaning in American culture.

National Holidays are also known as Federal Holidays

National Holidays

National Holidays are called that because they are celebrated across the country. Banks, post offices, schools, and other government offices will always be closed on these days. The 'S', which follows a few of these descriptions, indicates that retail stores may be closed as well. Many of the holidays listed below are not celebrated on a specific date. Rather, they are celebrated on a Monday close to the original date of the holiday to provide people with a three-day weekend.

January 1   New Year's Day
This first day of the New Year is a very busy travel day as families return home from the Christmas vacation. It is the day when many people take down their Christmas decorations and Christmas tree. It is an important sports day with (college level) American football games (called 'Bowls'). The largest floral parade in the United States, The Festival of Roses Parade, is televised in the morning. If American football does not interest you, you might try skiing, as the ski areas are often less busy this day. **S**

3rd Monday in January   Martin Luther King's Birthday
This holiday is the observance of the birthday of the charismatic American civil rights leader of the 1950's and '60's. Ceremonies are held commemorating Dr. King, who was assassinated in 1968. You will often hear excerpts from his "I Have a Dream" speech on this day.

3rd Monday in February   President's Day

This date is the observance of the birthdays of all forty-two former U.S. Presidents. George Washington and Abraham Lincoln, two of the best-remembered presidents have birthdates in February. No special celebrations are observed. Many retail stores have sales that employ advertisements that refer to the story of George Washington and the cherry tree. Desserts based on cherries are found in food stores.

Last Monday In May   Memorial Day

This holiday, first known as Decoration Day, was established as a tribute to men who had died in the Civil War. It has been expanded into a remembrance day for all those who have died in their Nations' service. A national ceremony is conducted at the Tomb of the Unknown Soldier, at the Arlington National Cemetery near Washington, D.C. Locally, ceremonies are held at the Vietnam Memorial, and parades are held in some towns and neighborhoods. Many people choose this day to place flowers and flags on the graves of loved ones.

It is also unofficially considered the first day of summer although school continues for another week or two. People spend this holiday by going away for the long weekend, holding neighborhood or family barbecues in the backyard, and catching up on yard work. Many stores have Memorial Day Weekend Sales.

July 4   Independence Day

Americans celebrate the anniversary of the signing of the Declaration of Independence (from England in 1776) with picnics, parties and barbecues with friends or family. Parades are held in almost every town. Some stores may be closed; others may have big sales. The day ends with fireworks at dusk in public displays in local parks. The Oregonian will list all of the venues for viewing fireworks. Fort Vancouver has the largest fireworks display in the area; they can be seen from both sides of the Columbia River.

From June 23-July 6, fireworks are sold in Oregon. The Oregon Safe and Sane law specifies the limits on fireworks that can be sold and used in Oregon. Fireworks sold in Washington State that exceed these limits can not legally be used in Oregon.

1st Monday in September   Labor Day

This day was established by the Labor Unions to recognize the social and economic achievements of American Workers; a yearly tribute to the contributions which workers

have made to the strength, prosperity and well-being of the country. Labor Union events and marches are held throughout the country. The day is spent much like Memorial Day with picnics, barbecues or a long weekend at the beach. It is unofficially considered the last day of summer because school usually begins the next day.

2nd Monday in October   Columbus Day

This day commemorates the Italian explorer Christopher Columbus' discovery of the American continent in 1492. No special celebrations are observed.

November 11   Veteran's Day

This day was initially known as Armistice Day. It was established after World War I to honor the cause of world peace. Now, after World War II and the Korean and Vietnam Wars, it is a day to honor veterans of all wars. Public ceremonies mark the day, with a minute of silence at 11 a.m. (local time).

Last Thursday in November   Thanksgiving

This holiday remembers the pilgrims (the first English settlers) and the local native Americans living in the area now known as Massachusetts. At harvest time in the mid 1600's, they shared the food gathered and raised during their early settlement years. Foods said to be a part of these first meals were turkey, cranberries, pumpkins, and corn. Today families get together for a large meal, which includes roasted turkey with (corn) bread stuffing, cranberry sauce and pumpkin pie.

For most people, Thanksgiving weekend is a four-day weekend, therefore people are able to travel to see family. The Wednesday before Thanksgiving is the busiest day in the year at Portland International Airport. If you are planning to use the four-day holiday to do some traveling yourself, you should plan to get your reservations as early as possible. If you stay at home on Thanksgiving, you can watch American professional football games on the television. Once Thanksgiving Day is over, the Christmas season 'officially' begins with decorations, lights and music. **S** (Stores are closed on Thanksgiving Day only, there are big sales the rest of the weekend).

December 25   Christmas

You may begin to see Christmas decorations and hear holiday music in stores as early as November 1, although the Christmas season does not really start until the day after Thanksgiving. Traditionally, holiday colors are red and green, silver and gold. Children are told that if they are good, Santa Claus, traveling in a sleigh pulled by eight reindeer, will come down the chimney on Christmas Eve. He will leave presents for them in their stockings (hung by the fireplace) and/or under the Christmas tree. Families open Christmas presents on Christmas morning. Later in the day, extended families get together to feast on turkey, roast beef or ham.

Other traditions during the month of December include:

- sending holiday cards to family and friends,
- baking and exchanging Christmas cookies,
- attending pageants of music and theater,
- workplace Christmas parties for employees. You may be asked to contribute a gift for someone (with a limit on value usually set), and
- Christmas parties at school.

Christmas stories and songs include both the classic subjects (based on the religious Christmas story) and popular subjects (based on Santa and other imaginary characters). Popular characters include Frosty the Snowman, the Grinch, and Rudolph the Red-Nosed Reindeer. Your library is a good source for stories about these non-religious characters who are part of the Christmas season for Americans. television stations will broadcast Christmas movies (some about these same characters) throughout the month of December. These movies are a good way to gain insight into this playful side of Christmas as celebrated in the United States.

In the weeks leading up to Christmas, there will be opportunities for your child to sit on the lap of a Santa Claus at a shopping mall, and to tell him what s/he wants for Christmas. Young children often write letters to Santa and mail them to the North Pole, telling him how well-behaved they have been this year and what gifts they especially want to receive.

Christmas lights of all different colors are an important part of the American celebration. There will be extravagant lighting displays throughout the city. Peacock Lane, the Oregon Zoo, the Grotto, and the Shilo Inn Headquarters are all 'destinations' for families wanting to view the lights. The Oregonian publishes a list of sites you can drive past or walk through.

Because there are so many cultures in American society, special foods for this time period differ by family cultural backgrounds. One item that will be found in every food shop is eggnog, a rich cream and egg based drink flavored with nutmeg. Peppermint candy canes can be found almost everywhere also.

Traveling during this time may be difficult for two reasons. First, many people are traveling to be with their families over the holidays. Second, the weather is unpredictable. In December and January, hub airports experiencing stormy cold weather (even if they are on the East Coast) can cause delays across the country. If you plan to travel try to arrange your flights through the southern state airports (Dallas, St. Louis or Atlanta) rather than through Denver, Minneapolis or Chicago. **S**

Days with Special Meaning

Below is a list of days that have special meaning in the U.S. calendar. A brief description is given of each and a short description of how Americans typically spend their time on that day. Your children will be exposed to some of these days in school. Some of them have a religious basis, and some are playful. Because these are not national holidays, stores will be open.

January

Last Sunday in January   Super Bowl Sunday

The winners of the two American football professional conferences play for the 'world' championship. Because of American football's popularity, this is a very significant game, with extensive media coverage in the weeks leading up to the game. Super Bowl parties in homes and at bars to watch the game are common. There is a tradition that companies, which advertise during the game, use more creative advertisements during the Superbowl than at other times of the year. Some people watch the game simply for the ads! Watching football is seen as a man's leisure activity, so many malls and shops will cater to women with special clothes, make-up, and hair fashion events.

The National Football Conference is the NFC and the American Football Conference is the AFC.

293

February

February 2   Ground Hog's Day

This day is of little importance, except that it is often indicated on calendars and mentioned in the news. The tradition is that IF the ground hog (a type of burrowing animal) comes out of its hole and sees its shadow, there will be six more weeks of winter weather. If it does not see its shadow, spring is only a month and a half away. The ground hog in question is named Phil and lives in Punxsutawny, Pennsylvania.

February 14   Valentine's Day

This popular holiday is a day for people to say "I Love You" to their loved ones including family and friends. Americans give cards (also known as valentines), boxes of chocolates, flowers, and other romantic gifts. Your sweetheart is also called your Valentine, hence the phrase "Be My Valentine". Taking your sweetheart out for a romantic dinner is popular. It is common for school children to have Valentine parties in their classrooms. The students exchange store bought or hand made valentine cards. Businesses are decorated with cupids, hearts, and all things red. Chocolates in red heart shaped boxes and sugary heart shaped candies with short phrases on them start to appear beginning in January.

March

March 17   St. Patrick's Day

This holiday commemorates St. Patrick, the patron saint of Ireland. Although not an important holiday in Ireland, much celebrating is done in the United States. Wearing green clothing, drinking green beer, and declaring yourself unofficially Irish for the day are common activities. Popular parades are held in major cities like New York City, Chicago and Boston. In Portland, the Shamrock Run is a 10K foot race through the city held in honor of this day.

March or April   Easter Season

You will see decorations, cards, and gifts for the Easter season after Valentine's Day. In addition to religious symbols, pastel colors, spring flowers, baby chicks and bunnies, and colored eggs are traditional decorations. Some people hang colored eggs from trees in their yard. Chocolate rabbits, marshmallow chickens, jelly beans, and cream

filled chocolate eggs dominate store candy shelves. The Easter Bunny is an imaginary character that delivers Easter baskets and hides Easter eggs around the house or yard. An Easter basket is a collection of sugary treats which family members find awaiting them on Easter Morning.

Friday Following Palm Sunday   Good Friday
Although not a federal holiday, many businesses will give their employees the day (or afternoon) off.

Sunday   Easter
On Easter day, children hunt for colored eggs and candy, reportedly left by the Easter Bunny, at family or neighborhood gatherings. Several large public Easter Egg hunts are held during the weekend of Easter (watch for ads). Extended families get together for a meal, traditionally of roasted ham, lamb or beef.

April

First Sunday in April   Day Light Savings Time
At 2:00 a.m., clocks are moved ahead one hour. Refer to Chapter 1, 'Basics' for more information on time zones.

April 15   Income Tax Day
Federal and State income tax returns must be postmarked by midnight. The U.S.P.S. main office in NW Portland is open until the last minute for late filers. You must file a form and pay whatever taxes you may owe, by April 15, even if you are asking for an extended time period to calculate them.

May

Second Sunday in May   Mother's Day
This day is used to express gratitude and appreciation for mothers. Children of all ages send flowers, gifts, cards, and/or telephone their mothers. Many restaurants offer special brunches or dinners to honor Mom. In some families it is a day of leisure for the mother, while the rest of the family takes over the chores.

June

Third Sunday in June   Father's Day

This day is used to express gratitude and appreciation for fathers. Children of all ages
send cards, gifts or call. It is also a day when the father is allowed to forgo chores.

October

Last Sunday in October   Day Light Savings Time

At 2:00 a.m., clocks are set back one hour.

October 31   Halloween

This day is based on pagan traditions from Europe. The U.S. interpretation is becoming more widely celebrated than New Year's Eve, as costume parties for children and
adults become more popular every year. Decorations include ghosts, witches, black
cats, spiders, spider webs and skeletons. It is a period of time where you are supposed to
enjoy being frightened by ghosts, witches, and other scary things. Movie theaters and
TV movie channels often show horror films. There are several places in Portland where
you can pay money to walk through a house and be frightened These events are usually a fund raising event for the sponsoring organization.

Children may celebrate Halloween at school with a party or costume parade. At dusk
and continuing until about 9:00 p.m. children (young children go with their parents)
walk from house to house Trick or Treating (asking for candy). Neighbors are expected
to be home to hand out the treats: store bought, pre-packaged candy. If you are not
going to be home, or simply do not want to be disturbed, turn off your porch light to
indicate that you are not interested in participating.

One tradition is the hollowing out of a pumpkin and carving a face into it to make a
'jack-o-lantern'. Candles (or flashlights) are lit in the jack-o-lanterns for a spooky
effect. Another is 'bobbing for apples' where you try to catch an apple (floating in a
pool of water) with only your teeth.

There are many pranks played this night. Teenagers may wrap a tree in toilet paper or
smash pumpkins in the street. If you want to protect your jack-o-lantern from vandals,
keep it in the house.

November

Friday after Thanksgiving   Christmas Season Begins

Because Thanksgiving always falls on a Thursday, many people have a four-day weekend. The Friday after Thanksgiving marks the start of the Christmas shopping season. Many stores open early with sales. It is a very busy day for the retailers. If you do not enjoy big crowds, you will want to avoid the stores on this day.

December

Mid December   Hanukkah

Also spelled Hanukah or Chanukah, this Jewish festival is known as the Festival of Lights. This holiday is celebrated around the world for the eight days and nights which begin with the 25th day of the month of Kislev, and ending on the 2nd day of the month of Tevet (all in the Hebrew calendar). Hanukkah is the celebration of the victory of the Jewish peoples over the Greek ruler Antiochus 2200 years ago. This Festival of Lights remembers the miracle during which one days-worth of oil lasted for eight days in a holy lamp in the temple of Jerusalem.

The Menorah is a special nine branched candleholder. Eight of the candles represent the eight days and nights of the miracle. The last candle is used for lighting the others. During the festival families sing songs, exchange gifts, and play traditional games. Jewish children will take time off from school. You will see menorahs and greeting cards in stores.

Traditional foods of this time are potato pancakes (latkes) and jelly donuts (sufganiot) or other foods fried in oil to commemorate the miracle of the festival of lights.

December 26 - January 1   Kwanzaa

This is a holiday celebrating the African-American community, heritage and culture. It was established in 1966. The name comes from the Swahili phrase of 'matunda ya kwanzaa' meaning 'the first fruits of the harvest'. In this celebration people honor the seven principles of Kwanzaa (also called Nguzo Saba). A seven-branched candleholder (called a Mishumaa Saba), with red and green candles, represents the principles of Kwanzaa. The candles are lit in a specific order each day.

Colors associated with this celebration are black, red, and green. Symbols of this celebration are corn and candles.

December 26   The Day after Christmas

The day after Christmas is a very busy shopping day as people return or exchange gifts or take advantage of after-Christmas sales. If you like to shop it is a good time to find Christmas wrapping papers, cards, and decorations on sale. It is also a time when many stores offer significant discounts to clear out their inventory.

December 31   New Year's Eve

New Year's Eve revelers celebrate the New Year in a variety of ways ranging from an evening of fine dining and ballroom dancing to parties at home with friends. Tradition calls for a kiss at midnight and a champagne toast. Fireworks have not, in the past, been common in the United States on this night, however after the extensive use of fireworks during the Millennium celebrations this may be changing. While it is only possible to purchase fireworks in Oregon during the weeks before July 4; you may light them at any time of year, provided that loud ones are not set off after 10 p.m.

More Information

Chapter 16

More Information

Books You Might Find Useful

Touring About Portland

The Facts of Life in Portland	Elaine Friedman
Rainy Day Guide to Portland	
Best Places Portland	Kim Carlson
City Smart Guidebook	Portland, Linda Nygaard
Around Portland with Kids	Judi Siewert Davis
Best Bike Rides Around Portland	Andy Wiselogle
Kidding Around Portland	Deborah Cuyle
Out and About Portland with Kids	Elizabeth Desimone
Papas' Portland	Bill Papas
Walking Portland	Sybilla Avery Cook
Portland's Best by Bus	Nancy Dendooven
Nature Walks in and Around Portland	Karen Whitehill
Event Resource Guide '98	Mary Lou Burton

Cultural Adaptation

Brit Think, Ameri Think	Jane Walmsley
American Ways	Gary Althen
Living in the U.S.A.	Alison Ranier
Culture Shock USA	
Hello USA	Judy Priven

Websites You Might Find Useful

Links to All Things Portland

www.el.com/to/Portland/links	Commercial site with many links
www.teleport.com/~samc/	Private site with links to many interesting things about Portland
www.pdxchamber.org	Official Chamber website for Portland
www.virtualrelocation.com	Site for people moving to Portland
www.portlandoregonhomes.com	Real-estate site with links
www.oregonlive.com	The Oregonian website with links

Travel sites

www.visitUSA.org	For information on any location the U.S.
www.travelocity.com	Airline, hotel, and rental car
www.expedia.com	Airline, hotel, and rental car
www.preview.com	Airline, hotel, and rental car
www.trip.com	Specializes in business travel
www.cruise4.com	Specializes in cruises
www.cruising.org	Site for 24 major cruiselines
www.placestostay.com	Hotels but not independent bed and breakfasts
www.priceline.com	Auction ticket travel agency
www.adventureseek.com	Adventure vacations - rafting, safari, etc.

Expatriate Resources

www.expatspouse.com	A free weekly electronic newsletter for expatriate spouses.
www.ozinamerica.com	A site for Australians living in the U.S.

Index

D

G

H

M

N

O

There is no need to 're-invent the wheel' each time a family moves into Portland. The shared knowledge of families who have been here before you can make the difference between feeling completely overwhelmed, and developing understanding.

Please send us your thoughts on how we can improve this book.

What did we leave out?
What has changed since we went to press?
What, in the book, do you think is unnecessary?
Have you had other types of experiences which we should include?

We would like to know.

Please write your comments down, with your name and telephone number, and forward to:

The Portland Handbook
RGM Group
2240 NW 113th Ave.
Portland, OR 97229

We will be in touch if we need clarification, and include your recommendations in the next edition.

About the Authors

Carol Cowan and Margie Rikert met while living in the Netherlands. They collaborated on a monthly newsletter for expatriates and their families. The Expat Life newsletter combined practical knowledge with cultural insight to give newcomers the tools they needed to settle into their adopted country quickly.

Now, living in the United States again, they observed the same types of practical questions and problems effecting their non-American friends in Portland. This book grew from a shared commitment to make the transition to Portland easier for international newcomers.

Carol originally moved to Portland in 1989. Her background includes an MBA in Health Care Finance from the University of Wisconsin-Madison. She has three children of elementary school age. She, and her husband Greg, use whatever free time they can find to remodel their home.

Margie moved to Portland in 1986. Her background includes an MBA in Marketing from the University of Massachusetts-Amherst. While in the Netherlands, she helped to create a video, Lets Go Dutch, and the rewrite of At Home in Holland. She has four adult sons. She shares the outdoors with her husband David through rock climbing, biking, hiking, and sea-kayaking,